NIGHT OF FIRE

NIGHT OF FIRE
The Black Napoleon and the Battle for Haiti

By
Martin Ros

Translated by Karin Ford-Treep

SARPEDON
New York

To she who inspired me,
with additional thanks to Vim Hoogbergen,
Paul Wartena and Herman Verhaar
who steered me in the right direction.

Published in the United States by
SARPEDON

First published in 1991 as *Vuurnacht:
Toussaint Louverture en de slavenopstand op Haïti* by Uitgeverij De
Arbeiderspers, Amsterdam, The Netherlands.

This publication was made possible thanks to, among others, the
generous assistance of the Foundation for the Production and Translation
of Dutch Literature.

Library of Congress Cataloging-in-Publication Data available.

ISBN 0-9627613-8-9 (cloth); ISBN 0-9627613-7-0 (paper)

Book and cover design by Libby Braden.
Cover and other illustrations courtesy of the Bibliothèque Nationale.

10 9 8 7 6 5 4 3 2 1

MANUFACTURED IN THE UNITED STATES OF AMERICA

Toussaint Louverture

Haiti, from its entwined sweetness,
extracts pathetic petals,
rectitude of gardens, grandiose
structures, the sea
lulls its ancient dignity of skin
and space like a dark grandfather.

Toussaint Louverture binds
the vegetable sovereignty,
the shackled majesty,
the mute voice of the drums,
and he attacks, blocks the way, rises,
commands, repels, defies
like a natural monarch,
until he falls in the sinister net
and is taken overseas,
dragged and trampled
like the return of his race,
cast to the secret death
of sewers and cellars.

But on the Island the cliffs burn,
hidden branches speak,
hopes are transmitted,
the bastion's walls rise up.
Freedom is your forest,
dark brother, preserve
your memory of suffering,
and let heroes of the past
safekeep your magic foam.

Pablo Neruda, *Canto General*
(from "The Liberators," 30th song)

Table of Contents

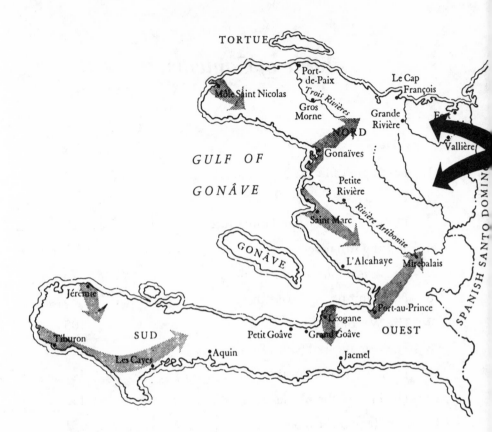

The Spanish and English invasions, 1793–94. The light arrows
indicate the English routes of advance; the dark ones the Spanish.
(Map courtesy of Thomas O. Ott, *The Haitian Revolution 1789–1804*,
The University of Tennessee Press.)

Preface

On the fourteenth of July, in 1989, the year of great commemorative celebrations for the French Revolution, the Presses Universitaires de France published a tome of 1,100 pages called *Dictionnaire historique de la Révolution française*. In their preface, editors Jean René Suratteau and François Gendron paid tribute to Albert Soboul, the editor in chief of the book, who had died before it was published. He had been the greatest French scholar of the Revolution.

The *Dictionnaire* was hailed as the definitive collection of facts about the period of the French Revolution. Many of the articles had been written by Marcel Dorigny of the Institut d'Histoire de la Révolution Française. One of these articles includes his presentation of the facts about Toussaint Louverture. It starts on page 1,043 and consists of 54 lines. The segment contains four errors.

Dorigny states that Toussaint had adopted a "policy of convenience," whereby he collaborated in turn with the Spanish, the British and Sonthonax. Toussaint never collaborated with the British. Dorigny classified Sonthonax as a Girondist deputy of the Convention; Sonthonax was instead a dedicated radical Jacobin. Dorigny could not refrain from emphasizing that Toussaint never intended to improve the fate of the slaves, and a few lines further down, he states that the uprising led by Toussaint turned the island into a ruin. Finally, Dorigny managed to include one more error. He reports that Toussaint "capitulated" on November 6, 1802, and was subsequently transferred to France; he was, in fact, seized by force on June 7.

This example of errors and inaccuracies in the standard work of the Bicentennial is typical of the tradition of French historiography about Toussaint Louverture, the slave rebellion in Haiti and the abolition of slavery by the Convention (whether written by scholars of the right or the left).

In his *Histoire de la Révolution,* which was reprinted to great acclaim in the Pléiade series in 1989, French historian Jules Michelet (1798–1874) simply forgot to mention the abolition of slavery. About the tragedy in Haiti, he wrote three lines and called it the most horrible uprising of savages that had ever been seen in the world. Both in the monumental *Histoire de la Révolution Française* by Louis Blanc (1811–82) and in the *Histoire socialiste de la Révolution Française* by Jean Jaurès (1859–1914) no mention is made of the abolition of slavery in 1794. Both authors dedicate just a few lines to the "horrible" slave revolt, viewing it as "a lamentable incident." In his voluminous *Histoire de France,* published in 1920, Ernest Lavisse (1842–1922) still described the rebellion of the mulattoes as part of the counter-revolution. Albert Mathiez (1874–1932), a contributor to *L'Humanité* magazine, who wrote a programmatic Marxist history of the Revolution, also forgot about the abolition of slavery. Reactionary colonial politics was attributed entirely to the Girondists, who supposedly occasioned the racial wars. Other than this, no word about the slave rebellion.

The *Nouvelle Histoire de la France contemporaine* (New History of Contemporary France), edited by French historians of great prestige and published in 1972, only mentions the abolition of slavery in its chronological table. The only statement about Haiti included in the book is clearly incorrect: "The abolition of slavery unleashed the uprising among blacks in the colonies."

Likewise, Toussaint and the slave rebellion hardly appear at all in modern British historiography about the French Revolution, which is otherwise very exhaustive. M. J. Sydenham remarks on Toussaint in only one line of his influential work *The First French Republic, 1792–1804.* Nor do Toussaint and the slave rebellion appear in the two most important and widely read translations of large works about the Revolution published in Holland before the Second World War. One is Louis Madelin's two-volume work, *De Fransche revolutie* (The French Revolution), which presents a typical rightist viewpoint. The other is Gabriel Deville's two-volume work, *Het Directoire* (The Directorate), which presents a classical view from the left (it is probably no accident that it was translated by the Marxist W. van Ravesteyn).

In 1989, I anxiously awaited the publication of what was

described as the first modern biography of Toussaint Louverture. The author was Pierre Pluchon, a former French ambassador to Haiti who had already written a series of books about the history of the Caribbean. This book of more than six hundred pages was published by Fayard under the title *Toussaint Louverture* and, significantly, the subtitle *Un Révolutionnaire noir de l'Ancien Régime* (A Black Revolutionary of the Old Regime). It was a great disappointment because it turned out to be not much more than an enlarged version of Pluchon's *Toussaint Louverture, de l'esclavage au pouvoir* (Toussaint Louverture: From Slavery to Power), which had been published in 1979. The subtitle of the new version is typical of the entire message of this book, which was written with a strong anti-Toussaint bias. Pluchon's nationalist combativeness is carried to the point where he presents Toussaint not only as a person who is consistently perfidious and who constantly foils the generally positive intentions of the French, but even as someone who implements the counter-revolution.

The new subtitle was obviously a surprise for the editors of the Saturday book supplement of the *NRC-Handelsblad,* a Dutch daily, as well. In the review, which highly praised this book that so greatly dishonors Toussaint Louverture and the slave rebellion, the Dutch editors of the "biography" category took it upon themselves to change the subtitle of the book into *Le Spartacus noir* (The Black Spartacus). Were they perhaps uneasy about the reactionary implications of the book's subtitle?

Pluchon's book contains, in the chapter on the period when Toussaint was in power, approximately twenty-five pages about the plantation economy and social developments. It appears that the extremely negative judgment expressed here by Pluchon is mainly based on testimonies by French officials and colonists who were enemies of Toussaint; in any case, these testimonies provided contradictory information. The greatest shortcoming in the literature on Toussaint and the slave war – which, as a war, is dispatched by Pluchon almost as a matter of minor importance – is the lack of a definitive social and economic history of this period. Numerous conflicting reports relating to these social and economic developments are to be found as well in the new studies from Clarendon Press written by the English authors David Geggus

(*Slavery, War and Revolution: The British Occupation of Saint Domingue 1793–1798*) and Michael Duffy (*Soldiers, Sugar and Seapower: The British Expeditions to the West Indies and the War Against Revolutionary France*). Even the number of casualties among the British soldiers is reported with the most widely divergent figures in these books, which were supposedly based on official sources. In his scathing judgment of Toussaint's socio-economic politics, Pluchon can therefore not maintain that the sources on which he relied are undisputed. On the contrary, his sources are the ones that are the most prejudiced. Pluchon questioned the significance of the slave rebellion and he considered Toussaint the person who completed its failure. It apparently did not occur to him to look for the cause of this failure in Napoleon's last invasion, which was launched for the purpose of reinstating slavery. It was this invasion that made it forever impossible to grant the benefit of the doubt to Toussaint's national restoration program. Toussaint, after all, was the one who tried until the very end to work together with the former colonists. The last possibility for a cooperative relationship between the colonists and the former slaves was eliminated by the invasion of the French and the fall of Toussaint.

Pierre Pluchon's book is part of a long anti-Toussaint tradition in France. This tradition has its origins in B. M. J. Dubroca's work, which was published as early as 1804, with the title *La Vie de Toussaint Louverture, chef des noirs insurgés de Saint-Domingue* (The Life of Toussaint Louverture, Leader of the Rebellious Blacks of Haiti). This book, written with a polemic anti-Toussaint bias, became very popular during the period of the Empire. Among Toussaint biographies written in France there are two that are the most important in counterbalancing those characterized by an anti-slavery bias. One is Gragnon-Lacoste's *Toussaint Louverture, général en chef de l'armée de Saint-Domingue, surnommé le premier des noirs* (Toussaint Louverture: Commanding General of the Army of Haiti, Also Known as the First of the Blacks), which was published in Paris in 1877. Particularly important is the second, entitled *Vie de Toussaint Louverture* (Life of Toussaint Louverture), written by Victor Schoelcher and published in Paris in 1889. In 1982, it was reprinted at Editions Karthala in Paris, with an introduction by Jacques Adélaïde-Merlande. In their exaggerated appreciation for

Toussaint, these books are a reaction, in particular, to the book entitled *Vie de Toussaint Louverture,* written by the mulatto Saint-Rémy and published in Port-au-Prince in 1850. This book is pronouncedly pro-mulatto and almost a hagiographical work on Rigaud – which makes it a continuous criticism of Toussaint. The most important work on Toussaint to come out of Haiti, *Histoire de Toussaint-L'Ouverture,* was only published between 1920 and 1934, in Port-au-Prince; this is the three-volume work by Pauléus Sannon.

A significant new impulse for the study of Toussaint's life was provided by the publication in 1938 of C. L. R. James' *The Black Jacobins: Toussaint Louverture and the San Domingo Revolution* (revised editions published in 1963 by Vintage, New York, and in 1982 by Allison and Busby, London). This book represents a re-evaluation of the slave uprising as a social revolution, presented from a radical-Marxist point of view. In a passionate narrative with a wide panoramic setting, James – who was born in Trinidad – conveyed an extremely one-sided vision that is highly attractive within a Marxist outlook. In his book, there is a close and direct interaction between the French Revolution and the slave rebellion, which, in its most radical development, constitutes a variation of the Jacobin phases of that upheaval. James suggests that Toussaint failed to integrate the black revolution with the class struggle. In his view, the definitive turning point occurred when Toussaint quashed Moyse's rebellion. The revolution was broken at that point and the counter-revolution got its last chance. Even in the context of James' ideological bias, the dynamics of the slave rebellion and the grandiose profile of Toussaint are unforgettably fascinating. It is to his shame and indicative of his reactionary bias that Pluchon does not even mention James' pioneering book in his bibliography.

The following five proven sources on the course of the uprising, the civil war and the invasion were also available to me: Antoine Métral's *Histoire de l'expédition des Français à Saint-Domingue,* reprinted by Karthala in 1985; the *Histoire militaire de la guerre d'indépendance de Saint-Domingue* by Colonel-General A. Nemours, a Haitian author and diplomat; the very objective autobiography of the French general Pamphile de Lacroix, *Mémoires pour servir à l'histoire de la révolution de Saint-Domingue*; the dry, but very thorough, military history by Colonel Poyen in *Histoire militaire de la révolution de Saint-Domingue*; and A. Dalmas' two-volume work, *Histoire de la révolution de Saint-Domingue*, which was published in 1814 and is indispensable for anecdotes and curiosities.

In addition, I was able to use the very rare *Histoire des révolutions d'Haïti* by M. Saint-Amand, which I obtained by chance. The first volume of this book appeared in 1860 at Dentu, a bookdealer in the Palais-Royal, Paris; a sequel was never published. Saint-Amand was an eyewitness to the founding of the free nation of Haiti, where he was a member of the Constituant Assembly for many years. I was also able to use the reprint of the famous historian Thomas Madiou's three-volume *Histoire d'Haïti*, published in Port-au-Prince in 1981. This work has an abundance of detail, but it is unfortunately very dry reading. In addition, it was written with an emphatically pro-mulatto bias and it, therefore, treats Toussaint and the slaves disparagingly throughout. Then there are the *Mémoires du Géneral Toussaint-Louverture écrits par lui-mème* (Memoirs of General Toussaint Louverture, Written by Himself), edited by the mulatto Saint-Rémy, who was also rather critical of Toussaint – to put it mildly. This book was published in reprint by Fardin in Port-au-Prince in 1982, but it is considered extremely apocryphal. A fantastic source, however, is *Toussaint Louverture à travers sa correspondance 1794–1798* (Toussaint Louverture, Seen Through His Letters, 1794–1798), edited by Gérard Laurent. It was published in 1953 for the anniversary year 1954, when the one hundred fiftieth year of Haiti's existence was celebrated.

In addition to Pluchon's book about Toussaint, two interesting monographs were recently published in France. In *Le Temps de Saint-Domingue, l'esclavage et la Révolution Française* (The Period of Haiti, Slavery and the French Revolution), published by Lattès, Jacques Thibeau presents, in a kind of day-to-day account based on the sources, a colorful picture of the period before and after the first days of the slave rebellion. A pleasant surprise was Yves Benot's *La Révolution Française et la fin des colonies* (The French Revolution and the End of the Colonies), published by Editions La Découverte. This is a revealing and sobering study about the slow pace of the contribution to the liberation of the slaves made by both the enlightened leaders and the Jacobins in France. The author demonstrates that there was practically no direct impetus from Paris in favor of the slave uprising. As far as this point is concerned, the book emphatically corrects James' much too orthodox Marxist viewpoint, although this book was written by a Marxist as well. (In James' book, there are also reflections of the permanent revolutionary ideology of Trotsky, whose theories James supported.) Quite a surprise was the publication in 1986 of Jan Pachonski's and Reuel K. Wilson's *Poland's Caribbean Tragedy: A Study of Polish Legions in the Haitian War of Independence 1802–1803* (Columbia University Press).

There has always been an interest in Haiti on the part of the Germans as well. A very unusual publication was that of *Die Revolution von Saint-Domingue* by Erwin Rüsch, which appeared in 1930. From a popular and Darwinist point of view, in which there is already a hint of fascism, Rüsch describes Toussaint as a black "Übermensch." Three books about Haiti were written by Hans Christoph Buch, the contemporary German author who is a descendant of German colonists in Môle Saint-Nicolas, where a German district still exists today. In his *Die Scheidung von San Domingo: wie die Negersklaven von Haiti Robespierre beim Wort nahmen* (The Separation of Santo Domingo: How the Negro Slaves of Haiti Took Robespierre at His Word), published by Klaus Wagenbach, he presents a rather traditionally Marxist history of the slave uprising, using excerpts and quotations from books and introducing a descriptive chronological table.

In two novels, *Die Hochzeit von Port-au-Prince* (The Wedding at Port-au-Prince) and *Haïti Chérie* (Dearest Haiti), both published by Suhrkamp, Buch portrays figures and events from the time of Toussaint, but his speculations – especially those about Sonthonax – are a little too outlandish. (Nor is he a good enough writer to be able to stand in the shadow of what has been accomplished by the great Latin American authors with the help of historical data.) The French novel about the slave uprising that continues to be reprinted and read is Victor Hugo's *Bug-Jargal,* a new edition of which appeared in 1985 at Presse Pocket, with extensive commentary by Claude Lémie and Robert Strick. For all his good intentions, Hugo produced a conventional image of the rebellious slaves as brutes and barbarians, just as was done by Germany's Heinrich von Kleist in his short story *Die Verlobung in St. Domingo* (The Engagement in Santo Domingo). Much more balanced and objective about Toussaint and the slaves is the French tetralogy *La Volupté et la haine* (The Voluptuousness and the Hatred), a popularly written novel by Robert Gaillard (Fleuve Noir, 1971).

A modern biography of Dessalines does not exist. Hubert Cole wrote about Christophe, however, in his *Christophe, King of Haiti,* published in 1967 by Eyre and Spottiswoode, London. Among the other historical figures around Toussaint, a modern biography was written about Leclerc only in 1990, under the title *Le Général Leclerc (1772– 1802) et l'expédition de Saint-Domingue,* published by Tallandier. Books about Pauline Bonaparte and her amorous exploits have continued to be published during the last few years, with new biographies by Geneviève Chastenet (Lattès), Antonio Spinosa (Tallandier) and Georges Blond (Perrin). A drama by French poet Alphonse de Lamartine (1790–1869) entitled *Toussaint Louverture, poème dramatique,* but originally called *Haïti ou les Noirs* (Haiti or the Blacks), was first published in 1850. It consists of sentimental rhetoric without any historical basis.

A monograph about Sonthonax, written by the American Robert Louis Stein, was published by the Associated University Presses in 1985 with the title *Léger Félicité Sonthonax: The Lost Sentinel of the Republic.* It is a surprisingly sedate book and also somewhat hagiographic. About Hédouville, we have only the first volume of a work by Michel Antoine that was intended to contain five volumes; entitled *La Mission du Général Hédouville à Saint-Domingue* (General Hédouville's Mission to Haiti), it appeared in 1929 in Port-au-Prince, where the author died in 1938.

In one of the most recent studies about Napoleon, *L'Homme Napoléon* (Napoleon the Man), by Louis Chardigny (published by Perrin), the name Toussaint does not appear. A monograph about Napoleon and Toussaint does not exist. As I completed the writing of this book in the summer of 1991, a new book on the bicentennial of the Night of Fire had been announced neither in France nor in the United States.

◆ 1 ◆

The Night of Fire

■——■

DURING THE NIGHT OF AUGUST 22, 1791, A WALL OF FIRE arose on the horizon in northern Haiti. It seemed to fan out in all directions, as if carried by the clouds, moving south, east, west and, in the north, all the way to the sea.

Far up the highest mountains the fire climbed. It almost seemed as if the peaks had become volcanoes spewing fire. The voraciousness of the flames turned night into day. Further, the immense fire created enormous gusts of wind that, in turn, drove the flames on, causing them to rage at incredible speed through the woods, over the plantations, into the sheds filled with cotton, over the fields thick with sugarcane, straight through the coffee plantations and sugar mills, and into the gigantic warehouses of the masters of the island.

The burning of the forests could be heard like the gurgling and bubbling of an antediluvian waterfall. Trees split apart, branches snapped, roots cracked underground. The green outline of the trees lasted only a moment once the flames had seized them and, in no time at all, their green dissolved into a reddish glow. Thick smoke enveloped the landscape, but the fire leapt up high through the dark roof of soot. Then, as the smoke was driven away by the wind, a shower of sparks rained down on the scourged earth.

The Pearl of the Antilles was burning!

1

"The colonists in Saint-Domingue are sleeping on the crater of a Vesuvius," Mirabeau had been heard to shout in the National Assembly of revolutionary France. The slaves in Haiti, the French possession of Saint-Domingue, totalled half a million, outnumbering the whites by a majority of nearly twenty to one. Already in the Caribbean, slave rebellions had broken out in Grenada, Dominica, Trinidad, Saint Vincent, Jamaica and Cuba. These islands had all experienced revolts to which were linked notorious names such as Cuffy, Fédon, Tachy and Boni. In Haiti itself, conspiracies and subsequent sentences and executions of slaves had taken place in 1679, 1691, 1703, 1704, 1758, 1775 and 1778. Violent unrest was no stranger to this crown jewel of the French economic empire.

During the first days of August 1791, the French newspapers – the *Gazette Générale de Saint-Domingue*, the *Moniteur Colonial* and a dozen other papers that were published daily to keep track of the island's bustling commerce – still issued their daily "wanted" lists of escaped slaves as if nothing was about to happen.

Miscellaneous Notices

LOUIS, 35 years old, who has scars all over his face and whose body is covered with welts from whippings.

MATHIEU, 14 or 16 years of age, whose left hand is missing and whose right hand is crippled as a result of burns.

JOSEPH, a Negro from the Congo, who has been branded with the Jesuit cross on his chest.

BOSSI, a girl of 24, who cannot speak and has a hole in the left nostril.

CADRUS the hunchback, who has a broken back.

DÉSIRÉ, the slave from Fort Dauphin, who can be recognized easily from the chain that ties his left arm to his left leg.

PHILIBERT, age unknown, whose left eye is missing.

JEAN BAPTISTE, whose body is covered with recent wounds and whose nails are all missing.

When a fire erupted on a plantation near Limbé on August 16, a slave was arrested who confessed under interrogation that, over a wide area, slaves were conspiring to burn down the plantations and strangle to death the whites. Weeks before August 22, the drums could be heard at night and, if anyone was foolhardy enough to venture into the woods, the monotonous and macabre repetitions of African wanga songs were heard as well.

For more than thirty years it had been whispered among the slaves that "Fire killed Mackandal, and fire will destroy the riches of Haiti." The renegade Mackandal had been burned at the stake on January 26, 1758, after organizing a band of escaped slaves, "maroons," who inflicted terror on a wide swathe of the countryside. It was said afterwards that his soul flew away like a fly from the fire in which his mortal remains were consumed. (The slaves believed that Mackandal had returned in the guise of mosquitoes that later brought the yellow fever.) On a sign next to the stake, the whites had written, "Seducer, blasphemer, poisoner." Part voodoo god, it was said that Mackandal had seduced many women whom he had visited on nights while they were chanting incantations. In life, he had taught the slaves how they could poison their masters without leaving a trace. He had preached the doctrines of the god Legba, who, with the approval of the Good God, had created the world as a place where the whites could indulge themselves like devils. Mackandal's plan, to poison the entire white population of Haiti all at one time, had failed. He had given in to his lust for a woman and had been betrayed by her lover.

Mackandal's diabolic life and downfall was portrayed in the *merengue*, danced in the Alligator Wood where, during the night of August 14, 1791, the prelude for the Night of Fire would be played out.

During that night, men and women first stood facing each other and then, following the staccato rhythm of the drums, jumped towards each other so that their bellies touched. Next, they jumped away from each other while making snapping movements with their bodies. Finally, they came together again, swinging their hips. As the rhythm increased, the movements became more intense and the gestures and expressions more passionate. The women turned around, offering their backs to the men. As soon as the men tried

to touch them, the women ran away screaming; then the men
chased them and jumped upon them with pent-up fervor. They
remembered what Mackandal had said: "God taught your children
how to dance while still in your wombs."

That Sunday, August 14, dozens of the slaves had gathered at
Lenormand, deep in the Alligator Wood. It was about seven miles
from Cap François, near the spot where Mackandal was burned at
the stake, and also close to the place where Ogé and Chavannes,
the first rebellious mulattoes, had been defeated and captured in
1790. Most of them had first been to church in L'Acul that morning,
where there had been a group of almost two thousand slaves
together with less than a hundred whites, the latter not suspecting
that anything was amiss.

In the woods, they had come from Port Margot, Limbé, Petite
Anse, Limonade, Plaine du Nord, Quartier Morin and Morne Rouge.
The giant voodoo priest, Boukman, led the service on behalf of
Baron Samedi and Baron Lentrenc, voodoo gods, who guarded and
protected the slaves.

"Dear God," they sang, "who lets the sun shine from up high,
who lifts up the sea, who makes the thunder roll, listen to us. Our
Dear God is hidden in a cloud; from there he looks down on us and
sees everything that the whites do to us. Our Dear God commands
the whites to do evil, but through us he wants to let the good
triumph. God, who is good, has charged us with his revenge. He will
hold our arms up and give us strength. Shatter the image of the god
of the whites who craves the light in our eyes. Listen to the freedom
that speaks in the hearts of us all."

It could not seem a coincidence to the secretly gathered slaves
that, during this night of prelude to the Night of Fire, a hurricane
arose, lightning flashed through the heavens, the earth was inun-
dated by rain in an instant and trees bent down under the fury of
the wind, some being uprooted.

The slaves moved aside to make room for an old woman who
was led to the center of the group by Boukman. Her body shook
with terrible shudders and she brandished a knife over her head.
It was the prophetess Roumaine. With that same knife, she would
lead many an attack on the plantations after the Night of Fire.

A black pig was brought. The animal's squealing was lost in

the noise of the storm. With one frenzied movement, Roumaine drove the knife into the animal's throat. The blood was collected and then passed around. They all drank of it and swore to obey the commands of the priest Boukman, the man with Herculean strength, until death should take them and lead them back to the land of their fathers.

The night in the Alligator Wood was not devoted simply to dancing and ceremony; deliberations were made and secret appointments arranged. Though to the naive eye possessed by devils, Boukman was the architect of an ingenious plan of attack, a plan conceived with the sure hand of a master creator of ruins. When the Night of Fire arrived on August 22, the sugarcane fields, the woods and the plantations all went up in flames simultaneously over a distance of hundreds of miles.

*   *   *

There is no twilight on Haiti, where the forces of nature are as quick as the passions of the people. Night is just as suddenly replaced by day as day is displaced by night. For the first time, however, it seemed that this Night of Fire on August 22, 1791, with its awesome fury, wished to hasten the advance of day. The sea of flames pushed up columns of smoke that gathered together to form smoldering ovens of clouds. Carried along by gusts of wind, they traveled for miles over the countryside and, finally, disintegrated in a rain of ashes that settled like tainted snow on the island. The clouds of smoke moved over not only Cap François, the terror-stricken capital of the colony, but also were seen as far away as the Bermudas.

After the Night of Fire, the light of day revealed a gruesome sight: toppled houses and buildings; screaming and moaning people. Fifty thousand slaves under the leadership of the priest Boukman had revolted and were celebrating their horrifying day of reckoning. With faces painted and bare chests smeared with ashes and blood, the slaves were finally taking revenge for centuries of humiliation, torture, terror and murder. Slaves dragged white planters from their homes and tore off their limbs one by one. They hanged the whites on their own ladders and riddled their bodies with their own guns, until nothing but crumpled masses of flesh were left. They strapped the whites to wooden racks and sawed them in half. They decapitated children and stuck the quivering limbs and heads onto their spears and swords like trophies. Young girls were raped repeatedly and murdered in front of their mothers' eyes – and then the mothers suffered the same fate.

Female slaves also participated in the outpouring of decades of silently harbored rage. They tortured the white planters who had so often punished, tormented and raped them, until the men were at the point of death; and then the slaves shouted at them, "No, don't die yet, you must suffer some more." Genitals were ripped out and stuffed into their owners' mouths as they lay bleeding, emitting the death rattle. The bodies were dragged to the Negro-gullies – ditches used by the planters to dispose of slaves who were gravely ill or near death, because they were not considered worth being cared for or buried in the usual manner.

Hadn't the whites claimed again and again that one could hit and torture the blacks as much as one wanted? They maintained that the blacks were actually insensitized to the blows and that they longed to die during their suffering because they would then go directly to the black heaven in Africa.

It lasted several days, this revenge of the fifty thousand, who, after weeks of preparation in the deepest secret, had unleashed the Night of Fire that held the whites paralyzed in dazed horror.

In a matter of days, two thousand whites were killed, 180 sugar plantations and 900 coffee plantations were destroyed, and two million francs' worth of damage inflicted.

Then the whites struck back in a way that was even more gruesome and indiscriminate. During their three-week-long counterterror, fifteen to twenty thousand blacks and mulattoes were murdered. Once the whites had shaken off their fear of the Night of Fire, they were possessed by a tremendous rage. Motivated by both revenge and policy, they believed that if only they had been even harsher, crueler and stricter with the slaves, the rebellion would never have been dared.

The whites continued for days to seize every black they could lay their hands on, whether old, young, male or female, both those whom they suspected of having been supporters of the revolt and those whose innocence was beyond doubt. All were literally slaughtered. The planters placed dozens of victims' heads on stakes surrounding their plantations, and they erected rows of crosses on which the slaves, often seriously wounded as a result of torture, were left to die.

In Cap François, the Paris of the Pearl of the Antilles, the bloody hunt lasted for days. The slaves were hanged in the streets and, on the squares in front of the houses, they were tied to wheels on which their bodies were broken. The whites put on their Sunday best to celebrate their feast of revenge. British flags were flown because Governor Blanchelande had immediately called the British in Jamaica, who obliged with their own brand of assistance. The British were the best slave hunters in the world and they did not hesitate to bring their specially trained hounds to help crush the rebellion.

The whites in power also murdered other whites because they found that, among the revolting slaves whom they had captured, there were Frenchmen who had blackened their faces and joined in the mayhem. Slaves were not the only ones in the colony to have chafed under the autocratic rule of the planters in these first years after the French Revolution. Poor whites confessed to having incited the slaves with news about the escaping King of France, who, near Varennes, had been taken hostage by his subjects because, they said, of his plan to abolish slavery.

For days, the rebel army, still comprised of thirty to forty thousand, ranged along a zigzag course over the plains in the north, through the woods, along the plantations, and straight across the restricted military area that the French had set up against possible attack by the Spanish. Rebel slaves also roamed about in smaller groups, joining bands of maroons in the hills who had been living on the run for years. Although they had practically no weapons, at one point they threatened to surround Cap François and actually succeeded in setting fires within the city itself.

On September 3, 1791, the National Assembly met in the capital. Lieutenant Touzard declared that he was now able to guarantee safety again with his army—though barely 2,500 fully armed men, they had heavy cannons at their disposal. The effect of the Night of Fire had subsided. The slaves were already retreating. It had been the largest, bloodiest, most terrifying slave revolt ever to take place in the Caribbean, but the white ruling class did not succumb, responding instead with murder and terror of its own to maintain the upper hand. The lesson the whites had learned, in fact, was that despite all the euphoria about the revolution in France, with its motto of equality (*égalité,* as well as *liberté* and *fraternité*), the system of slavery had to be fostered and maintained in a harsher and more ruthless manner than ever. Only then would a disaster such as the Night of Fire be prevented from happening again.

* * *

The blaze of the Night of Fire was also visible on the Bréda plantation, which was managed by Bayon de Libertad on behalf of Baron Noé, the owner, who had been living in France for years. The plantation was situated in the Plaine du Nord, half an hour on horseback from Cap François.

Libertad and his wife managed the Bréda plantation in an untypically liberal and tolerant manner. In fact, there existed an expression, "as happy as a Negro at Bréda." Pierre Dominique Toussaint had spent a peaceful, relatively happy childhood on the Bréda plantation, despite the fact that he was a slave.

Toussaint was the eldest son of Gaou Guinon, who was said to be the descendant of an African king. Born on May 20, 1743, he took the name Toussaint because, on Haiti, the feast of All Saints was celebrated on May 20. He was a boy of slender build who walked with a stoop, gaining him the nickname, *"fatras-bâton"* ("fragile little stick"). His godfather was the priest Simon Baptiste, who taught him to read and write, and even some Latin.

Bayon de Libertad had taken a liking to *fatras-bâton,* and the boy was allowed to read books from Bayon's library. Among these was Abbot Raynal's *Histoire philosophique et politique des établissements et du commerce des Européens dans les deux Indes* (Philosophical and Political History of the European Trading Establishments in the Territories of the Two Indies). In this book, there was a prediction of a "Black Spartacus" who would lead a revolt of the slaves.

Time and again, Toussaint would get Father Baptiste to tell him the story of Spartacus of ancient Rome, who nearly became victorious but, in the end, was crucified with his thousands of rebel slaves along the Appian Way. Toussaint derived a mysterious feeling of strength from Raynal's prediction. Overcoming the frailty of his youth, he grew to become an extremely tough man with supple strength and rare stamina. He had an astounding memory and learned so much about herbs and plants from Father Baptiste that he was considered an accomplished medical practitioner before he was twenty. When Bayon de Libertad realized, with some amazement, that he could have a conversation with his slave Toussaint about the classics, he upgraded the young man's status. Although an official document of manumission was never drawn up for Toussaint as a "freeman," he was granted complete liberty within the territory of the plantation.

Bayon de Libertad gave Toussaint forty acres to manage for himself and thirteen slaves to supervise. Toussaint was thus able to build his own farmstead and small coffee plantation. In addition, he remained in charge of Libertad's household personnel and acted as his permanent coachman. By the time he was twenty, Toussaint was already a marvelous horseman who, as the saying went, could "talk to horses," so that they were seen to follow him and seemed to go wherever he wished.

Toussaint was nearly thirty when he married Suzanne Simon. Because only one in a thousand slaves on Haiti was married, this too indicated Toussaint's unique status. Slaves were generally prevented from marrying by their masters, who could more easily exchange human property among themselves if they were not impeded by marriage or family ties.

Suzanne Simon, who was a few years older than Toussaint and who had a considerably fuller and broader figure, already had a son by a mulatto who had deserted her. Toussaint was extremely fond of this boy, Placidus. In time, the couple had two more sons, Isaac and Saint-Jean. During his later campaigns, Toussaint would nostalgically tell his soldiers about the almost idyllic life he had lived on the plantation with his family.

Toussaint and Suzanne were both devoutly Roman Catholic, and on Sunday mornings they would walk to church hand in hand. Toussaint always carried his missal, which he read devotedly. When he drove Bayon de Libertad to church in his coach, however, whites would often force him to wait outside near the horses, and they also forbid him to mount a horse in their presence. Once a planter took Toussaint's riding whip away and gave him a severe beating with it.

When the blaze of the Night of Fire forced even the slaves on the Bréda plantation to either flee or join the rebels, Toussaint instructed his brother Paul to take Suzanne and the children to Santo Domingo, the eastern part of the island, where the Spaniards ruled. He himself drove Bayon de Libertad and his wife in a coach along narrow backroads, and got them safely to the coast from where they left at once for America.

Toussaint returned to the Bréda plantation to find most of it burned and destroyed. Several of Libertad's slaves, who had apparently tried to resist the rebellion, had been beaten up or murdered. It was long rumored that Toussaint first sought out the planter who had beaten him with his own riding crop, and then killed the planter with a stick. Perhaps, on viewing the destruction, his thoughts dwelled only on the storied exploits of Spartacus. What is known is that Toussaint decided to leave the Bréda plantation to join the army camp of the slaves.

◆ 2 ◆

The Slaves

▬ —— ▬

"*SIRE, VOTRE COEUR EST CRÉOLE!*" ("SIRE, YOUR HEART IS CREOLE!")
Shortly before the French Revolution, Guy d'Arcy could still
say these words to King Louis XVI. Speaking as the representative
of the Club Massiac of the French planters on Haiti, he assured the
king, "Lord, your Haiti is the Pearl of the Antilles."

By 1791, one-fifth of France's foreign trade consisted of
commerce to and from Haiti. Besides providing year-round work
for 15,000 sailors, a full forty percent of France's trade balance
consisted of the processing and transportation of coffee, sugar,
cocoa, indigo, cotton and tobacco from its prize colony. By the end
of the 18th century, there were at least 7,000 plantations, spread
over a total of forty-three percent of the soil of Haiti, and seventy-
five percent of the population worked on the plantations. The
coffee plantations alone, situated mostly in higher regions, covered
a total of 800 square miles. The sugar plantations, located mainly
in the lowlands, required a total of 1,235,000 acres.

Immediately before the French revolution, there were only
some six million trees left on Haiti, less than ten percent of the total
that had existed in 1700, and one million of these were banana
trees. (The banana was a staple of the colony, along with the sweet
potato, which was cultivated extensively by slaves on the little
plots of ground set aside for production of their own food.) Even
in the 18th century, there was talk about the problems of soil

erosion that resulted from radical and sudden deforestation of the land.

Sources dating from the end of the 18th century provide disparate figures for the size of the population. Some give predominance in numbers to the whites, as compared with the mixed-race people known as mulattoes; others show the number of mulattoes being greater. It is probably safest to assume, for the period before 1791, a total of 25,000 to 30,000 whites and a total of 30,000 to 35,000 mulattoes. The vast majority of the population, however, was black – and slave. The number of slaves stood at a minimum of 450,000 and a maximum of 500,000. Every year, four thousand ships delivered at least 30,000 new blacks from Africa, but there were also years when between 50,000 and 100,000 were delivered.

The planters of Haiti were considered to be the richest people in the Caribbean. They were, in fact, called the "Lords of Haiti," while the planters on Martinique, for example, had to make do with the appellation "Gentlemen of Martinique," and those on Guadeloupe were simply called the "Good People of Guadeloupe."

Within its total area of 12,000 square miles, Haiti had almost two hundred small cities and towns. The largest were Cap François and Port-au-Prince, with 18,000 and 10,000 inhabitants, respectively. Though the cities and towns had received their share of benefits from the wealth of the colony, the greatest trappings of luxury were to be found in the buildings and homes of the planters in the countryside.

During the wettest period of the rainy season – lasting from October to March, a favorable time for the cultivation of sugar – the roads, even those in the cities, were completely impassable. Visitors often complained about constant leaks in the houses; even in the theaters, people had to keep their umbrellas at the ready. Almost forty percent of the land in Haiti lies above an altitude of 1,400 feet and at least twenty percent of the remaining land lies at or above 550. The countryside often reminded visitors of Switzerland, the only difference being that the climate, despite an average temperature of eighty degrees Fahrenheit, was considered extremely unpleasant. Only in the highest mountains, which reached to heights of 10,000 feet, did the temperature fall as low as around forty degrees Fahrenheit at night. The weather was almost always humid, damp and oppressive – a climate that, to Europeans, signaled licentiousness. Barbé de Marbois, the French lieutenant governor (*intendant*), once remarked: "Laziness and debauchery are the inevitable results of a protracted stay on Haiti."

Haiti was of course a paradise for flies, mosquitoes and other insects, and in the ongoing battle to get a sound night's sleep, inhabitants had learned to fashion elaborate, ingenious nets around their beds and furniture.

* * *

On December 6, 1492, Columbus officially discovered the island we now know as a combination of Haiti in the west and the Dominican Republic in the east. On behalf of the sponsors of his exploration, he called the island Hispaniola, or "Little Spain."

During their first scouting expeditions on Hispaniola, the Spaniards came in contact with Indians whom they called Arawacs. These lived as inhabitants of four small kingdoms that were spread over the entire island, one of which was ruled by a sweet-natured old queen. The Indians had an extremely peaceable disposition and hence approached their discoverers without guile. In his later years, while living on Hispaniola, Columbus praised the friendly curiosity of the Indians in one of his letters to the Spanish court: "These people are so loving, so obedient and so peace-loving that I can assure Your Majesties there is no better nation on earth, nor a better land."

Like wolves tormented by hunger, however, the Spaniards pounced on these gentle and good-hearted natives. Initially on the excuse that the Indians would not provide them with food, the Spaniards created terrible bloodbaths. For years, the Indians were persecuted, tortured and massacred. The Spaniards roamed the countryside in squads of no more than a few dozen soldiers who, heavily armed with European weapons, were more than a match for the unwarlike Indians they encountered. More than once, in honor of the Feast of the Twelve Apostles, the Spaniards agreed among themselves to each "take care of" at least twelve Indians every day. They split the heads of men, women and children as if they were cutting firewood. The Indians, who sometimes had first been forced to be baptized, could not help but wonder if they should long for a heaven in which there would also be Spaniards.

The priest Bartolomé de las Casas, who was born in Seville in 1474, accompanied Columbus on his third voyage and reported on the deeds of terror done by his Catholic countrymen in his now famous *Short Account of the Destruction of the West-Indian Lands*, published in 1552, in which he took the side of the natives. According to some estimates, by this time millions of Indians had already been killed by the Spanish in Central and South America and the Caribbean. On Hispaniola, only a few hundred of the estimated 300,000 original inhabitants were still alive.

De las Casas, an honest and fearless eyewitness, reported extensively on the events of his time. Now that the five-hundredth anniversary of Columbus' discovery has passed, it behooves us to listen to some of the things he said:

> The Spaniards attacked [the Indians'] cities and towns showing no regard for either children or graybeards. They spared neither pregnant women nor women about to give birth, but tore open their bellies and hacked everything to pieces. The Indians were attacked like lambs resting in their pens. The Spaniards took bets among each other that they could cut people in half with one blow of their swords or split someone's head or rip his intestines from his body with their pikes. They grabbed newborn babies by their two little legs and pulled them from their mothers' breasts to fling their heads against the rocks, or they threw them over their shoulders, laughing and joking all the while, and then threw them in the river, shouting, "Keep on suckling over there, dirty little rascals!" Others put mother and child to the sword and kicked them with their boots as they went. They also made wide gallows in such a manner that the victims' feet almost touched the earth and, every time, they hung thirteen Indians on each in honor and for the glory of our Redeemer and the Twelve Apostles; and they put wood and fire underneath the gallows so as to burn their victims alive. Others again they bound tight and wrapped dry straw around their bodies, lit it and burnt them alive. Others they let live specifically so they could cut

off both of the victims' hands and hang them around their necks, saying, "Go spread the news about this and tell your countrymen who have fled to the mountains." Gentlemen and nobles they generally killed in the following manner: first they made gratings of bars which they put on top of forks, then they tied the unfortunate people onto these and made a small fire underneath until they died screaming and shrieking in despair about this unspeakable torture.

I was there once when they were broiling four or five prominent Indians on such gratings. I think there were another two or three similar gratings on which people of lesser rank were roasted. They shrieked so horribly that it bothered the captain, maybe disturbed his sleep, and he gave orders to have them strangled. [But] the bailiff was even more cruel than the executioner who was burning them. He did not have them strangled, but he himself shoved a piece of wood in each of their mouths so as to keep them from screaming and he poked up the fire so he could broil them at his ease, just the way he liked. All the cruel deeds described here and innumerable other ones I saw being committed with my own eyes.

All who could flee went to hide in the mountains, climbing the steepest rocks to escape these abominable, merciless, predator-like people. But the exterminators, mortal enemies of the human race, trained their vicious hunting dogs so that they would tear every Indian who came into their field of vision into pieces in less than no time – in less time than required for the Lord's Prayer. The largest of these hounds caught Indians as if they were wild boars and devoured them.

The tragedy of Bartolomé de las Casas was that his plea for the Indians – who turned out to be unfit for labor either in the tin, silver and gold mines that were soon set up by the Spaniards or on the first plantations that were being designed – caused an acceleration in the importation of slave labor from Africa, which had already been initiated by the Portuguese at the beginning of the 16th century. Eventually, a total of at least thirty million blacks, including Senegalese, Babaras, Arandas, Congolese and Angolese, would be transported to the Caribbean islands, the United States and the Latin American countries.

* * *

In the middle of the 17th century, a rapid development of the plantation culture would turn the western third of Hispaniola into the economic "Pearl of the Antilles." Originally called Saint-Domingue by the French, after the holy Dominic (1170–1221), who had converted so many people to Christianity, the slave-driven production of the west far exceeded that of the eastern part of the island. (Haiti is an Arawac Indian word.) The colony's sugar, cocoa, tobacco, indigo, coffee and cotton contributed enormously to filling European coffers, though it was only during the 18th century that the French increased the number of slaves on the island from five thousand to half a million.

In 1697, as a result of the Treaty of Rijswijk that concluded the Nine-Year War, the western third of the island was taken over by the French from the Spanish. For dozens of years, the French had already had bases there in the form of settlements and pirates' nests along the coast that had been set up by buccaneers.

The buccaneers, or "buffalo hunters," lived like freebooters and traded mainly in smoked meat. They were noted for their long hair and beards and were generally covered with blood as a result of their work as butchers. They always carried five or six knives on their belts. For the most part, they were men who had been banned from France after having committed misdeeds and who, as the sources state, "had forgotten the God of their fathers." At the end of the 17th century, the French on the island imported some fifty women – prostitutes and condemned prisoners – for these buccaneers and pirates.

The Compagnie de la Providence et de l'Isle de l'Association, already founded in 1631, made sure after the Peace of Rijswijk that a ship arrived every day in the little Haitian ports that were developing. Louis XIII gave his royal permission for a more drastic importation of Negro slaves. The king was convinced that in so doing he was advancing the cause of Christianity because, in this manner, far more blacks would quickly become Christians than was possible in Africa. According to Louis, this was a great service to humanity, which was more important than the lowly desire for riches and money that also perhaps played a role.

As early as the first decade of the 18th century, there were eight thousand planters on Haiti, while forty small cities had been founded and fifty churches built. The twelve thousand slaves were easily kept in check – the planters had complete military juris-diction. Only in the second half of the century was a colonial government organized from Paris and set up with a governor and a lieutenant governor who had military police at their disposal. The police could be called upon by the planters in cases of unrest or riots when the usual punishments did not seem to be enough of a deterrent or sufficiently effective. However, on most of the scattered plantations – the majority of which were never visited by the authorities – the planters ruled supreme with their guns and their whips, without anyone checking on them.

The *Code Noir* (Black Code), a set of guidelines for slave owners, gave the planters the right, at all times, to dispose of the possessions of their slaves. The Code forbade the slaves to gather together at any time or place. It prescribed that fugitive slaves who were caught had to have their ears cut off. They would also be branded on their shoulders. On a second attempt to flee, further brandmarking would be done and their hamstrings would be cut. If they tried to flee for a third time, they would be put to death. According to the Code, the slaves were to be considered nothing more than the furniture of their owners. The Code left it up to the owners to judge whether slaves who misbehaved should be tied with chains as their punishment, or beaten with the whip or the rod.

The various sources that provide information on the slave trade – the most shameful chapter in the modern history of the West – still provide, unfortunately, the most divergent statistics. In any case, the annual importation of slaves from Africa to Haiti stood at a minimum of thirty thousand and a maximum of one hundred thousand throughout the entire 18th century.

Their suffering would start in Africa, as soon as they were captured by the slave hunters to be transported, chained to each other, on foot or by canoe over the rivers, to the slave ships moored off the uninhabited coastal areas. Hundreds died during these transports. Those who could no longer drag themselves along to the coast were left behind, still in their chains and a prey to animal and/or human predators.

While waiting to receive clearance, the slaves were held–or rather, stored–sometimes for days, in barracks. These were the so-called "trunks," where the heat and stench were so unbearable that here, as well, many dozens succumbed. Before being loaded into the ships, the slaves were branded and received names that were recorded in a notebook. They had to make desperate efforts to remember these names, for the French were derisively inventive when left to their own devices, assigning names such as Without-Name, When-It-Pleases-Me, Ear-Pain, Fresh-Air, Pleasant-Disposition, Good-Heart, etc. There were always some slaves who succeeded in freeing themselves by, for example, diving into the sea to end their lives. The hunters were forever complaining that, with some blacks, one had to constantly be on the alert against attempts to commit suicide.

During a crossing that would last at least forty days, the slaves were housed under the decks. For safety's sake, they were chained, and often they were not able to sit upright. When the weather was stormy, the portholes were closed. The slaves would fall against and on top of each other, wounding and soiling those next to them. At the most, twice every 24-hour period, they were given some water and beans. Twelve to fifteen percent of the slaves did not survive the crossing. Those who became seriously ill were thrown overboard alive–a total of several thousand per year. Some slaves succeeded in ending their lives by banging their heads against the walls or against each other. Numerous slaves, among these many women and children especially, died of hunger and grief during the crossing. When slaves tried to starve themselves, the slave hunters foiled their attempts by forcing their lips open with burning coals. During the periods that they were aired on deck, once every 24 hours, the slaves were forced to dance and sing.

The females were regularly brought abovedeck at night to be raped. The terrible moral dilemma thus presented to the females was that, if they became pregnant, they would be considered more valuable in the slave markets and so would receive more careful treatment while in the hands of the slave traders. One source simply states, "Especially at night, it did not matter if a face was white or black and, besides, the Negresses had ways and manners to encourage lovemaking that were much appreciated by the Europeans."

* * *

Haiti had the best slave markets in the world, which meant that the slaves who were considered to be the strongest and healthiest were sent to Cap François or Port-au-Prince, where they would fetch a higher price than in other colonies. Nevertheless, on Haiti, the mortality figures for slaves were the highest in the entire Caribbean area. One out of every ten slaves died within four years of arriving there.

Once they had been disembarked in Cap François, Port Dauphin, Môle Saint-Nicolas and Port-au-Prince, the slaves – men, women and children – were branded again when they were sold. Less than five percent of the slaves were sold as house personnel; ninety-five percent were immediately put to work on the plantations, from sunup to sundown. On Sundays, no one needed to labor, but the planters had the right to cancel the Sunday rest if they still had work to be done. If slaves then missed work because they went to Mass, they would get thirty lashes with the whip.

Up to the moment when the newly arrived slaves arrived at a plantation, some would continue with their suicide attempts. In his unequaled work, *Saint-Domingue, La société et la vie créoles sous l'ancien régime, 1629–1789* (The Society and the Life of the Creoles under the Pre-Revolutionary Regime), French scholar Pierre de Vaissière reported at least 2,500 suicides per year among the newly arrived slaves. Sometimes old female slaves provided the new slaves with poison so they could end their lives. They also administered these poisons to newborn babies if requested to do so by the mothers. Some women also had very fine needles that they would push into the brains of babies immediately after birth so as to end their lives. Vaissière reports that, on one plantation, thirty slaves succeeded in hanging themselves, all on the same day. The planter had the bodies decapitated and placed the heads as decorations in his rooms.

In 1788, the Lejeune case became famous. This planter had suspected some of his female slaves of having wanted to poison themselves (mistakenly, as was shown later). To punish them, he had them beaten so badly that they became totally crippled invalids and subsequently died of their wounds. Something that hardly ever happened did occur in this case: the other slaves who worked for Lejeune filed suit on the basis of the Black Code. Lejeune's guilt was incontestable but, upon pressure exerted by the planters, he was absolved and the slaves were punished for having filed charges against him.

One German traveler, the Baron de Wimpffen, who wrote an exhaustive report of a trip he made across Haiti before the French Revolution, noticed that almost all the slaves would curse loudly and at length as soon as it turned light in the morning. They cursed the beginning of every new day. It was also the observation of the baron that the wives of the planters were even more cruel than the men – and these men were considered the most cruel in the entire Caribbean. To his consternation, Baron de Wimpffen witnessed a white woman ordering her Negro cook thrown into the oven because he had served her a pie that was slightly burnt.

Many slaves became ill shortly after their arrival in Haiti. This was nearly always fatal. Slaves were not treated in hospitals, not even those – a few dozen per week – who lost fingers or hands performing the dangerous work in the sugar mills.

The slaves – men, women and children all together – slept in thatched huts without windows or window openings. Baron de Wimpffen noted that the stench in and around the huts was terrible. Before they could reach their huts, the slaves had to walk past tall racks on which hung whips: symbols of the sinister power of the whites. Small hooks or pellets, filed so they would be angular, were attached to some of the whips. The planters of Haiti had the reputation of being accomplished "cutters," which meant that they were able to use the whip in such a manner as to cut the skin and flesh of the slaves into ribbons.

The Black Code prescribed fifty lashes as the maximum penalty for laziness and transgressions, but the masters themselves were to judge the nature and the extent of the laziness or other transgression. They had also obtained the unwritten right to smear the wounds with salt, ash or aloe or to pour hot water on them after a few lashes. They wanted the slaves to remember the punishment so that it would serve as a deterrent for future offenses.

A slave who attacked or wounded his master was irrevocably doomed, as was the slave who repeatedly escaped. In some cases he would be roasted alive, and his flesh given to the dogs. A certain Champenoix was known as a great fancier of roasting. He was so good at it that his victims, once they had died, looked as if they had sneered in anger while in the throes of death. There were also reported cases where the masters, in disciplining their slaves, would bite them or even eat them.

Even pregnant women were flogged; however, if they were already in an advanced stage of pregnancy, they were allowed to sit in a pit while being disciplined so that they could rest their bellies. A favorite punishment of some planters was to let gunpowder explode in the anus of a slave or on the genitals of a female slave. At the end of the 18th century, the cutting off of ears had been almost completely replaced by the chopping off of the nose. The reason was that the slaves could easily cover up the missing ear, and thus their "guilt." Vaissière also mentioned the habit some planters had of locking condemned slaves in barrels and letting them roll down the hills. The barrels would then be opened and the seriously wounded or dying slaves abandoned to the dogs.

Often, the planters had their slaves disciplined by other slaves, preferably by those who had been condemned to death themselves and were allowed to prolong their lives only by serving as executioners. In Haiti's shops, torture instruments were displayed in the windows: chains, handcuffs, neck clamps, neck rings, instruments to open the mouths of the blacks, throat rings with sharply pointed teeth and thumb screws being some of the more popular items.

* * *

It was said of colonists who returned to France at ever longer intervals that they "had fallen into the Negress." In any case, the erotic attraction that the black women exerted on the planters had as a result that, toward the end of the 18th century, the population of mulattoes exceeded that of the planters on the island. Of course, the French rarely actually married black women. It could have cost them their rank, they would have had to give up their titles of nobility as a result of such racial disgrace, and they would have been despised and isolated. In fact, in 1778, the law in France ended all uncertainty in this matter by forbidding marriages between whites and blacks under any circumstances. The law was not able to forbid, retroactively, that there were already almost thirty thousand mulattoes and that approximately eight thousand female mulattoes were by then living as the concubines of whites.

A meticulous classification was put together for the close to 130 shades of color between totally white and totally black that French anthropologists had identified, and this was added to the Black Code. At the top were the light-colored *capre, griffe, mestif* and *quarteron* (quadroon), who, just like the ones further down in the classification, were all – without exception – grouped in the class of mulattoes.

Mulattoes were officially declared free on their twenty-first birthday. But, although free, there was considerable discrimination against them. They were all Catholic, because every child of a mulatto was baptized at the age of two. Afterward, the clergy did not bother to check whether they fulfilled any of their religious duties. The priests asserted that the mulattoes could simply not understand the Holy Trinity and the mystery of the Son of God. For the slaves, on the other hand, it was considered easier for them to fathom the mysteries of the Catholic religion because of their African background and familiarity with voodoo. So the priests gave regular attention to the slaves, while leaving the mulattoes to live their lives as they saw fit. By the beginning of the 18th century, Catholicism was being practiced so intensely by the slaves, who were so often desperate for solace, that it was becoming a mania. The French authorities then quickly announced a prohibition on images and chapels so that the slaves would no longer waste precious work time by praying.

As generations succeeded each other in the colony, at least half of the mulattoes had attained a strong economic position by the time of the French Revolution. Ten percent even owned more slaves than was the average among white planters, though the latter group still contained the richest individuals. The mulattoes' energy and commitment to economic upward mobility were enormous; although subject to discrimination, it had by this time become apparent that, as a class, they were second in economic power to none – an impressive accomplishment. Denied political rights, commerce and the plantations were their only avenues of improvement.

The Black Code forbade them to become physicians, jewelers, priests, judges, lawyers, officers and teachers. In churches and theaters they had to stand if there were whites present, and they were not allowed to eat, drink, dance or sing in the presence of whites. They were also officially forbidden to wear clothes or ride horses that were more beautiful than those of whites. In the cities, they could only lead their horses by the reins, not ride them. They did not have the right to file suit against whites; they were not allowed to loan money to whites, nor were they allowed to swear under oath. A separate Code had, in fact, been written providing punishments for offenses by mulattoes against whites. The manual for the judge was as simple as possible: for example, the penalty for hitting a white person was that the mulatto would have his hand cut off.

* * *

Between the Fourteenth of July, 1789, and the autumn of that year, the French Revolution blew in like a storm over the land of Haiti. The new slogans of freedom, equality and brotherhood were acclaimed by most of the planters. The rich ones, or "big whites," were waiting for the abolition of the *exclusif métropolitain,* which greatly limited their freedom of trade. The "small whites," on the other hand, were convinced that now things would finally get to the point where plantations and land ownership were going to be reapportioned. Provincial Committees organized dozens of revolutionary meetings, at which the small whites began to call already, even louder than the Jacobins in Paris, for abolition of the monarchy. Slogans of independence could be heard from the big as well as from the small whites. However, the majority of the big whites soon detached themselves from such radicalism out of fear for a second, social revolution of the small whites. The latter had rather early on begun to make attacks on big whites who were suspected of supporting the reactionary movement, and the first lynchings took place. Governor Peinier was far too weak-kneed to keep Barbé de Marbois, his lieutenant governor, who fiercely defended the sovereignty of Paris, in his position. As early as October 26, 1789, Barbé, who had received death threats, fled to France.

From that moment, the Colonial Assembly in Cap François adopted a more conservative policy of "wait and see." The word "independence" was not even allowed to be used in this Assembly. A meeting of revisionists in Saint-Marc, who called themselves the National Assembly, did declare for Haitian independence and drafted radical articles for a new social and economic policy. With one stroke, all the ports were made into ports of refuge for unlimited trade. This was done in the hope of generating favorable reactions abroad. Dozens of rich, conservative planters decided to flee to Santo Domingo, the Spanish part of the island, with their families.

For a short time, it seemed that there would be a strong reactionary move against the radicalist thinkers. This happened prior to the coming of the new governor, Blanchelande, when the officer Duplessis de Mauduit arrived from Paris with a small army that had been financed completely by the Club Massiac – the Paris stronghold of the rich planters. Although the details on Mauduit's appointment were not totally clear, it had definitely been authorized by King Louis XVI. Mauduit immediately began to prepare for a counterrevolution, and an actual civil war between the Cap François and the Saint-Marc forces ensued. Mulattoes and slaves watched, amazed and bewildered, as the whites undertook to settle scores with each other.

The mulattoes began to experience feelings of desperation. They worried that the turbulent circumstances would not allow for any serious and respectful interest in their own favorite cause: the quick granting of equal rights to colored people. After the first proposals for granting of rights to the mulattoes were submitted to the Paris Constituant Assembly in March 1790, the National Assembly in Saint-Marc immediately advised that they would never grant anything at all to "that degenerate race of bastards." At the same time, work was begun on drafting a decree adopting slavery in Haiti for all eternity. In Paris, even the Society of Friends of the Blacks, whose members included Lafayette, Mirabeau, Brissot, the abbot Grégoire, Pétion, Lameth and the nucleus of the future

Girondists, was not anywhere near ready for a serious debate about the abolition of slavery.

All that happened during the year 1790 in the General Assembly was that radicals connected with the Society of Friends of the Blacks hesitantly recommended a gradual improvement in the conditions of slavery. The Massiac Club, however (officially called the Corresponding Society of French Colonists), was able to exert much more influence. Its members managed to block all new delegations from Haiti, stating that they themselves represented the interests of the mulattoes as well.

The same fate befell the delegates from the Assembly of Citizens of Color of the French Islands and Colonies, which had been founded by the mulattoes as early as September 12, 1789. These mulattoes were a total of a few dozen very rich planters who even offered to pay off a part of the French national debt with their riches. They subsequently placed all their hope on the forceful statements being made in the Constituant Assembly by people like Charles de Lameth and Jérôme Pétion. In March 1790, Lameth declared, "I am one of the largest landowners on Haiti and I can tell you that, even if I should lose everything I own there, I would rather make that sacrifice than abandon our principles, which are based on what is right and on the respect for human dignity. I declare myself in favor of admitting the coloreds to all administrative bodies and to the National Assembly of Haiti, and I also declare myself in favor of emancipation of the slaves."

The reason for this pronouncement was probably that these future Girondists had ulterior political motives; and, in fact, they later went back considerably on their opportunistic statements, which were mainly aimed at bringing about the fall of the monarchy. However, such statements still fueled the illusions and the courage of the mulattoes.

Abolition of slavery was something that the mulattoes themselves did not even consider. This was explicitly emphasized once more by Vincent Ogé, who, in early 1790, dared to plead for the mulattoes in the Massiac Club itself. In Haiti, a mob had lynched the mulatto Lacombe, a rich planter who had drafted, in the name of the Father, the Son and the Holy Ghost, a modest petition for the granting of equal rights to his class. The same fate at the hands of a mob befell the progressive white planter Ferrand de Baudière, who had dared to plead on behalf of the mulattoes only for some reduction in discrimination.

In Paris, the mulatto Ogé, along with another, Jean Baptiste Chavannes, had come to the conclusion that radicalism would quickly take hold after all and, upon their return to Haiti, they finally dared to cast the die. In early October 1790, Ogé, who was the owner of a plantation in Dondon, sent a list of demands to the National Assembly in Cap François. In careful wording, he stated, for the first time, that giving in to the mulattoes at that moment might prevent a possible rebellion of the slaves later on. Governor Blanchelande understood, of course, very clearly what the actual message was: if the mulattoes' demands were not met, they would unleash a slave rebellion.

Ogé and Chavannes did not even receive a reply, and they eventually assembled a group of about 250 armed men and marched on Cap François. Near Grande Rivière they succeeded, at first, in surprising and routing an army detachment of 600 men from Cap François. In that city, a mad fury erupted among the population at the news that the mulattoes, among these a certain Rigaud and other men who had fought in the American War of Independence against the British, had killed white planters. Hundreds of volunteers came to enlist. Under the command of a Colonel Vincent, who was later to become a sincere admirer and supporter of Toussaint Louverture, a massive attack was launched against Ogé and his men. The mulattoes escaped to Spanish Santo Domingo, where the local whites did not hesitate for a moment but immediately delivered the captured mulattoes back to Cap François.

The French dealt with them summarily. It was to be a demonstration of revenge meant to make the "bastard race" tremble for a long time to come. For weeks, Ogé and Chavannes, as well as others, were extensively interrogated in order to force them to betray the names of as many other participants in the rebellion as possible. After having been subjected to a variety of tortures, they admitted to what they had really not been planning at all: the unleashing of a slave rebellion under their leadership. At the beginning of March 1791, twenty-one mulattoes, among these Ogé and Chavannes, were condemned to death and thirteen were sentenced to the gallows.

Ogé and the other condemned men were forced to kneel in the parochial church of Cap François with a noose around their necks and with burning candles weighing two pounds in their hands, to ask the whites for forgiveness. They were then taken to the scaffold that had been erected on the main city square and around which a crowd had gathered. First, their arms, legs, shoulders and hips were broken. Then they were tied onto wheels with their faces turned to the sky, so they could beg God to keep them alive as long as possible. When the unfortunate men were finally dead after many hours of suffering, the bodies were decapitated and the heads were placed onto poles. Not until three years later, after Toussaint Louverture and the rebellious slaves had concluded a peace accord with the French, were the heads of Ogé and Chavannes taken down from the poles and solemnly buried by order of Toussaint.

* * *

By the beginning of March 1791, anarchy among the whites on Haiti was spreading at an accelerating pace. Lieutenant-Colonel Mauduit, the royalist head of the force dispatched by the Massiac Club, fell victim in Port-au-Prince to a popular rebellion of radicals. It seemed as if the "small whites," bent on having a revolution but, at the same time, fearing for their lives if the mulattoes and slaves should rebel, furiously wanted to anticipate the killings in Paris that were to set off the Reign of Terror two years later. Mauduit and his staff were murdered, Mauduit himself knocked down in the street and beheaded as a female citizen held his feet. On May 15, the Constituant Assembly in Paris finally declared the granting of equal rights to the mulattoes. Joseph Barnave, an influential planter who was a member of both the Massiac Club and the Jacobin Club, declared in the Constituant Assembly, "You do not know the island! If you yourselves had lived there for a while, you would see things differently."

In the fall of 1791, this same Barnave would succeed in scaling back the decree of May 15, to the great disadvantage of the mulattoes and with the result that barely 400 of their total number of 28,000 profited from the granting of equal rights. By the time the Constituant Assembly presented this "dressed-down" version of the granting of equal rights, both the mulattoes and the slaves had for some time become participants in the general rebellion. Nor did a publicity campaign among the whites against every single part of the decree have much significance, although it seemed for a while that it would, just this one more time, bring together the big and the small whites into one movement.

On August 20, two days before the Night of Fire, the mulattoes, under the leadership of three of their number – Rigaud, Pinchinat and Beauvais – proclaimed a rebellion. Their conspiracy took place in the woods near Port-au-Prince and they would profit from the panic caused by the Night of Fire among the big whites in the west. This despite the fact that their rebellion was militarily much less significant than that of the slaves.

A number of the whites soon concluded an agreement with the mulattoes. At the end of September, there were even cordial demonstrations, with whites and mulattoes going arm in arm in Port-au-Prince. However, the cordiality did not last long. The small whites, who called themselves Jacobins and who nurtured a terrible hatred for the mulattoes, fueled largely by economic jealousy, seized power in Port-au-Prince and immediately organized massacres among the coloreds. Dozens of mulatto women and children were murdered before they could flee the city. At this point, the mulattoes began a policy of constantly alternating cooperation between the big whites, whose main ambition was acquiring wealth, and the rebellious slaves, who sought freedom.

◆ 3 ◆

The Rise of
Toussaint Louverture

■— ■

AUGUSTE BOREL, NICKNAMED THE "LAND PIRATE," WAS THE MOST irreconcilable of the Pompons Rouges (Red Topknots), who were adopting an ever more radical attitude toward the Pompons Blancs (White Topknots). The latter were the royalist gentlemen who counted on a counterrevolution in France or, in the event this failed, on Haiti's becoming independent. Under the leadership of Hanus de Jumecourt, they went about concluding pragmatic alliances with the mulattoes, to whom they promised completely equal rights. De Jumecourt, a rich planter and a royalist to the core, assumed that the counterrevolution in France would triumph and that the *Ancien Régime* would be restored. He argued that the planters should arm themselves and the mulattoes to the teeth in order to resist a possible slave uprising on the island. In fighting in the south, the mulattoes had already proven their ruthless sense of solidarity. Their battle hymn sounded determined indeed:

Look at those mulattoes
who used to be called cowards,
see how they fight
camped deep inside the woods.
These "Negroes" are soon going to
make you take flight!
Long live independence!

29

Borel's Pompons Rouges, on the other hand, were among the poorest riffraff of Port-au-Prince. They were the "small whites" who had already settled their score with Mauduit and then presented the people of Cap François with the challenge of their lawlessness. They felt a special solidarity with the French Revolution, particularly those principles that called for an overthrow of the first and second estates – the nobility reeking of wealth and the planters with large holdings, and the clergy. (The third estate was the bourgeoisie.) In Port-au-Prince, they founded a club of Jacobins and erected a statue of the revolutionary journalist Jean-Paul Marat. Even more than the first and the second estates, however, the Pompons Rouges hated the fourth, which, on Haiti, was that of the mulattoes. There were planters among the mulattoes who were so rich that they could offer enough money to their puppets at the French trading companies – operating in Nantes, Bordeaux and La Rochelle on the basis of imports from Haiti – to equip an entire army of mercenaries for the purpose of crushing a slave rebellion in the east and the north of the island.

The Pompons Rouges dreamt of becoming the new ruling class in Haiti in conjunction with the rise of the downtrodden in France. Removed to the lowest end of the social scale, the mulattoes and the blacks would then be made to live in unshakable submissiveness and slavery.

As revolutionary ardor spread, some of the Pompons Blancs, also called "*bossus*," or "hunchbacks" (the Pompons Rouges were called "*crochus*," or "crooks"), began to doubt that absolute monarchy would return. They also doubted that their alliance with the mulattoes, which they actually found distasteful, could be maintained. Dozens fled to the east in order to serve in the Spanish army, which, they hoped, would one day attack Haiti (this would indeed happen). Hundreds fled to Jamaica, where, in October 1791, their spokesman, the Marquis de Cadusch, suggested to the British that their assumption of sovereignty over Haiti would be welcome.

It was no coincidence that all three men, Borel, Jumecourt and Cadusch, continued to engage in intrigues for, with and against the mulattoes, who, as a moneyed class situated between black and white, were pulled back and forth between the parties. This continued until after the conquest of Port-au-Prince on June 5, 1794, at which time the Pompons Blancs were put back in the saddle to wield their former power for another four years. The British army had landed in southern Haiti toward the end of 1793, adding another ingredient to the turbulent stew with the substantial resources they brought to bear behind the Pompons Blancs in the south. Slavery, officially abolished in February 1794 by the French National Convention, was of course reinstated in British-held territory. Later, the royalists were dispersed by the victories of Toussaint and his armies of ex-slaves, but they did not disappear entirely. The last remaining representatives of the great class of planters, who were the richest people in the world during an entire century, did not finally meet their doom until after the final French invasion, in 1802. After the French had been thwarted and the free black state of Haiti had been newly founded, the Pompons Blancs were killed to the last man by Toussaint's successors.

By that time, it had been years since there was any trace of the Pompons Rouges, the red Jacobins, or small whites, who had been the most violent slave haters and sworn enemies of the mulattoes. They embarked on the road to their final destiny between 1792 and 1794. In and around Port-au-Prince, their forces, under the leadership of Borel, broke the unstable peace with the mulattoes that had barely been maintained by show of arms. Desperate, as well as furious, the mulattoes then joined up with the slaves, whom they had helped incite to rebellion. In Ouanaminthe, the mulattoes attacked a church and murdered all the white Creoles who were attending Mass there. Borel and his dragoons arrived while the bodies were still writhing in death throes among the pews and over the altar. Dipping his banner in the blood of the victims, Borel exclaimed, "From now on, this color will be the symbol of our new hope!" He then attacked the towns and plantations of the mulattoes with his dragoons. Men, women and children were first undressed and then killed. "They will only be allowed to die naked, like slaves," he said.

Borel subsequently received help from one of the many shadowy figures thrust into sudden prominence by the revolution in Haiti, a man by the name of Praloto. He had arrived from Malta together with his wife, who dressed and behaved like a man. Despite the age-old prohibition forbidding Jews to settle on the island (the French were unprogressive in this respect as well), he had been able to establish himself in Port-au-Prince during these chaotic times. Praloto felt greatly inspired by news of the Reign of Terror in France. Imagining himself the new Julius Caesar, he carried with him at all times Caesar's book about his campaigns in Gaul. Being an expert cannoneer, he acquired considerable authority among the Pompons Rouges, who were sometimes called the "Léopards," after the name of the ship in the port of Saint-Marc where they had their meetings.

Praloto soon had a chance to strike against both the mulattoes and the slaves at the same time. Incited to rebellion by the mulattoes, the slaves in the southern region had advanced up to the walls of Port-au-Prince. The city had, meanwhile, been rebaptized Port Républicain by the Pompons Rouges, who were following as best they could the examples set from the storming of the Bastille on July 14.

The leader of the slaves was the nineteen-year-old Hyacinthe, who is reported to have looked the way Jesus Christ would have looked if he had been black. To his approximately two thousand followers, Hyacinthe described the heaven that would be waiting for them after their deaths as heroes on the battlefield. There would be enough to drink for everyone, there would be no whites and no one would have to work. There would be a few white women and they would always be at everyone's disposal. Armed with sticks, axes, knives and iron bars, Hyacinthe and his men charged at Praloto's army, encouraged by voodoo priests, who promised them they would go to the African heaven immediately upon death. Deeming himself invulnerable to bullets and swords, Hyacinthe had taken as his only weapon the tail of a cow, to which he ascribed magical powers.

The blacks threw themselves at Praloto's cannons. They thrust their arms and legs into the barrels thinking that this would stop the firing of the bullets. After they lost their primitive weapons, they still had their teeth and they clamped them onto the bodies of the Pompons Rouges. One hundred of the white radicals died, their bodies ripped apart. Hyacinthe and his followers, however, died almost to the last man.

The punitive expeditions of Borel and Praloto proved to be a watershed separating the blacks and whites in the south and west. Until then, it had seemed that, in some areas, the planters in the south could remain totally divorced from all the uprisings and hostilities. Overcome now by fear and despair, these planters too engaged in a war of destruction against the mulattoes, who were the only ones to have weapons at their disposal that could truly be used to wage war.

The clash between the whites and the mulattoes ended in unimaginable tragedies. White fathers strangled the bastard mulattoes whom they knew to be their own sons. Mulattoes murdered sleeping planters whom they believed to be their fathers. Inside plantation houses, sometimes at the table, historic accounts were settled in bloodbaths. One father cut down his bastard son in front of the eyes of his legitimate children. Another father dragged his son onto the table and shouted while raising the knife, "I want to see once and for all if you have the blood of a white man." In Jérémie, on the tip of the country's southern peninsula, a planter hacked open the belly of a pregnant mulatto woman "to see if there is a little mulatto in there."

News about the Night of Fire only came to Paris at the end of November 1791. Mainly still as a reaction to what Parisians saw as "the irregularities caused by the mulattoes," Roume, Mirbeck and Saint-Léger were dispatched from France to Haiti as citizen-commissioners.

An immediate request for an army against the slaves meanwhile had been made by the Massiac club, whose function it was to promote the interests of the planters. Although his Jacobin friend, Barnave, was a member, Brissot despised this club and he made a fiery speech in the National Assembly in the hope of getting a discussion started about the granting of equal rights to the mulattoes. A discussion about slavery was not yet on the agenda.

It was only on September 28, 1791, that the Assembly had abolished slavery on France's soil. It should therefore not be a surprise that it was only on March 24, 1792, that the (renamed) Legislative Assembly issued the first decree that was to lead to general political freedom and equality for the mulattoes. From June 3, 1792, up to the days of the Reign of Terror, slave owners Messrs. Page and Brulley held dominant positions as delegates of the official

Assembly of Cap François, in the Legislative Assembly of Paris, and in the Jacobin and Massiac clubs. It remains one of the riddles of the French Revolution that, even during the period of Robespierre's radical reign, the two men were not liquidated or at least revealed as die-hards of the old order of slavery. They were believed to have been converted to the revolution in Cap François; this opinion, however, had provoked peals of laughter in the Haitian Assembly.

Page was probably the richest planter in Jérémie. During the month of Thermidor (July, as renamed by the revolutionaries), 1794, he published a militant pamphlet in two parts arguing for restoration of the old order: *Traité d'économie politique appliqué aux colonies* (Treatise of Political Economy as Applied to the Colonies). Brulley was mayor of Marmelade. As late as 1814, he managed to publish a book arguing for the restoration of slavery in Haiti!

Brulley and Page had ample opportunity, all the necessary freedom and the support of at least as many Jacobins as Girondists, as well as all the different small parties in between these two, to win the Haitian Assembly over to an incredible decree. With this decree, slavery was proclaimed for all eternity. The decree was announced in Cap François on May 12, 1792, at a time when all eyes in France were on the war being waged in Europe, defending the Revolution against Austria and Prussia.

When commissioners Roume, Mirbeck and Saint-Léger arrived in Cap François in November 1791, they made the acquaintance of this reactionary assembly. They also found that they had to deal with Toussaint Louverture, whose name had appeared for the first time in an official capacity as signer of a letter to the assembly. In this letter, the leaders of the slave rebellion offered peace on certain conditions, including a partial and gradual abolition of slavery.

Meanwhile, during a bold but undisciplined attack on Cap François, which was easily repulsed, the original instigator of the slave revolt, Boukman, was captured. He was tortured to death and his head exhibited on a spear above the gate to the city. Attached to it was a sign that said, "Head of Boukman, leader of the rebels." An eyewitness noted that never before had the face of a dead person continued to have such an intense expression. The eyes were open and seemed to shine as if attempting to give the slaves the courage to renew their fight.

At this moment the two most important leaders of the slaves were Jean François and Biassou. Jean François was a runaway slave, a light-skinned and graceful maroon who had never been treated inhumanely by his master, Papillon, as he himself admitted. The fact that Papillon's wife had often looked with satisfaction at the very handsomely built Jean François may have played a part in the matter.

Jean François used the title of General of the Negroes and Grand Admiral and Commander-in-Chief of the Royal Army. There was a persistent rumor that he had received this appointment from the Spaniards. He was supposed to have shown a letter containing his appointment as royal commander by the Spanish functionary Don Alfonso to Gros, a French provincial administrator, who left a compelling account of his stay as a captive in Jean François' camp.

According to another rumor, going around from the very beginning of the slave uprising, the rebellion was supposedly instigated by anti-revolutionary aristocrats who were preparing a counterrevolution in secret consultations with the Spaniards of eastern Hispaniola. The fact remains that Jean François and his followers were being provided with weapons and ammunition by the Spaniards more than a year before they openly chose sides for Spain (whose rulers were of the French Bourbon line).

Jean François' standard was the white of the Bourbon kings with the legend "Ancien Régime" on the one side and, on the other, "Long Live the King." On his shiny uniform (Toussaint was amazed that it fit him so perfectly, because the slave women were not able to do that kind of sewing or embroidery) he wore the Order of Saint Louis. Gold epaulets decorated his jacket, and his boots were equipped with musketeer-like spurs. Jean François was not a good horseman (one reason for his respect for Toussaint, the master horseman), but he could not get enough of his coach, which had a royal appearance. According to Gros, he had the coach ride regularly around the army camp; it was pulled by black stallions sporting lily-blue plumes.

Jean François spoke French and Spanish reasonably well and his written French was excellent. In particular, the irony evident in his manifestos and letters was later imitated by Toussaint, who was to become a truly fanatic writer. Toussaint undoubtedly saw

him as a rival with whom he might have difficulty competing.
However, when Toussaint abandoned Jean François for good, it was
not at a time when he had the upper hand in the overall situation,
so personal enmity probably did not play a role.

Even on November 28, 1794, when Jean François wrote his last
taunting letter to the French general and governor, Etienne Laveaux,
the northern territory of Haiti, between Gros-Morne and Fort
Dauphin and Mirebalais, was still totally in the hands of the
Spanish, who had the support of the slaves who had not joined
Toussaint. To an offer of conciliation from Laveaux, who had
become even then Toussaint's admired "white father," Jean François
replied:

> Your letter of the 30th Brumaire [October], Year III of the so-
> called French Republic, which I have just received, displays
> the noble feelings that you have tried to express in this writing.
> It starts out with the disgust that you and yours, as always, feel
> for people of my skin color. I have the honor of being called
> general by my friends as well as my enemies. It is an illustrious
> title, obtained by me on the basis of my deeds, my good
> leadership, my honesty and courage. But, at the start of your
> letter, you immediately take this sign of honor away from me
> by calling me emphatically and condescendingly Jean
> François, as in the wretched days gone by when your
> haughtiness and delight in tormenting us equated us with
> horses and cows and with the lowliest animals in the field. And
> now you turn up at a time when you need me. What you are
> proposing to me represents the blackest treason and you
> attempt to disguise it with deceitful wordiness. In so doing,
> you only manage to emphasize to what extent you consider
> my behavior and character devoid of all rank and worth. My
> decision is immovable and irrevocable. I will live and die for
> our just cause. This is separate from the business that the
> Spaniards have in mind here for their own benefit. All I can
> say in their favor is that they have always honored their
> agreements, without any oratory about equality and
> brotherhood. There is no need for me to address in detail all
> the minor points in your letter since I have extensively set
> forth the opinions of my countrymen in a manifesto which,

of course, you have not read because you feel that you have long since owned the truth with all those beautiful words of liberty, equality and brotherhood. Only when I see Mr. Laveaux and all other Frenchmen of his rank giving permission to their daughters to marry Negroes, will I pay some attention to your phrases about equality.

Such was, at a time when the reaction was already in full swing in France, the reply sent by a rebellious slave to a Frenchman — whose revolutionary announcement received a message in kind.

In fact, the clear and simple truth was that the French were the ones who had occupied and plundered Haiti, brought hundreds of thousands of Africans to Haiti as slaves and subjected them to total exploitation. Jean François' motto was: "If you shake hands with a Frenchman, you must make sure that you always have a knife in your other hand, behind your back." Toussaint adopted this motto from him. When Jean François wrote the above letter of rejection to Laveaux, and it was a clear indication of his strength of character, he and Toussaint had already come to a parting of the ways and had even become adversaries in a subsequent stage of the slave rebellion. But that was a long way off — during the winter of 1791–92, Toussaint was still a slowly rising star in the bands of Jean François and Biassou.

At Jean François' side, Biassou turned out to be only a very faint shadow of the voodoo high priest Boukman in terms of leadership. He had a short, squat figure and his face seemed a mask that had collected all the hatred and suffering in the world. He had indeed suffered, though he grew up in Cap François with the good priests and friars of Christian charity whose reputation was that their slaves lived the longest of all the slaves in the Antilles. That is why they were able to supply slaves to the plantations, where the mortality figures towered in high peaks above the number of births.

Biassou called himself "Generalissimo of the Conquered Territories," and he was, in any case, somewhat less bloodthirsty and rapacious than a certain Jeannot, who, in the beginning, had been the third of the trio that had been leading the slaves since the Night of Fire.

Jeannot liked to take responsibility for all the atrocities that had been committed during, and also still abundantly after, the Night of Fire. He had been terribly battered by Bullet, a planter who collected as many Negro heads as possible, in order to put them like trophies on the poles surrounding his plantations. During the Night of Fire, Jeannot had stuck the body of a white child on the tip of his standard. For days afterwards, he continued to ride around with the remains of the small corpse, using it like a personal banner. His favorite method of treating prisoners was to hang them on hooks so that they would slowly bleed to death, while he would take the opportunity to gouge out their eyes with a corkscrew. Further, he was reported to slash the throats of his prisoners and drink their blood while closing his eyes and exclaiming, "How delicious, how delectable does this white blood taste."

Indicative of his capriciousness (although Jean François and Biassou were also accused of such dealings) was that Jeannot sold the wives and children of slaves who had disappointed him in the fighting to planters and Spaniards as "bad citizens."

* * *

The army of slaves was clad in rags and tatters and, since many were only recently arrived from Africa, did not all speak the same Creole dialect. After battles and forays, the slaves would assemble the plundered goods in the camps of Jean François and Biassou. Among the items found there by Toussaint were bloody harnesses, expensive watches, mathematical tools, iron kettles, all kinds of pots and pans, porcelain sets, animal skins, exquisite diamonds, stuffed animals and skulls. But only one in three slaves had a firearm at his disposal.

They fought mostly with knives, sticks with sharp points and old sabres and swords stolen from the houses of the planters. Only the officers – and one in five slaves called himself an officer – had horses at their disposal. The slaves sometimes sat three or four at a time on the backs of donkeys and mules.

Approximately one-fifth of the train of slaves consisted of women and children. The first scene to catch Toussaint's attention when he was led into the camp of Biassou were warrior-like women who, completely drunk from the bad tafia rum, were roasting goats and sheep on the spit while singing voodoo songs to Beelzebub.

When he wrote to Laveaux later on, Toussaint did not voice his suspicion that the women were possibly also roasting captured whites.

The slaves who, like Toussaint, were good horsemen – riding without saddles over terrain strewn with broken stones, straight through bushes or, like circus performers, zigzagging through the trees – constituted an elite corps of about five hundred men. The nucleus of this group would become Toussaint's faithful guard, the men with mustaches and beards that would turn gray during the long years of fighting. These were the men who cried as they said good-bye to Toussaint in 1802, shortly before he fell into a fatal trap set by the French.

Toussaint learned many of his guerrilla tactics from the Spaniards. It was, in fact, no accident that the Spanish showed themselves to be masters of this type of warfare in their continental war against the French. However, as he later wrote to Laveaux, with whom he liked to correspond about military strategy, Toussaint owed most of his ideas to the spontaneous actions of the first slave army.

The slaves almost always avoided a direct encounter with their opponents. They formed squads of ten to twelve men who had undergone training in creeping stiff and taut close to the ground. They were preceded by the women and children, who would dance and sing loudly and then suddenly fall silent as they disappeared in bushes and undergrowth. This alternating of mass singing and dancing with sudden silence had a frightening effect. Opponents knew that the men were hiding nearby – but where?

The slaves had a small number of cannons at their disposal which they had obtained at the time of the many surprise attacks during and immediately after the Night of Fire. They did not know how to handle these, however, and Toussaint never became an expert in their use either; he was even wounded a couple of times as he tried to tinker with his own cannon.

As an attack got underway, the first squads would creep toward the firing line, staying close to the ground where they could not easily be hit. One squad would be strictly occupied in trying to put a cannon out of action, and the slaves never hesitated to throw themselves as a group in front of or even onto the barrel in order to render a cannon harmless. Meantime, another squad that had come creeping in would suddenly appear for the hand-to-hand battle. All the while, the slaves would sing warlike songs while the women and children who had survived the fire would continue with their sinister alternation of noise and silence. Again and again, new squads would appear from different directions, and this would convey the impression of superior numbers whereas, in fact, the slaves were often outnumbered.

Toussaint adopted this strategy, invented variations on it and improved it. For a decisive encounter with the enemy, he always chose a battlefield where he could have mounted soldiers and foot soldiers advance in various groups, so they would be able to link up with a few quick maneuvers.

The reports of English as well as French military sources make mention of constant confusion on their own side. In their battles with Toussaint, they always seemed to be faced with overwhelming masses. Although they eventually became familiar with his tactics, and knew he would have his columns come charging past several times successively in order to convey an exaggerated impression of strength, they would still be awed time and again.

Those blacks who were seriously wounded in these battles, where no mercy was shown on either side, were doomed to die. In Biassou's camp, Toussaint found large pits where the bodies of the dead were deposited together with those of the seriously wounded, who actually begged to be burned with the dead.

*   *   *

When Toussaint saw Biassou for the first time, he became aware of an appalling stench. It emanated from Biassou's right foot, where a terrible wound was festering and rotting. Toussaint immediately began to treat the wound and the stench disappeared within a few days, although Biassou later had to have the foot amputated after all. Biassou, who practiced voodoo, gratefully called Toussaint the "Catholic Mackandal" and appointed him physician of the blacks' "Royal Army."

At first, Toussaint was especially impressed by Biassou's audacity. His most daring raid was the one in which he had managed to free his wife, who was being held in the residence of the

Augustine monks in Cap François. Biassou and four of his comrades had disguised themselves as policemen (the French had an entire detachment of blacks serving as policemen), and the five of them had ridden into town in broad daylight. As Biassou told the story he always added proudly that, during this successful raid, he had also managed to hang a few priests while he was at it.

In camp, however, Toussaint immediately established good relationships with various priests whom he found among the slaves. They enjoyed much greater liberty than the other captured whites – a fact that, to some, reinforced the suspicion that they were scheming to use the slaves to their own advantage. Father Delahaye, the parish priest of Dondon, had drafted the first few letters and manifestos for Jean François and Biassou. He turned out to be a true friend of the slaves.

Toussaint, who knew the heroic story of the priest Las Casas, called him "the new Las Casas." In addition, he became great friends with the priests Bienvenu, Sulpice and Boucler, who would later be among those church leaders who, in 1801, declared themselves completely loyal to Toussaint's constitution and his absolute sovereignty.

Toussaint, who often showed himself to be rather sanctimonious, also used the priests for confessions. He himself chose two permanent father confessors and took advantage of his relationship with the others who heard confessions from the slaves to set up a kind of secret service.

Toussaint liked to engage in voyeurism and eavesdropping. He often appeared suddenly from behind a tree, hid in tents and huts and, later in his villas and palaces, behind curtains and highchairs before participating in conversations or receptions. His reputation for piety was never adversely affected by this behavior. Even the devoutly Catholic Marquis Hermonas, who was said by the Spanish General Cabrera to be able to summon the Good Lord off the cross with his prayers, was stunned by Toussaint's piety: "Never have I seen anyone with a purer soul than Toussaint Louverture." It was rumored that Toussaint knew the *Te Deum* by heart; the Marquis Hermonas did not know it.

The Mass could never be too long for Toussaint. He loved the High Mass with three priests, whom he referred to as "gentlemen," at the main altar, to which luster was added by constant new supplies of incense that extended the service endlessly. During the Mass, he liked to sit and memorize Latin texts from his missal. Biassou and Dessalines were extremely impressed by the rapid Latin with which Toussaint would bombard them when he got angry. To these two primal personalities, whose robust natures left little room for culture, it seemed to pack all the force of a punch.

As reported in all testimonies, Toussaint was unattractive. "Even for an old Negro," Jean François had stated, "he really is very ugly." Toussaint had a somewhat prominent chin, hollow cheeks, and his head seemed to taper into the form of a flattened pear. By the time of the slave revolt, he no longer had any teeth in his upper jaw and his face was marked by three large scars, remnants of battles. In addition, his right jaw was somewhat lopsided.

Toussaint liked to wear a madras as headgear. When he did, he looked like one of the buccaneers who achieved the first footholds in Haiti for France. Toussaint was not very agile or limber. He walked stiffly and with a slight limp that, oddly, conveyed an impression of frivolity.

The white women, dozens of whom would later vie for his favors, liked to imitate his way of walking. When he saw them doing this, he would double over with laughter. Toussaint told Bonaparte's aide-de-camp, Caffarelli, who tried to interrogate him shortly before his death in the fortress of Joux, that he had ten children, of whom seven were illegitimate. In the framework of his crusade – as dictator and as the father of his country – against licentiousness, concubinage and prostitution, he described his marriage to Suzanne Simon as a truly idyllic one. In Biassou's camp, however, both Toussaint and Father Delahaye advised the captured white women to prostitute themselves voluntarily if, by so doing, they could save their children's lives. In Limé, twenty-five women had been killed on orders of Biassou because they had refused to embrace him and his officers.

At some point, Toussaint is reported to have said to the priest Delahaye, "I understand how I must live in order to govern: by showing two faces and by nurturing two souls, the face and the soul that show who you are and the face and the soul that you keep to yourself. With one hand, I will wield the sword because it is necessary, while with the other I will openly and honestly offer friendship because it is sometimes possible."

It can be found in all the existing historical sources that Toussaint opposed atrocities and terror wherever he could. He did this first and foremost based on the conviction, maintained throughout his life, that a free Haiti would need all its people if it was to continue to exist. It would need the blacks, in the first place, but also the whites and the mulattoes who had once so terrorized the blacks.

From the very beginning, he took action against Jeannot, who once went to Mass after – as he himself proudly stated – having first washed his hands in the blood of a white man whom he had butchered in front of the man's children. Toussaint, who was enraged, obtained permission from Jean François to surprise Jeannot in his sleep and to tie him to a tree. Toussaint insisted that he be legally prosecuted. Jean François subsequently allowed Toussaint to choose the method of execution.

Faced with death, Jeannot behaved like a terrible coward. He cried, begged and screamed for his life, and said he was willing to become Toussaint's slave. He was condemned to hang on the same hook on which he had caused so many of his unfortunate victims to die.

* * *

In Cap François, terror reigned supreme during the first weeks after the Night of Fire. There were those among the whites who suggested that it would be best to exterminate all the Negroes once and for all: "Dear mother Africa will provide us with new slaves."

With an estimated one hundred thousand supporters throughout the northern areas, the slaves, however, felt strong enough to begin attacks on the large coastal cities, where they would kill or chase away all the whites. Less than a week later, the whites in the west concluded an alliance with the mulattoes, whom they temporarily sought to turn into allies.

On September 4, 1791, Governor Blanchelande received the most radical letter yet from the slaves, with the request that it be read in the Assembly. The letter said:

With due respect, Mr. Blanchelande, in order to show you that we are not only cruel but also sensible, we urgently request that you gather together all the whites from the municipalities as quickly as possible and have them withdraw to places where they can turn in their weapons. They may take their gold and jewels with them. Until our last drop of blood, we want only one thing: our freedom. We have also taken up arms to defend the King, who has been taken prisoner by the whites in Paris because he had decided to free the blacks, his faithful subjects.

The Assembly reacted with a short, jeering and crushing reply. Jean François and Biassou were ordered to immediately surrender unconditionally, together with all the slaves under their command.

The last letter from the slaves to Blanchelande and the Assembly was the first one to include Toussaint's signature. This letter was delivered by two slaves who were barely able to get away with their lives because they were threatened by planters, foaming with rage, who wanted to kill them on the spot. In this letter, without doubt drafted by the priest Delahaye, the slave leaders had already gone back considerably on their demands. They no longer asked for the immediate and total abolition of slavery, much less the removal of all whites from Haiti. They wanted three free days per week for the slaves. They wanted those slaves whose names were recorded on a list composed by them to be given their freedom; on this list there were, at first, four hundred names and later only fifty, among these Toussaint's. Eventually, an arrangement would have to be made, upon consultation, for a gradual abolition of slavery.

Roume, Mirbeck and Saint-Léger, the French commissioners who had arrived in Haiti on November 22, urged the Assembly to hold a meeting with the slaves. Toussaint also believed in negotiations: "Even if we use rocks while we talk, it is better to talk to them, because then we will have talked at least."

He was convinced that the negotiations would fail and that, subsequently, Jean François and Biassou would end up in a weakened position. Indeed, Jean François behaved in an incredibly tolerant way during the meeting with the commissioners. He even dismounted from his horse and knelt in front of the whites. He must have held the grim hope that the whites would be willing to buy off the uprising by accepting him into their governing hierarchy.

Then, a white man ran up and hit Jean François with his whip. It was Bullet, Jeannot's former supervisor, who shouted at Jean François that he would cut up his wife, who was a prisoner in Cap François, until there was nothing left of her. He even spat in Jean François' face.

After the failed negotiotions, Biassou wanted to kill all the whites then being held in the blacks' camp, but Toussaint was able to prevent this, subsequently managing to arrange a prisoner exchange instead. With himself as escort, one hundred women and children were delivered to the whites. But the French did not keep their word and Jean François' wife was not freed. At that point, Jean François humbled himself even more by offering, in exchange for his own freedom and that of a few others, to make the slaves again subjects of the whites. He did not even receive a reply to this proposal.

After this, the slaves began to plunder anew, moving far into the western zones. They even laid siege to Fort Dauphin and Môle Saint-Nicolas. Again many houses went up in flames, again plantations were destroyed, and fire storms were ignited above the burning fields of sugarcane.

Toussaint, always riding his horse Bel-Argent (he continued to call every horse he subsequently rode by that name), quickly acquired a reputation as the leader of quick and deadly hit-and-run raids. In between forays, he drilled his men in small-scale and guerrilla tactics. His most ardent follower in these maneuvers was Jean Jacques Dessalines, a gigantic fighter of about thirty, who always fought bare-chested. He had been a carpenter and, during and immediately after the Night of Fire, had taken a devilish pleasure in having people tied onto trestles or placed gagged inside chests and then sawed in half. His skin color was pitch black, but his face also had Indian features. Dessalines, who had taken the name of the planter from whom he'd escaped, had been cared for by Toussaint a few times when he was slightly wounded.

Dessalines liked to sing and dance, though he did not know how to read or write. He had a brutish sense of humor and liked to sit around and enjoy atrocities at his ease. Whenever he was ashamed, he would bow his head and close his eyes. He had boundless admiration for Toussaint and blindly supported his proposals, which he always considered decisions. When speaking to Toussaint, he hardly dared to look at him, as was also the case with Biassou. Much later, when Dessalines had become emperor of Haiti and was flinging mud at Toussaint's name and honor, he said, "It was as if he looked through my eyes into my soul."

* * *

During the period between the fall of 1791 and the spring of 1792, a rapid succession of petitions arrived from Nantes, Bordeaux, Le Havre, Brest and Rouen. Organizations of farmers, manufacturers and merchants declared with emphasis that a decrease in the wealth of Haiti, which was based on the plantation system and slavery, would rob the French of their daily bread. The citizens of Nantes presented a plea to the King on March 17, 1792. They pleaded for the transfer of at least twenty thousand soldiers to Haiti in order to restore order and safeguard the wealth. Not until the end of 1801 would this request be accepted – by Napoleon.

In the south, the civil war between whites and mulattoes continued unabated. Within one year, the whites would get the help that they had been continuously requesting: an invasion by the British. Looking ahead toward a transfer of sovereignty to the British, the southern planters did not consider it a sensible course of action to continue to produce cash crops, most of which were still going to France. They believed that if they would let the economy in Haiti collapse completely, it could prove to be the final blow for the revolution in Paris.

Governor Blanchelande also seemed to be thinking in terms of a counterrevolution. He assigned a considerable part of his army to help bring the radical "small whites" in Port-au-Prince, Saint-Marc and Léogane back under the authority of the "big whites" in Cap François. It almost seemed as if Blanchelande attached more importance to this fight for power in the wasps' nest of Port-au-Prince than to intensifying the war against the slaves.

In the National Assembly in Paris, the basic decision to grant equal rights to the mulattoes had finally been taken on March 24.

A month later, on the outbreak of war against Prussia and Austria, a delegation of mulattoes represented by Jean Raymond arrived to propose to the astonished Assembly that a corps of mulattoes be accepted into the French army. Or, if it was easier, the mulattoes could take on all the expenses of the war.

The obdurate refusal of Haiti's white majority to give in to any of the mulattoes' demands, let alone those of the rebellious slaves, was the reason that the government in Paris decided to send three new commissioners to the colony. Sonthonax, Polvérel and Ailhaud were men of a more radical persuasion than their predecessors and they were given considerably more authority. They landed in Cap François on September 17.

Léger Félicité Sonthonax, born in Oyonnax in 1763, had diligently been publishing radical political writings since before the Revolution. He was a great admirer of Rousseau and he had also contributed to the magazine *Révolutions de Paris,* where he wrote, in 1790, "We confidently predict that the day will come – and it is no longer very far off – when we will see kinky-haired Africans, who will then be judged only on their virtues and talents, participate in all our political processes and address our national assemblies."

Sonthonax had obtained a degree at the age of nineteen, writing a thesis in Latin, and had quickly become an influential lawyer. However, like his father, he also made many enemies. At the beginning of the 19th century, Pierre J. J. Tacon, a lawyer, published a voluminous defamatory work in which he revealed all the misdeeds of father and son, who (and this made matters worse) were almost certainly of Jewish origin.

Sonthonax was a friend of Fabre d'Eglantine, whose stance as an orator he imitated whenever he could. But Sonthonax was better at carefully drafting letters, articles and pamphlets than at public speaking. Although he had become a member of the Jacobin club early on, he scarcely ever came to the meetings of the Assembly. He just could not bring himself to waste his time listening to "all those boring speeches." He became a real Brissotin, that is, he played up all radical pronouncements and proposals for more liberty, equality and brotherhood, but the national interest was always of the greatest importance to him. This national interest would be served by a citizenry that worked hard, expanded its energies in the areas of commerce and economics and could, with the support of the politicians, further France's interests outside its borders. This meant, among other things, that there was no call for any kind of anti-colonialism but rather for a fierce nationalism.

In his viewpoints on society, Sonthonax was close to the Hébertists, and his friendship with Pierre Chaumette played a part in this. In any case, even before he left for Haiti as a commissioner (he had once paid a private visit to the colony), he was in word and deed a Jacobin for whom Jacobinism might have been invented; he was, in fact, a radicalist, a nationalist and an idealist to the extreme.

Compared to Sonthonax, the other commissioners did not have much influence on the course of events. Once he understood that Haiti was a vipers' nest, Ailhaud soon returned to Paris. Polvérel followed Sonthonax's lead in everything and Sonthonax let him operate in the south while he himself traveled constantly back and forth between Cap François and Port-au-Prince, the two focal points of the white politicians, while they lasted.

It was Sonthonax's intention to implement the Jacobin revolution on Haiti, slowly but very surely. To accomplish this, he wanted to have the mulattoes on his side, and drew the line with his first proclamation:

> We have come here with unlimited authority and, if necessary, we will use it to the fullest extent. As far as we are concerned, there are two clearly defined classes of people on Haiti at the moment. The one consists of free individuals against whom there is no discrimination, no matter what the color of their skin. The other is made up of the slaves. We declare that only the Assembly that was created on this island in accordance with the Constitution has the right to decide the fate of the slaves. We declare that slavery until now has been essential to the economic well-being of the colony and that neither the Assembly in Paris nor the King had the right to strike at any of the privileges of the inhabitants of this island.

Sonthonax arrived with six thousand troops, commanded by the generals Laveaux and Rochambeau. Now that the monarchy had been abolished, the Republic felt confident enough to be able to go on the counteroffensive – not only against the reactionaries, but against the rebellious slaves as well.

For a whole year, the situation had remained about the same. The various slave armies, altogether still approximately thirty thousand men operating in more or less organized units, continued to dominate large areas of the countryside in the north, from which they sometimes made attacks to the west and even to the southwest. Most of their weapons were obtained from eastern Hispaniola, where the Spanish were eagerly awaiting the war against France, which was to begin officially in Europe only on July 9, 1793. Until then, the slaves could not officially serve in the Spanish army.

The French whites' attitude toward the blacks did not change as a result of the arrival of Sonthonax, who immediately set up his own Jacobin club in Cap François and proceeded to build the first scaffolds for the aristocrats of the colony. In fact, Sonthonax was not at first planning to do anything about slavery.

Neither would the Spaniards, as the slaves knew very well. But they hoped that an all-out rebellion against the French could still be unleashed with the support of the Spaniards, who were aching to conquer the entire island, and who would at least do anything possible to irritate the French. Once the slaves had shaken off the French yoke, they would force the Spanish to grant them permanent concessions or they would settle the score with *them* as well. When, for a time, the slave leaders based their forces on Spanish-held soil, it was a pragmatic alliance in which both sides' ideology was moot.

It was obvious that the new French commissioners, with their six thousand men, could not quell the rebellion. The nucleus of the slave army was by then tried and tested in its new guerrilla tactics. The slaves ruled over territories where maroons had had their own plantations and cattle ranches for many years. Hence they were not plagued by hunger. All they had to do for the moment was to wait and see what would be the result of Sonthonax's battle against the white separatist movement in Port-au-Prince and against the mulattoes, who, under the leadership of Rigaud, were in the process of creating a free state in the south and, subsequently, against the Spanish – because that war would certainly come.

* * *

Sonthonax brought with him two generals of quite disparate character to command the French army in Haiti.

Count Donatien de Rochambeau is known to history primarily for having led the French troops sent to aid the Americans in the Revolutionary War. After Yorktown, he fought against the slave rebellion on Martinique, as well as the one on Guadeloupe, which was crushed after a heroic effort of suffering and fighting on the part of the slaves. Sonthonax was unfortunate to have been saddled with Rochambeau, who prided himself on the fact that in the Caribbean he never took prisoners of war. Every black who capitulated to Rochambeau was immediately executed by this general, who sometimes decapitated prisoners himself. He was one of the first Frenchmen to declare that there was only one solution for the entire problem: to kill all the rebellious blacks and mulattoes and then quickly begin the importation from Africa of fresh slaves who had not been imbued with the desire for rebellion.

Etienne Maynaud Bizefranc, Count of Laveaux, lieutenant-colonel of the dragoons while serving the King, on the other hand, had come to take part in the Revolution strictly propelled by motives of idealism. He was probably one of the most noble personalities to play a role on the bloody stage of Haiti. As a soldier, he had stood fast against the Prussians at the battle of Valmy and against the Austrians at Jemappes. Different from Sonthonax, for whom the national interest was always still more important than the revolutionary interest, as was appropriate for a Jacobin, Laveaux had pronounced himself to be, out of principle, in favor of the abolition of slavery. He had done so the moment he set foot on Haiti. Sonthonax was fortunate to have Laveaux as a commander of his armies.

Sonthonax liked to call the big and the small whites "aristocrats of the upper layer of the skin." He immediately had their so-called Jacobin club closed, it being a place where racist declarations were made under the guise of revolutionary speeches. Obsessed with French politics, it never occurred to Sonthonax that he might take some initiatives toward solving the problem of the rebellious slaves.

Only a few short weeks after Laveaux's arrival on the island, contacts were made with Toussaint, probably again through the offices of Catholic priests. At that point, Laveaux considered Toussaint nothing more than a rebel leader. He felt that, first of all, the rebellious slaves had to be returned to French authority. Laveaux considered it dishonorable that they allowed themselves to be supported and provisioned by the Spanish, thereby indirectly bolstering the illusions of royalist and anti-revolutionary whites. (The latter still dreamt of an independent Haiti under their leadership, which would come about once the contending parties of the moment would have eliminated each other on the battlefield.)

So Laveaux determinedly made war on the slaves, and Toussaint even remarked on the new French fury that had been unleashed. While Jean François and Biassou suffered a heavy defeat at Morne Pelé, Toussaint managed through smart maneuvering to barely escape an almost fatal French encirclement. It must also have been during this period that Laveaux is reported to have said, after yet another miraculous escape by the black leader, "That blasted Toussaint always manages to find an opening." From then on, Toussaint was no longer Toussaint Bréda but became Toussaint "Louverture," the man who could always find an opening.

Meanwhile, Toussaint and his cavalry went about defiantly dressed in uniforms they had seized from the French. In the early 1790s, it was not clear to anyone what France would stand for once the revolutionary smoke had cleared. Laveaux, for his part, was greatly perturbed the first time he was attacked, during a battle near Dondon, by slaves who were unmistakably singing a somewhat mutilated version of the *Marseillaise* as they rushed out from the undergrowth.

* * *

After the spring of 1793, the year that would bring such climactic events in France, a situation quickly began to develop that caused Sonthonax considerable anxiety, despite the fact that Laveaux seemed to have gotten the slave rebellion under control. After Port-au-Prince had finally been subdued for a while by Blanchelande, the Marquis Borel managed to disunite the city again from Cap François. Again there were lynchings and killings on a large scale among the blacks and mulattoes. Near Platon, in the south, a new uprising of slaves and mulattoes took place as well, and Blanchelande was not able to quell it. On his return to Cap François, he was deposed by Sonthonax and sent back to France. During the Reign of Terror, he would be condemned to the guillotine on the basis of Sonthonax's accusations and imputations.

In the meantime, Sonthonax was hoping that a new petition, submitted by a group of cities led by Nantes asking that an army of twenty thousand men be sent to Haiti, would meet with a positive response from the Constituant Assembly. But the Republic had its hands full just conducting its revolutionary wars. And the royalist Malouet, formerly in charge of Haiti's navy, had meanwhile offered sovereignty over the entire island to Great Britain. This offer was made in the name of the colonists on Haiti who shared his opinion – and, according to his statement, that meant practically all.

Sonthonax continued to issue proclamations on his pet Jacobin themes: persecution of priests who refused to swear an oath on the Republican Constitution; prohibition of all activities of the Dominican and Capuchin friars (with no thought given to the fact that the entire educational system was in their hands); and, of course, the imprisonment or transportation to France of anti-revolutionary conspirators.

Sonthonax's greatest challenge arrived in June of 1793. After Blanchelande's successor, Desparbes, had quickly been deposed once he turned out to be someone who gave in too easily to the Jacobins, the Convention in Paris sent a more decisive man. This general, François Galbaud, arrived with some four frigates carrying at least two hundred soldiers. The general had possessions on Haiti as well, which fact the Convention considered to be a positive portent for his commitment. However, they had overlooked the regulation that no one with possessions could become governor. When Galbaud was immediately expelled by Sonthonax, he lowered his anchors in the harbor that was filled with ships ready to depart for France with Sonthonax's prisoners. Having suddenly decided that he wasn't much of a revolutionary after all, he gave orders to free the prisoners and to assemble all the sailors (who were ready for any kind of an adventure), as well as all the anti-revolutionaries, wherever they could be found. He then sailed off with his small fleet and returned in the third week of June, his ships filled with men straining at the bit to fight for the counter-revolution.

It would become the last act of what has been called the *Léopard*, the predator that had been stalking its prey around Haiti since 1789, intent on just two goals: maintaining the state of slavery for the blacks and that of inequality for the mulattoes, on the one hand, and independence from revolutionary France on the other.

Galbaud now had an army of about five thousand men. Using a ruse, he managed to seize cannons during the night and, early the next morning, his men surprised the garrison of Cap François. Sonthonax prudently escaped, leaving the city to be defended by the mulattoes. It became the beginning of a reverse Night of Fire as, during that night of June 21, 1793, a repeat of the historical St. Bartholemew's Day Massacre took place on Haiti.

Galbaud and his men pillaged and murdered in an all-out hunt for mulattoes and blacks. Laveaux's only advice to Sonthonax was to call on the slaves for help! Sonthonax hesitated. If he should let the slaves into the city, he would lose the chance to obtain what he had aimed for – an alliance with the mulattoes. And wouldn't the slaves then attack him in the end?

It just so happened that, at that moment, there was a small slave army in the vicinity of Cap François, led by Macaya and Pierrot, which did not recognize the authority of Jean François and Biassou. Sonthonax met with Macaya in an historic spot – the very place where Boukman had sworn his voodoo oath for the Night of Fire. Macaya and Pierrot decided to invade the city on the strength of Sonthonax's promise: "You will be the equals of all other people, white or whatever color. I guarantee you the rights and privileges of all French citizens."

The slaves were in luck. As they approached the city, the cannons remained silent. The reason was that, in the middle of the night, the sailors, together with the royalists, had conquered the city warehouse containing the wine and tafia. Now, the reverse Night of Fire became the Day of Drinking.

It all turned into a grandiose, drunken party, and the blood-thirstiness of the men was overcome by their intoxication. The sailors, in particular, were no longer able to man the cannons, although those who stayed aboard their ships in the harbor were able to witness the thousands of slaves streaming down from the hills toward their doomed mates in the town. Galbaud, who was almost insane with rage, had to retreat before the black onslaught. The drunkards in Cap François suffered sudden disenchantment when the slaves burst in to hack them down with the legs of the tables at which they were drinking.

Galbaud tried to steal everything he could as he retreated, including seizing as many of the ships lying in the harbor as possible. His fleet of seventeen, now with a total of ten thousand whites, was turned into the Noah's Ark of white supremacy; for years to come, goods stolen from Haiti would continue to turn up for sale in markets in Massachusetts, Maryland and Virginia. Galbaud managed to take Polvérel's son with him as a hostage. First he went to America, where he lost his fortune. Returning to France, he later participated in Napoleon's campaign in Egypt, where he died.

Sonthonax and his government had squeezed through the eye of a needle, and he felt he had to keep his word. On August 29, 1793, he proclaimed the abolition of slavery for the entire northern part of the island. He included, however, a condition to this freedom, namely, that the slaves return to the plantations and go back to work under supervision. He also addressed the question of the revenues that would be obtained from the plantations, almost half of which, at that time, were not in operation or had been destroyed by fire and the effects of war. His solution was very simply that they would be divided four ways, with one quarter of them each to go to the owner, the state, the middlemen and the plantation workers – the former slaves. This combination of three elements – paid labor, sharing of the profits and paying taxes – would later become an example to be followed by Toussaint in his efforts to save, to whatever extent possible, the large plantations that were the vital revenue producers. Only these large plantations would someday enable Haiti to restore its economy.

* * *

One month later, the British landed in the south of the island. Balcarres, the governor of Jamaica, had received another urgent request to this end from the planter Charmilly, on behalf of the whites. By September 22, even Môle Saint-Nicolas was in the hands of the British, who were received with open arms by the whites. "Long live King George!" was shouted.

The arrival of the British was hailed also by those mulattoes who did not want to join the banner of Rigaud, who had begun to steer a pro-French course. One of their leaders was Lapointe, who would follow a policy of treasonous opportunism until he was forced to flee Haiti in 1799.

The French lines began to cave in and the British conquered Léogane, Saint-Marc, Verrette, Bombarde, L'Alcahaye and Petite Rivière. The Spanish, using Toussaint's slave army as their spearhead, also went on the offensive, and conquered Plaisance, Terre Neuve, L'Acul, Limbé, Borgne, Gonaïves and Marmelade. The French were pushed back to the small towns around the harbors on the north shore. In Port de Paix, Laveaux found himself under siege by a combination of British, slaves and Spaniards.

Wherever they arrived, the British immediately reinstituted slavery. This led the slaves to decide to abandon their siege of Port de Paix. Despite a shortage of food and water, Laveaux stood fast. He also resisted a bribery attempt by Whitelock, the British general who later was to enrich himself enormously in the occupied territories. Laveaux's words to the British general were, "The fact that you are my enemy, and seemingly so much stronger than I, does not give you the right to consider my honor as a secondary matter."

Pitt once called Haiti "The Eden of the Western World." After the British had also conquered Martinique, Guadeloupe, Saint Lucia and Tobago, he saw for a brief moment one large British West-Indian territory looming on the horizon. On June 1, 1794, while the British were celebrating a grand triumphal feast after their conquest of Port-au-Prince, the church bells in London were kept ringing throughout the entire morning.

Until that point, the military campaign had cost the British less than six thousand dead, one-fifth of whom were Negro soldiers who had been shanghaied into service. By 1796, however, the British had begun to suffer enormous losses from the "sickness of Siam"–later termed "yellow fever." Combined with the devastating campaigns of Toussaint, yellow fever succeeded in costing the British 25,000 dead by the time their expedition was abandoned.

The British soldiers complained that Toussaint's men "fought like apes and were worse than the Arabs." Eventually they all knew by heart the infamous variation on the *Marseillaise* that Toussaint's soldiers would sing at night:

Les Anglais, ces foudres de guerre
ont éprouvés nos bataillons.
Leur sang a rougi la poussière
Leurs corps ont comblé nos sillons.
Armé d'un courage intrépide
Toussaint partout guidait nos pas
Et dans l'action de nos combats
Son panache était notre guide.

Terrible aux ennemis
humain pour ses amis
Toussaint, Toussaint, reçoit nos vœux,
par toi, tout est heureux.

(The English, those great warriors
have tested our battalions.
Their blood has reddened our soil,
Their bodies have filled up our furrows.
Armed with an intrepid courage,
Toussaint has everywhere guided our steps
And in the action of our battles
His flamboyance has been our guide.

Terrible against enemies,
Humane toward his friends,
Toussaint, Toussaint, receive our gratitude.
Because of you, everything is joyous.)

◆ 4 ◆

Shifting Alliances

▬▬——▬▬

EVEN BEFORE 1793, TOUSSAINT'S CHARISMA WAS SUCH THAT, TO the slaves, he had become known as Father Toussaint. His small, elite army had grown from five hundred to five thousand men. The slaves were attracted to him for three reasons in particular. The first was that Toussaint knew what to do when they got wounded. He had a box which he always carried on his back, kept hidden underneath the jacket of the uniform that he had stolen from the French, so that some people even thought he was hunchbacked. Inside this box were simple, small-sized knives and tweezers to use in mini-operations, as well as herbs, leaves and fruit that he mixed for use as salves, ointments and pain-killing powders.

The second reason was that Toussaint projected those characteristics that the slaves realized were so painfully missing in Jean François and Biassou – authority, knowledge and insight. He alone actually made time to read the books that were looted from the homes of the whites or the libraries of the municipalities. Toussaint did not speak French fluently and his English and Spanish were very poor, but he could read all three languages, and – something that made an enormous impression – he could speak some Latin. Whenever he did not get what he wanted during a conversation with Jean François or Biassou, he would switch into Latin, and he would then get his way. He was Catholic to the point where he would sometimes act like a priest and preach or even hear confessions, which increased his aura as "Father" Toussaint. The priests remained well disposed to him because they expected that the power of the Church would one day be increased through Toussaint's patronage.

In addition to the goodwill of the priests, Toussaint had the help of two "secretaries," Pascal and Mars Plaisir, who were his most trusted confidants. He made them exercise their skills daily by copying texts from the books he lugged along with him. He himself moved into the foreground as a writer of letters only in 1793. However, in the slave camp, memos written by Pascal and Mars Plaisir were already being sent to Jean François and Biassou. In these short letters, Toussaint was often ambiguous, saying both yes and no. He confirmed agreements that had been made orally and, at the same time, allowed for variations on what had been agreed. In so doing, he cunningly created a certain degree of confusion in the minds of Jean François and Biassou, whom he set against each other in small, subtle ways. Toussaint had even been taken prisoner by both of them. Toussaint implied to Biassou that Jean François, the dandy, made fun of the uncouth manners of Biassou. Jean François, on the other hand, was given the impression that Biassou, jealous of his knowledge and manners, was deliberating how to get rid of him. The truth is probably that Toussaint did indeed want Biassou to rob Jean François of his leadership role so that he himself could, subsequently, take power by surpassing the weaker Biassou.

The third reason why the slaves were attracted to Toussaint was his regimen of discipline, which resulted in his holding out against the French when, toward the end of 1792, the slave rebellion was for a while threatened with complete defeat—partly due to the fact that the mulattoes were supporting the whites.

Toussaint subjected the slaves to hard and intensive drills. He started by having them walk, or creep and stalk, for hours at a time with baggage, provisions and weapons. In addition, he had them construct depots—log cabins or hideouts in the mountains—where provisions and weapons could be stored. Toussaint was the only one who knew the exact locations of these reinforced supply dumps, which he had marked on an area map that he had drawn up himself. In the 18th century, the French had set up a restricted military area to protect the Haitian part of the island; it consisted of a series of forts and casemates that were meant to withstand an attack by the Spanish from the east. Starting in 1793, the British, too, had built up a chain of fortresses, mostly in the central region of Haiti. But both the French and the British continued to be amazed by the raids and forays that Toussaint conducted with great speed and from the most surprising directions.

Where did Toussaint obtain his weapons, his provisions?

This remained his secret. Only after Toussaint's (partial) surrender to the French in 1802, did he supposedly entrust the map to Dessalines, who, with the help of Toussaint's system of secret hideouts, was eventually able to win the all-out war against the French.

In his two-volume book, *Mémoires pour servir à l'Histoire de la Révolution de Saint-Domingue,* published in Paris in 1820, General Pamphile de Lacroix extensively described Toussaint's new drilling and guerrilla tactics, praising them highly. In his opinion, Napoleon would have benefited greatly if he had studied and imitated these tactics. He would have had better results, especially in Russia, where lack of discipline and insufficient depots for provisions had dealt the final blow to the Grande Armée. "No European army," De Lacroix wrote, "was ever better disciplined than Toussaint's troops."

Toussaint always had his officers give commands with their pistols in hand. Obedience was therefore always a matter of life or death. It was astonishing how he had trained the blacks to take their ammunition, musket, sword, sabre and chopping knife wherever and whenever they went. As they arrived in some small town, on their way back from a campaign during which they had sometimes eaten nothing more than a few grains of corn, they would touch absolutely nothing of the provisions in houses or barns. They trembled before their officers, who managed to command the respect of their soldiers and the local inhabitants alike.

The fact that he was able to impose such discipline on his troops was perhaps Toussaint's most formidable achievement and the key to his eventual success.

Toussaint was very much aware of this remarkable feat when he told Maitland, the English general upon whom he had forced the total retreat of the British troops, "I want to emphasize to you to give total precedence to the strictest obedience and most complete discipline. These are the main military virtues that, in antiquity, made the Romans the most warlike and most powerful people in the world. And these are the virtues that, in the end, helped our armies to triumph over those of the Europeans. Only if we continue to cherish these virtues, will we continue to record victories."

Pamphile de Lacroix came to an additional conclusion. Between the years 1795 and 1798, during the period when Sonthonax also worked together intermittently with Toussaint and wholeheartedly praised his part in implementing the French Revolution in Haiti, the papers in France published scores of articles commending Toussaint. The former planters, ex-royalists and other has-beens continued to publish pamphlets against Toussaint and his Negrophile politics that they said were ruining the country, but the press totally ignored them. L. Adolphe Thiers wrote that, at the time of the Directorate, "France craved and longed for great men."

In the territory of the Greater Antilles, Toussaint Louverture suddenly seemed to be such a man. In later years, the mood changed and the Napoleonic press took a radical position against Toussaint. This only happened after Sonthonax had returned to France for good, where he began to spout his disparaging insults against the Haitian leader. He was joined in this by his successor, Hédouville, who had tried in vain to increase the influence of France by playing the mulattoes against the blacks.

During the period when Toussaint was in favor, he was praised especially for his military genius and his novel approach toward guerrilla warfare and lightning actions. Pamphile de Lacroix made it abundantly clear that he was convinced that Napoleon had internalized the image of the mythical war hero Toussaint as well as the accounts of his campaigns. These, said De Lacroix, helped to inspire Bonaparte to undertake the expedition to Egypt, which – and this was no accident – began after Toussaint had almost completely, and very brilliantly, defeated the British. Even at the time of his first campaign in Italy, Napoleon is believed to have thought of Toussaint. Said De Lacroix: "Toussaint unleashed a new dynamic by channeling the slaves' passionate longing for freedom with iron discipline." Bonaparte's desire for adventure drew extensively on the nationalist and revolutionary feelings of his own ragged masses, who longed for a promised land after almost ten years of revolution.

* * *

Even before they went into the service of Spain in July 1793, there had never been any doubt for Jean François and Biassou on whose side they should be and remain. Only a king could be the friend of the Negroes. The republicans, disguised as fowlers, proclaimed the business of the devil.

In their last letter to Sonthonax, Jean François and Biassou wrote, "We cannot suddenly accept the will of a so-called nation while, ever since the beginning of the world, we have done the will of the King. We have lost the King of France but we are now held in high esteem by the King of Spain, who has held out the promise of great rewards to us and who never ceases to support us. For this reason, we are not able to even recognize your existence until after you, Mr. Commissioner, have found another king."

Macaya, together with the mulatto Candy as deputy commander, had shown himself to be rather independent from Jean François and Biassou during the slave rebellion. He wrote something even more remarkable: "I am the subject of three kings. They are: the King of the Congo, who is the king of all blacks; the King of France, who is our father; and the King of Spain, who is our mother. The three kings are the descendants of those who, guided by the star, set out to worship the divine child. Therefore, I cannot serve a republic, because I do not want to be at odds with all my brothers who are subjects of these Three Kings."

* * *

The population of Santo Domingo, the eastern part of Hispaniola, was only 125,000, including 15,000 slaves – this despite its size being twice that of Haiti when measured as the crow flies. There were only twenty-five sugar plantations and Santo Domingo even had to import tobacco and coffee. Instead of a plantation culture, there was some cattle-breeding; but it was not an important export industry. Many slaves were house slaves and the slaves were traditionally not subjected to severe beatings.

There was often famine in the colony of Santo Domingo, partly because there were serious problems with transportation. Between the towns, all very small in size, there were no roads; people simply drove straight across the fields and estates. During the rainy season, all transportation ceased. The only export of some significance, conducted by the Spanish settlers and the mulattoes, was the slave trade. Santo Domingo served as a place of transit for slaves from Africa destined for Cuba, Jamaica and Puerto Rico. The African slave trade continued to record practically no decrease in total numbers until the spring of 1793, even on Haiti. This was accounted for by the constant stream of petitions from ports and commercial towns on the western coast of France, urgently requesting that slavery not be abolished.

Shortly after the beginning of the Haitian slave uprising, a proclamation by Don Pedro Acuna, Secretary for Colonial Affairs, was sent from Madrid to Don Joaquín García, the governor of Santo Domingo. It decreed that the leaders of the rebellious Negroes should be persuaded to go into Spanish service in exchange for their complete freedom and Spanish citizenship. "They should also be offered large plots of land so that, once they have become rich, they will keep the rest of the Negroes subject to us as slaves. We will find the land for them in Haiti."

Toussaint was familiar with the contents of this proclamation from Madrid. Practically on the same day that Sonthonax proclaimed the abolition of slavery for the northern part of the island, Toussaint addressed the people with a proclamation of his own for the first time. Its content was an extremely subtle challenge to the French, who were still holding back by limiting themselves to the northern zone, as well as to the Spanish, to whom he made clear that the proclamation from Madrid would not be heeded. For the first time, and also the last, Toussaint signed his name as Toussaint L'Ouverture; subsequently it was always spelled Louverture.

Brothers and friends:

I am Toussaint L'Ouverture.

Maybe my name is already known to you. I have taken on the task of revenging you. I demand that freedom and equality reign on this entire island. It is the only goal that I want to attain. Come and join me, brothers, and fight on our side for the same cause.

Toussaint L'Ouverture
general of the armies of the King for the public good

It was the priest, Father Sulpice, who managed to keep Toussaint thinking about the interests of the Spanish for a long time. In July 1793, he was able to persuade the black leader and several others to sign an official document committing them to enter into the service of Spain. The others were: Moyse Bréda, who came from the same plantation as Toussaint and was sometimes referred to as his cousin [or nephew], Dessalines, Belair, Maurepas (who was closest to Toussaint in intellectual abilities), Clervaux, and Toussaint's brothers, Paul and Jean-Pierre. During those days, Toussaint went regularly to San Raphael near the border with Santo Domingo in order to negotiate with the Spanish. This was done at the headquarters of General Cabrera, who had remarked that Toussaint handed out a thousand roses every day while always concealing a knife in his hand. In San Raphael, Toussaint was especially amazed to see that so many planters and royalists had already gone over to the Spanish. It looked as if he would actually become an ally of those against whom he most wanted to fight!

In San Raphael, Toussaint was decorated with the Order of Queen Isabella, and perhaps this event transported him to a higher spiritual level. On a hill in San Raphael, with the scent of incense from all the *Te Deums* and holy Masses still in the air, Toussaint experienced a vision. A black Madonna came floating in on a cloud while scattering roses, Toussaint's favorite flowers. He heard the sound of trumpets and then the black Madonna said, "You are the Spartacus of the Negroes, as was predicted by the abbot Raynal. You shall revenge the evil that has been done unto the people of your race."

Among the Spanish, Toussaint saw yet another instance of this evil. The Spanish had imported specially trained bloodhounds from Cuba which they used to hunt down the slaves and maroons who had escaped from Haiti, in order to then sell them to plantations on other West Indian islands.

In a lightning campaign on behalf of the Spanish, Toussaint

conquered La Tannerie, Morne Pelé, Ennery (where he took possession of a plantation for himself), Plaisance and, finally, the entire territory to the south of Cap François. Upon this accomplishment, Hermonas called him, "the benefactor of Santo Domingo." After a particularly brilliant maneuver by Toussaint, even the French general De Brandicourt, a famous tactician, was taken prisoner by the Spanish, as were a large number of his officers.

After this event, Brandicourt, who had remained a royalist in his heart, chose the side of the Spanish, who then assigned him and his men to join Toussaint's guards. They would certainly have been happy to hear the reply that Jean François and Biassou had given earlier to the representatives of Sonthonax, who sent suggestions to the slaves for an agreement and promised them their freedom: "We have lost the King of France, but now we cherish the King of Spain. We cannot recognize you as commissioner unless you restore the King to the throne in France. We will spill our blood only for the Bourbons."

The letter that Sonthonax received was also signed by Toussaint and Moyse, nicknamed Adonis, who served Toussaint as tactician and would become his right hand. Moyse, who had been severely battered in the past, continued to hate the planters with a fierce intensity. He suggested to Toussaint that he change allegiance and join the revolutionaries.

Toussaint had, in fact, kept quiet about what he really longed to do: turn his back on the Spaniards and their retinue of has-beens and slaveholders. The fact is that his head always prevailed over his heart and, all along, he had only had one thought, namely, to make his army as strong as possible, too strong for the Spanish to tackle and, then, for all other adversaries as well; only then would he be able to finally complete the slave rebellion.

*   *   *

On days when there were no raids to be made, Toussaint trained his four thousand infantry and eight hundred dragoons for hours on end. While Napoleon's troops were never able to march more than seventy kilometers per day during their most famous campaigns in Germany and Austria, Toussaint's armies seemed to fly, and could attain a total of eighty kilometers per day. Toussaint's soldiers could now profit from the experiences they had had as slaves, which had trained them to suffer hardships. They now had a head start because they could go for days without food. They were also able to remain hidden in an ambush for twenty-four hours without food or drink. They never felt the weight of their weapons and ammunition, no matter how hot, hungry or thirsty they were. They remembered what their Father Toussaint had told them: "If you ever again stand in front of the whites without weapons, the hour of slavery will have returned."

Toussaint now had a whole collection of uniforms at his disposal, both looted from the French and received from the Spaniards. He himself preferred to ride his horse dressed in a shirt that was open at the collar, always with a kerchief wrapped around his head, a long sword at his side and pistols in his belt. Neither he nor his cavalry needed saddles, and they were invincible in cavalry battles as a result of their being able to perform stunts like circus riders.

In the towns where Toussaint established his authority, he issued his first decrees designed to increase agricultural production. Maroons and slaves roaming around the countryside who were willing to work again on the plantations would receive statements from Toussaint in which he personally guaranteed that they would receive one quarter of the revenues in return for their work. They would not become owners of the plantations; the planters would be allowed to remain. Toussaint was firmly convinced that restoration and preservation of the plantation system was dependent on the maintenance of large enterprises. He appointed Vollée, whom he judged to be an expert on economic affairs, to strictly supervise the revenue-sharing.

The planters practically worshipped Toussaint now that they would finally have workers again, be protected against attacks, and could once more look to the future with some optimism.

Vollée also laid the basis for Toussaint's private fortune, which, in those days, had already reached the formidable sum of 450,000 francs. Toussaint used it mainly to buy weapons from the Americans, with whom he made his first contacts in the coastal areas. He jeeringly asked the Americans why they weren't coming to help the French: "Didn't Mr. Washington promise, in gratitude for the support of the French during the War of Independence against the British, to come and help the French if they should be attacked by anyone at all in their West Indian territories?"

But the Americans had one fear: that either France or England would become the dominant power in the Caribbean. Their interest was therefore in playing the two powers out against each other. They welcomed the slave rebellion as a potential hornets' nest in which the British and French would both become entangled, leading to their mutual exhaustion. The spread of such a rebellion to their own shores did not seem imminent.

On December 6, 1793, Toussaint attained his greatest triumph as ally of the Spanish by conquering Gonaïves. The town had long been defended for Sonthonax by the mulattoes, many of whom now joined the ranks of Toussaint's armies. Gonaïves became Toussaint's headquarters, where he also brought his wife and his sons. When he traveled to Santo Domingo to bring Suzanne to his new quarters, he had not seen her for two hundred days. She barely recognized him and thought he seemed to have grown younger. She marveled at the letters he was continuously writing and the respect he was shown by the Spanish. How was it possible that they held *Te Deums* for El Marito (her husband), the new Caesar, and concurred with everything he said although they often did not understand a word of his perorations in Latin? Fortunately, he was still the devout Catholic that he had been in the days of the Bréda plantation.

Biassou warned Cabrera and Don García against Toussaint's religious devotion. The result was that Toussaint himself had Biassou temporarily imprisoned once he had obtained an order to that effect from the Spanish. Once he had been freed, Biassou began to incite Jean François, who also complained about Toussaint to the Spanish, who then adopted a wait-and-see attitude.

Among the French who were fighting on the side of the Spanish, an anti-Toussaint coalition was formed with Laplace, former secretary to Blanchelande, as the key person. More and more, they took over the task of continuing to incite the treacherous Biassou.

*   *   *

The Spanish now saw as within their grasp the conquest of all Haiti. Fort Dauphin, Cap François and Port de Paix were in fact the last bulwarks of the French. A test of the two opposing powers took place in the battle for Fort Dauphin. The Spaniards had been attacking it regularly for almost a year. The town was mainly defended by mulattoes, led by Vilatte, and by Candy, who had left Jean Francois to rejoin the French.

The mulattoes were fighting with great conviction and commitment. Jean Vilatte considered the idea of subduing the French in the north and then offering to make peace with Rigaud and Beauvais in the south, who would march from their base at Tiburon. These two also had a dream: a mulatto government in Haiti that would then sell itself as ally to the foreign power who would pay the most to have its dirty work done. There was another reason still, and it went deeper than all the speculations relating to the economy and the attainment of power. The mulattoes wanted to take revenge and punish those above as well as those below them. They wanted to put the whites to work in the plantations next to the slaves, who had to go back to where they belonged.

Toussaint was totally familiar with the entire area in and around Fort Dauphin, including terrain, access roads, strong and weak points. With Belair on the left wing and Moyse on the right, he accomplished in nine days what the Spanish had been trying to accomplish for almost three hundred days: the fall of Fort Dauphin. After its surrender, he magnanimously decided to reward the mulattoes and the slaves who had fought so courageously against the Spaniards. He would let them go free, and their heroism would be symbolized by the flags of the Holy Catholic Majesty of Spain that were hoisted everywhere.

Concentrating his thoughts now on the grand-scale final offensive against Cap François, Toussaint set out for that city. On his way there, he was overtaken by a blood-spattered messenger, the mulatto Vasques, who came to report that the Spaniards had not followed Toussaint's orders. Led by Jean François, who wanted to punish Candy's slaves, they had invaded Fort Dauphin and occasioned an enormous bloodbath. All the mulattoes and all the French defenders of the town had been murdered, the women raped and the children thrown into the air to be caught on the Spanish lances.

*　*　*

The situation continued to be in flux from the moment that Sonthonax had abolished slavery. But he had done it. The Spaniards had been telling Toussaint again and again that in France itself nothing had yet been done. The only—neither radical nor shocking—measure on the part of the National Convention had been the revenue-raising stipulation of putting an additional tax on slave ships. However, the slave ships themselves, although fewer than before, continued to embark on their voyages, continued to pick up their shameful loads from Africa and continued to transport them to the Caribbean islands, including Haiti. Meanwhile, the Convention, with all those Jacobins shouting their radical slogans, did not give any indication that it would confirm Sonthonax's decision for all of the colonies governed by the French Republic.

Still, on that black day at Fort Dauphin, January 28 of the year 1794, the day of yet another massacre on the unfortunate island of Hispaniola, Toussaint made his decision to go over to the French.

But when? While Toussaint came, saw and conquered, Biassou had not been sitting still. He had obtained support from the French captains Laplace and Thomas for his plans to set a trap for Toussaint on his return for the celebration of his new conquest for the Spanish. Toussaint fell into the trap, together with Pierre, his youngest brother, who was killed, as were seven of Toussaint's officers. He himself barely escaped with his life.

Toussaint took immediate revenge. In the middle of the night, his forces surrounded Biassou's camp. He killed most of Biassou's followers and plundered Dondon. Biassou was able to flee at the last minute, with the help of some of his concubines. In Biassou's tent, Toussaint found the text of a letter that Biassou had sent to the Spanish on behalf of Jean François and all the French who collaborated with Spain and who lived in Gonaïves, Saint-Michel, Ennery, Plaisance, Marmelade and Dondon—all towns that had been conquered for the Spanish by Toussaint. Toussaint now realized that, even as he commanded the most powerful military force on the island, he could never trust his former allies. The letter read:

Toussaint is an instigator. He talks to the slaves on the plantations and tells these scoundrels that they are free. He preaches disobedience and insubordination. He wants to become the sole leader of the uprising and he has even made an attempt on Biassou's life who, thanks to the intervention of providence, was able to escape. We are completely in agreement with our loyal Biassou and, together with him, we demand Toussaint's head.

Toussaint managed to suppress his terrible anger and only succeeded in expressing his fury by "looking cross-eyed," as Sonthonax once put it. Toussaint had a real talent for feigning and he loved to express himself in letters; he immediately wrote one to García and it was typical of his style of writing. He would say both yes and no, think out loud and announce by means of intermediate steps what would be the end result.

Biassou, who enjoys having his friends – the French planters – call me an old Capuchin monk, sells slaves to the Spanish plantations, without your knowledge, I presume. He wants all the slaves on Haiti to return again to the plantations that I have conquered. The slaves are coming to me to complain while Biassou proclaims me to be a monster. I can no longer work together with such a man and such allies. It is also impossible to work together with Biassou and Jean François because they come to me in their jealousy and constantly accuse each other of the most terrible crimes. I call the Good Lord Jesus Christ to witness that I have born all this with great patience and that I want to remain loyal and faithful to Spain. Without them, I could have long since conquered Cap François for you. I am determined to continue to serve God and the King with my life.

The Spaniards García and Cabrera, who were experts in detecting cunning in between the lines, easily understood this evasive and at the same time threatening language of diplomats. Employing the leap of a panther, Cabrera made an attempt to stay one move ahead of his opponent. He had Moyse arrested while he was recuperating in San Raphael from wounds he had sustained at Fort Dauphin. And he put Mrs. Toussaint under house arrest.

Again Toussaint forced back his fury, going to García to register a protest. He succeeded in persuading García to force Cabrera to release the prisoners and to cancel the house arrest. Once his people were safe, Toussaint humbly thanked Cabrera for his solicitude and vigilance.

Cabrera replied that Toussaint could only prove that the last sentence he had written in his letter was true by going on another grandiose campaign against the French, who only needed to be given a small shove – by Toussaint, indeed – to cave in completely.

Toussaint consented at once. However, when he called together Dessalines, Moyse, Belair, Maurepas and Clervaux – the pick of his deputy commanders – they were only told that they were standing on the threshold of an important new turning point, one that would be decisive for the future of Haiti.

Toussaint read aloud the letter of inquiry he had received from the French General Laveaux, to whom he owed the name Louverture that by then was being used by everyone. The letter expressly stated that Laveaux had received the first notices from Paris confirming that the Convention had officially abolished slavery! Six blacks and mulattoes had become members of the Convention. This meant that there was only one place where Toussaint belonged: next to the French; next to Laveaux.

Toussaint requested, in a short letter, containing few concrete and many noncommittal statements, that Laveaux send a negotiator. The man, a certain Chevalier, arrived and spent a whole week holding secret discussions with Toussaint.

Meanwhile, Toussaint's lieutenants were tirelessly preparing their coup, which ended with the Spaniards falling into the trap of this new Cesare Borgia. "They think that if you open the skull of a typical Negro you will find the genitals of a woman; open my skull and you will find the three-cornered hat of a general," Toussaint remarked.

The discussions with Chevalier were the deciding factor. In Europe, France was now spearheading the Revolution for all the have-nots. Using the same battle cries, Toussaint should be able to join the slave rebellion and the French Revolution in the Caribbean both at the same time, to form one tidal wave that would sweep all of the old order away.

At the very moment that the British and the Spanish seemed to be whittling away the authority of the French on Haiti, Toussaint had to carefully consider his future course of action. He imagined the situation as in a vision, picturing the dangerous threat like a giant on feet of clay. The Spanish stakes depended entirely on him, Toussaint. The British were upholding slavery and continuing to fight against the mulattoes. But France had an entirely new and powerful weapon at its disposal, different from firearms and soldiers: a fascinating, revolutionary ideology that could turn people into fanatics. Toussaint made his choice – he would fight on behalf of France.

* * *

On Sunday, May 6, 1794, blacks and Spaniards hastened to church in San Raphael. The latter were preceded by their women in flaming red mantillas, looking like gems as they ascended the steps leading inside. General Cabrera and his staff sat down in the front pews.

Suddenly Toussaint rode up with one hundred horsemen. Trumpets sounded as he climbed the steps, with Dessalines on his left and Moyse on his right. They slowly walked the center aisle toward the altar, past Cabrera and his staff, and sat down to the side in front. Before sitting, his face looking solemn, Toussaint called out, *"Ad majorem Dei gloriam!"*

During the Mass, Toussaint followed silently along in his missal, moving his lips while reading, as always. A faint smile on his face, with his slightly protruding lower jaw, he looked somewhat like an alligator. It seemed a mystery that this extremely unattractive man, this *fatras bâton* (frail stick), had become the centaur of the savannahs.

Toussaint became absorbed in the Mass, constantly making the sign of the cross with great diligence. He took communion and then devoutly kept his hands in front of his face for at least ten minutes.

After the *"Ite, missa est"* had been said, Toussaint and Cabrera left the church, walking next to each other as if to emphasize Toussaint's prestige with the Spanish. They stopped to talk in front of the building. The Spaniard invited Toussaint to have a drink with him.

"I never drink."

"Then you have bad taste."

"*De gustibus non disputandum.*" (There is no accounting for tastes.)

Cabrera asked mockingly where Toussaint had learned all those Latin expressions. With a wide smile, Toussaint replied that he had learned them from an old Capuchin priest, whose horse he had saved. "I asked him not to give me money, but to write down for me all the important Latin phrases and expressions that Capuchin priests exchange with each other all day long."

While mounting his horse, a little stiffly as usual, almost as if to emphasize even more the mystery of his great equestrian skill, Toussaint's last words to Cabrera were, "*Jou' malhe, lait caille, casse tete ous,*" which meant something like "You might have an unlucky day, so that you could even get a hangover from a glass of milk."

Then Toussaint blew on a whistle. There was a flash of swords and sabres, and musket shots were fired. The trap had closed.

It turned out that, during the Mass, the church had been completely surrounded by Toussaint's men-at-arms. The unsuspecting Spaniards were taken by surprise when suddenly they were attacked from all sides. Cabrera, who was shouting a stream of curses, managed to flee during the confusion. He returned with more men, gathered quickly from the vicinity of the town, but his counterattack was a failure.

The San Raphael trap was another black day with yet another bloodbath. Toussaint gave his soldiers free reign and was without mercy in his revenge. If he had not arranged this trap, he and his men would shortly themselves have become victims of a coup.

Dessalines and Moyse were able to have their fling. The former re-earned his nickname "the Tiger" as he set upon the Spaniards with a fury. The latter may have truly resembled Adonis, but was known to be consumed by hatred for the whites. Women were not spared in the sudden rush to kill as many of the enemy as possible. As Dessalines proceeded, he sang voodoo songs for the god Legba: "*Papa Legba, ouvri barrière poru moins.*" ("Father Legba, open destiny's door for me.")

Toussaint subsequently marched on Marmelade and opened an intense and systematically executed offensive against his former slave allies who had conspired with the Spanish. He knew the exact composition of their troops, he knew where their provisions were stored and he knew the roads leading to their secret hideouts. Jean François and Biassou themselves barely escaped. In the case of Biassou, as Toussaint jeered, "because he always manages to find bushes behind which he can hide."

Turning to deal with the Spanish, Toussaint's elite formations of slaves proved masters of the battlefield. During the attack on Gonaïves, which he would turn into his permanent headquarters, however, Toussaint was seriously wounded in the right hip. During the following days, he neglected the wound. Since the joint itself was probably damaged, he was never able to lie on his right side again or walk without pain. He often stumbled, but he refused to use a walking stick, "and lying on one side for two hours is no problem. I never sleep more than two hours anyway," he would insist.

Toussaint conquered Gros Morne, Limbé, Brogne, Grande Rivière, Limonade and Quartier Morin, and repulsed the forces that threatened Port de Paix and Cap François. The Spanish armies began retreating all across the length of Haiti, and it became clear that only with the help of Toussaint had they been able to remain on the offensive for so long. The slaves kept going with grim determination, fighting battles day and night, and walking thirty to forty kilometers per day. Compared to the Spanish, they were much better able to withstand the heat, the many hours without water, and the mosquitoes and other insects that attacked without interruption all night long.

The Spanish were fortunate at least in that they did not become victims of an epidemic of the yellow fever which would be such a terrible torment for the British in the southern and western zones and which, eight years later, would strike a fatal blow at the French during their last campaign.

During these battles, Toussaint experienced his finest hours. He had been freed from the burden of having to play a double game with the Spaniards, and he felt as if he had wings. What a privilege it was to look forward to the end of a century that would open up such a new era of freedom and justice!

• 5 •

The Aristocracy of Skin Color

■━ ━■

ON MAY 18, 1794, WHILE THE REIGN OF TERROR IN PARIS WAS ringing in its last phase before Thermidor and the reaction sprang unannounced from the wings, Toussaint wrote his first long letter – the first of many dozens that would follow – to Laveaux:

You probably remember that, even before the unfortunate situation in which you found yourself in Cap François, I approached you several times, fervently hoping that we would be able to unite our forces and fight the enemies of France together. Unfortunately for both parties, the ultimate condition that I proposed, i.e., official recognition of freedom for the Negroes, was always rejected. Under those circumstances, I could only accept the Spanish offer for protection and freedom, at least for all those who wanted to fight in the service of the King. I accepted their offers, but I felt terribly deserted by my true brothers, the French. Now I have seen the National Convention's decree, dated February 4, 1794, with my own eyes. Slavery has been abolished; it is the most wonderful news for all friends of the human race. Therefore, let us now unite and remain united forever, while forgetting the past. Let our joint endeavor be only to defeat our enemies and, in particular, let us obtain our revenge on these false and perfidious Spanish neighbors.

On June 4, 1794, Port-au-Prince fell to the British after the work performed by a type of fifth column in the city, in which the treasonous mulatto Lapointe had participated.

Sonthonax now felt intense hatred toward the mulattoes, who had formerly made up his "Legions of Freedom." As a nationalist and a Jacobin, he remained consistent and, now, suddenly proclaimed the slaves to be the perfect segment of humanity on whom to build the revolution. In Paris, the planters Brulley and Page, who also called themselves revolutionaries and Jacobins, succeeded in casting suspicion on Sonthonax: "He was hit by the British invasion and, in despair, he abolished slavery while the slaves supported the Spaniards."

Sonthonax was recalled and Laveaux was appointed interim-governor. He would be the last one. Still, on behalf of Sonthonax but already against his own wishes, Laveaux appointed the mulattoes Vilatte, Rigaud and Beauvais to the rank of brigadier general. In the south, the mulattoes now strongly supported the French and they were again the strongest bastion in Cap François.

In France, preoccupied with its own turmoil and out of touch with events in the Caribbean, it was clear that the abolition of slavery would not be an easy or natural result of the revolution. Voltaire had pronounced his opinion that, in the tropics, at some point apes had "subdued some of our girls" and that the Negro race had thus come into existence. Montesquieu had once stated: "It is improbable that we should have to assume that those black beings over there are human, because, if we have to consider them human beings, we might as well believe that we ourselves are no longer Christians."

The Abbot Raynal (1713–1796), who had predicted the advent of a "black Spartacus" in his writings, had enriched himself through the slave trade even during the early stages of the Revolution. In 1791, he was one of the reactionary members of the Constituant Assembly. And he later called Napoleon, who would reinstate slavery, "the greatest giver of dreams ever known by the human race."

Condorcet (1743–1794), whose *Réflexions sur l'esclavage des nègres* (Reflections on Negro Slavery), published in 1781, had supplied the agenda for the Society of Friends of the Negroes, advocated a very gradual program for effectively freeing the slaves in careful stages, "that had to be regulated in accordance with strict laws."

Abbot Grégoire (1750–1831) deserves our respect as a magnanimous fighter, even well before the Revolution, against discrimination toward the Jews and the "Coloreds." But his long letter of June 1, 1791, with arguments against the colonists of the Club Massiac – who opposed all forms of equality for the mulattoes – was addressed to them and to the free Negroes – not to the slaves.

Mirabeau and Brissot, spokesmen for the Society of Friends of the Blacks, courageously proclaimed themselves to be against the slave trade and against discrimination toward the mulattoes. But they did warn, in 1790, against granting the slaves equality with the mulattoes. As long as Joseph Barnave, that soul of fire in a body of ice, was able to exert a dominant influence on the Constituant Assembly (at least until the beginning of 1792), he criticized the colonists abundantly. But he did not do much more than attempt to weaken the first carefully worded proposals for granting equality to the mulattoes. His theory was in concurrence with a conviction that, at first, had found broad support also within the Convention. It was that the colonies themselves should be left to decide how they wanted to adapt the ideas of the Revolution in their relationships with the mulattoes and the slaves. Naturally, this meant that even a gradual abolition of slavery would never have a chance. Meanwhile Barnave, typically, managed for a considerable period of time to be a member of the Club Massiac as well as of the Jacobin club. In this latter club, the principle of slavery had until the year 1793 never been a point of discussion. Camille Desmoulins had said indifferently, "Let's forget about the Negroes and our principles, as long as our citizens won't cut their bonds and their alliance with us."

After the King had finally, in April 1792, sanctioned the decree of the Legislative Assembly that made equality of the mulattoes a fact, Robespierre and Marat kept their silence about slavery from then on.

In 1789, the total number of slaves in Haiti, Guadeloupe, Martinique, Saint Lucia, Tobago and Guyana stood at seven hundred thousand. By 1791, it had increased by another sixty thousand, who were brought over from Africa as if the Revolution had never happened. The last slave ship entered the port of Cap François on July 27, 1793, more than a month after the Hébertist Chaumette and Abbot Grégoire had finally proclaimed, in a pamphlet, to be radically in favor of the abolition of slavery.

The big dilemma for the nationalist radicals was that, if slavery were abolished, the colonies would be threatened by such chaos and confusion that they were likely, in time, to be taken over by the British, who maintained or restored slavery everywhere. Furthermore, continuation of the Revolution was dependent on the radicalist citizens, who had many interests in the colonies, and especially in Haiti, that produced profits which determined almost one quarter of the French trade balance.

In his famous report on foreign policy of 1793, Robespierre accused the Girondist Brissotins of committing a crime with their, albeit careful, attempts to abolish slavery. A true believer in the Revolution was easily able to reconcile the idea of slavery with those of the Revolution. Even ten days after the official abolition of slavery on February 4, 1794, a Jacobin pamphlet was published that contained the following message: "The uprising of the blacks in Haiti is a true Vendée, which is maintained, incited and rewarded by foreign agents and the commissioners Polvérel, Sonthonax and Delpech. The blacks of Haiti have broken their chains only to plunder for booty and drink blood and to obtain a new king."

So it was no accident that Polvérel's son, who had been kidnapped in Haiti by the reactionary Galbaud, was imprisoned immediately upon his arrival in Paris in 1794; he was only saved from the scaffold by the events of Thermidor, July 27, 1794, which ended the Terror.

* * *

Was it possible for the rebellious slaves, after the French Revolution of 1789 and the Night of Fire of 1791, to look with any kind of confidence to the policies enacted by the French in Paris? It should be no surprise that Sonthonax, prompted to abolish slavery only by his desperate strategic position, did not immediately invite all the slaves to join him on the side of the French while the Convention in Paris kept silent.

Nevertheless, Sonthonax's act on August 29, 1793 – the partial abolition of slavery – certainly had put the Convention and, subsequently, the Reign of Terror under pressure. The British landings in Haiti in the fall, which followed the acceleration of events caused by Sonthonax, prompted the decisive change in the Jacobins' position. In their report to the Convention, spokesman Danton finally requested the abolition of slavery. This was done in the firm conviction that the Jacobins would be able to convince the Convention that the consequences meant a blow to England, because slave rebellions could be expected to occur in the British colonies as well. At this point, Robespierre preferred to have the reverse of Desmoulins' words attributed to himself: that the citizens and the colonies could be lost as long as the principles of the Revolution could triumph.

On February 4, 1794, the moment had finally come. The Convention received the six delegates from Haiti who had been sent by the commissioners. They were the whites Dufay and Ganot, the mulattoes Laforêt and Mills and the blacks Belley and Boisson. The Convention reacted with a standing ovation to the following words of French representative Chamboulas: "In 1789, the aristocracies of birth and religion were abolished, but the aristocracy of skin color continued to exist; now its final hour has come and the equality of all people will become reality."

The president of the Convention embraced the delegates from Haiti. The applause grew until it was deafening and almost all the members were standing on the benches. Representative Levasseur said again what had been stated already, but this time with more honesty and more emphasis: "When we drafted the concept of a constitution for the people of France, we forgot the unfortunate Negro people. Future generations will reproach us for this. Let us now correct this oversight by proclaiming freedom for the Negroes. May the president never allow the assembly to have any more discussions on this subject."

A black woman, one of the people who had regularly been attending the meetings of the Convention, fainted. Ecstatic, representative Cambon requested that this incident be recorded in the minutes of the meeting and that the woman be given a place of honor on the dais, as soon as she had been revived.

This splendid day for the Convention and for humanity ended with a ceremony dedicated to the Supreme Being, held in Notre Dame Cathedral, which had been rebaptized as the "Temple of Reason." The ceremony was led by Chaumette, the Hébertist who, at least since early 1793, had been the most radical among those agitating for the direct and total abolition of slavery. To their shame, the leaders of the Revolution had needed to debate about this for four sinful years. "Never before," Chaumette remarked, "have the people hungered so much for our religion."

History's tricks are often bizarre. It was later found that the black woman who had fainted at the Convention was a mulatto who had collapsed when she realized that her husband's possessions in Haiti would now be lost forever to the slaves. (Also, Belley would return to Haiti in 1802 as a member of the expedition of General Leclerc and there he would participate in the invasion *against* the slaves—as a member of the police.)

Sonthonax had written enthusiastically to people in Paris that, since he had abolished slavery, many planters had married their colored concubines and many creole women had married blacks. In Paris, however, pamphlets were circulated on and after February 4, 1794, that showed evil caricatures and insinuations of blacks, especially of black women, represented as animal-like beings. "Look, these will now be your fellow citizens."

Persecutions of the radical Hébertists would begin in March 1794. Next, the moderate Dantonists and then the center party of the Jacobins with Robespierre became the target. On November 11, 1794, the Jacobin Club was closed.

* * *

On December 19, 1793, a young artillery officer named Napoleon Bonaparte gained popular attention and respect with his conquest of the anti-revolutionary city of Toulon. In 1795, he saved the remnants of the Revolution during street fights in Paris, where he appeared on horseback like a surrogate Robespierre. On March 30, 1796, while Toussaint was engaged in a spectacular campaign to chase the British out of Haiti, Napoleon began his first triumphant campaign in Italy.

On May 5, 1796, having achieved a striking series of victories,

Napoleon gave a speech in Milan, in which he addressed himself for the first time not just to his soldiers and to the Italians but to the world: "People of Italy, the armies of France have now broken your chains; the people of France are the friends of all nations, so approach them with confidence."

"The people of Europe," the French historian Louis Madelin remarked, "saw with amazement how here, in a matter of days, a star began to rise that would change the image of the earth."

But it would not quite get to that point. Napoleon's adventurous attempts to straddle the globe would fail first in the sands of Egypt and later in the Russian snow. But when Bonaparte announced on December 13, 1799, a few weeks after the coup of November 9, eliminating the Directorate, that the Revolution had ended, there were already signs of the chains that he himself would put in its place.

On May 20, 1802, at a time when Haiti seemed to be subject to France again as a result of the French invasion under Napoleon's general, Leclerc, Napoleon enacted the law that restored the slave trade and reinstated slavery.

About a month later, a new law forbade all blacks and mulattoes from whatever part of the world entrance onto French soil. But that was part of the final phase of the duel fought by France under the leadership of its newly risen star against the slaves of Haiti under the leadership of Toussaint Louverture.

◆ 6 ◆

The Triumph of Toussaint

▬——▬

L AVEAUX WAS JUBILANT AS HE ADVISED PARIS THAT HE NOW HAD
an entirely new weapon at his disposal: Toussaint Louverture
with his five thousand iron fighters who were possessed by the new
ideal of freedom that had been given to them by the Convention.

He requested that smart revolutionary uniforms be sent to him
immediately. For Toussaint, it would soon have to be the uniform
of a general. He also asked for the songbooks of the revolutionary
army to be sent as soon as possible, so that the former slaves could
sing revolutionary tunes while marching, thus becoming distracted
somewhat from the heat and deprivation.

At that point, Laveaux had no idea that, eight years later,
Toussaint's soldiers would be defeating the French invasion army
while singing the *Marseillaise* and other French military songs of
the new era.

Laveaux truly did his best for Toussaint and the slaves. Many
blacks were appointed officers and, even in Cap François, the
higher ranks were quickly taken by the blacks. Laveaux was totally
consistent in applying his policy of equality; any display of racism
on the part of the whites was condemned and punished.

Laveaux also saw another problem looming, now that equality
was the word of the day. The mulattoes led by Jean Vilatte, who had
long been Laveaux's main support against Toussaint and his men,
were beginning to grumble and sulk. In their daily behavior and

use of language, they were much more racist than the whites. They could hide and conserve their hatred against the whites for long periods of time, convinced as they were that their day of reckoning would come. But they had always been able to trample on the slaves. Now the slaves were standing right next to them after first having supported the Spaniards and also after having destroyed many plantations, including some of the mulattoes' own. The mulattoes in the south, in contrast, except for a few traitors such as Lapointe, had not for a moment considered making a pact with a foreign power such as the British.

Laveaux could see things coming to a climax – a confrontation between the slaves and the mulattoes. Toussaint was confident that, if such a conflict ensued, it would end with the mulattoes having to submit to the blacks. He had made this conviction perfectly clear to Sonthonax as well.

With this uncompromising, red-haired Jacobin, who had arrived on the island with his slogan of "Slavery must remain!", Toussaint had never had a good relationship, despite the fact that he and Sonthonax were able to have a reasonable conversation in Latin. The case was very different with Laveaux, whom Toussaint gradually began to treat like a father. In person, though he had a fiery temperament, Toussaint was always correct and formal in conversation. His letters to Leveaux, however, were sometimes excessively sentimental, as if the black leader were musing on paper, finally airing his gentler feelings.

* * *

In the fall of 1794, Toussaint began a series of attacks against the British, for which he used his new weapon: the abolition of slavery. For the blacks on the plantations, the news did not come from Paris, nor was it brought by the French, but rather by Toussaint, who was the remaining principal hero of the slave rebellion now that Jean François and Biassou had been eliminated and the Spanish had become the new enemies.

Jean François left toward the end of 1795 for Spain, where he later became governor of Cádiz. He was an extremely rich man when he died in 1820, in the arms of his last mistress. Biassou fled to the United States, where he lived a life of poverty until he was murdered in a bar.

Wherever he obtained authority through force, Toussaint not only abolished slavery, always with a solemn ceremony, but he also expropriated the plantations that the whites had abandoned in their flight and bestowed ownership of them on the former slaves in partnership with the French Republic, represented by himself.

This did not mean that the whites were chased away. Toussaint protected them against the blacks who wanted to settle accounts with them, allowing them to return and again become the owners of their own plantations for a maximum one-third of the revenues. There would be substantial taxes on their output–Toussaint assessed an average rate of twenty percent–but the whites were assured that from then on the monies would be spent in Haiti instead of being sent to Paris. To some extent, this was a change in the relationship with Paris that the colonists themselves had always sought to obtain.

In all the territory that the British came to control, they maintained or reinstated slavery. At the high point of their invasion, this comprised the area between Gonaïves and Port-au-Prince, as well as extensive bridgeheads around Jérémie in the extreme west and Môle Saint-Nicolas in the extreme northwest. But there were always fifth columns working for Toussaint in the British zones and, during all his raids, he was always supported by the populace. And so he conquered Lascahobas, Grand Bois, Trou de l'Eau and Mirebalais, a key location and the most idyllically situated of all the small towns in Haiti–a tropical oasis amidst waterfalls and parks.

From Mirebalais, Toussaint wrote many letters to Laveaux, who was generally confronted with situations after they had become accomplished facts. For example, Toussaint did not pay any attention to the revolutionary edict that the white planters had to be entirely expropriated. On July 22, 1795, the Peace Treaty of Basel was concluded whereby, according to its Article 9, Spanish Santo Domingo was ceded to France. This meant that Toussaint had even more of a free hand to play against the British. In August he had brilliantly outmaneuvered the Spanish, who were engaged in their last attempt to make an agreement with the British for a joint effort in eliminating the resistance of the French. They had lost the hubs Saint-Michel and Dondon and were already in full retreat from the north when the Treaty of Basel was concluded.

* * *

The battle against the British lasted during all of 1795. Led by Williamson, Governor of Jamaica, the British twice carried out new offensives. However, they were not fighting only against Toussaint. Rigaud and Beauvais were constantly attacking from the south with their mulatto troops. Also, under their leader, Vilatte, a strong mulatto colony had settled in Cap François. In addition to Toussaint, Laveaux had also appointed Rigaud, Beauvais and Vilatte brigadier generals.

In the west, the mulattoes came up with a third ace, Pinchinat. According to what was said by his soldiers, he had killed more people than he had hairs on his head. Pinchinat strove for cooperation between mulattoes and blacks – meaning that he tried to force as many blacks as possible to join the mulatto armies. Toussaint considered this simply an attempt to acquire more power for the mulattoes and to purposely cut off all influence exerted by Toussaint and his ex-slaves.

Toussaint had become convinced, as a result of the efforts of his spies, that the Spaniards continued to support the British with food and weapons despite the Treaty of Basel. He proposed to Laveaux that they begin a large-scale attack on Santo Domingo so to cut off the entire head of the Spanish army. And didn't the provision of the Treaty of Basel entitle them to complete annexation anyway? Laveaux refused, explaining that Spain was now again an ally and that, therefore, annexations of Spanish territory would not be proper without strict orders from Paris. Gnashing his teeth, Toussaint had to put away his dream of one greater Haitian state for another five years.

Toussaint regularly showed that he could also act ruthlessly, whether the French liked it or not. He was, for example, cunning and merciless in settling accounts with Dieudonné, the leader of yet another small army of slaves, who suddenly seemed to become very influential in the west. And the citizens of Verrette, who balked at obeying Toussaint's new social programs, were told that slavery had indeed been replaced by a system based on an honest division of work, but that everyone had to work extremely hard. Anyone persisting in continued idleness could be sentenced to death.

* * *

At the beginning of March 1796, the mulatto Pinchinat began an intrigue in Cap François. He is supposed to have stated to Vilatte, an extremely handsome, power-hungry but not very intelligent man, "We must now dip our already bloody hands in the hearts of our enemies." According to Pinchinat, Rigaud's troops were ready to move in from the south. And so the first important attempt to seize power on the part of the mulattoes began.

On March 20, Laveaux mustered a parade on the Place d'Armes in Cap François. After the parade, he retired early to his bedroom. Dressed in his nightshirt and slippers, he received an engineer with whom he sat down to discuss the defense works of the city.

Suddenly the door was thrown open. Vilatte burst into the room with a dozen heavily armed mulattoes.

"Citizens, what has gotten into you?"

Laveaux was thrown to the floor and a dagger was pointed at his throat.

"Citizens, I am not armed; you are acting like murderers."

"We have come in the name of the people and we will take you to your own scaffold."

After receiving a beating, Laveaux was dragged along and thrown into a cell, where he found other members of his staff. All were tied up and had been physically mistreated. Among them was his financial wizard, Perrod.

Vilatte also had Laveaux's officers arrested. Mulattoes were patrolling the streets. In the harbor, a ship was ready to take Laveaux back to France. Vilatte had himself proclaimed governor-general and commander of all the troops on Haiti. He also appointed co-rulers, and Toussaint received a commission as well, as if he had participated in the plot.

The surprise element of the attack seemed to work in Vilatte's favor. Pinchinat had the rumor circulated that chains had been found on ships in the harbor, an indication that Laveaux had secretly been preparing to reinstate slavery. Mulattoes were running through the streets shouting, "Death to Laveaux!" But the blacks reacted just as quickly.

Colonel Pierre Michel, an ex-slave, soon had barricades erected at vital points in the city and he also occupied the most important buildings. In addition, he called the populace to action with the battle cry, "The mulattoes want to subjugate us, long live Laveaux!"

The combined actions of Michel and his men and the black masses proved too much for the mulattoes. Vilatte fled from the city and, once outside, hurriedly set up a revolutionary opposition government, which never amounted to anything. Laveaux, badly battered, was freed within 24 hours.

Toussaint had remained in Gonaïves, where he had been informed about the coup, remarkably soon as it turned out. At first, he did not react other than ordering his black generals, Dessalines, Moyse and Belair, to surround Cap François. But it has never been clearly established what role he played during the first days of the coup. Pinchinat always maintained that Toussaint knew about the coup and had wanted to join them if Vilatte had been successful. Reportedly, Toussaint wanted to get rid of Laveaux even then, despite the father complex that he so busily displayed in his letters.

Maybe Toussaint had given the impression to Pinchinat and Vilatte that he might join them; nevertheless, he really wanted to wait and see whether Rigaud would let himself be persuaded. In any case, Rigaud did not lift a finger to help Vilatte.

Only after a few days passed did Toussaint set out with his main forces to take over Cap François from Michel, who by then had settled all the problems in the aftermath of the coup. Toussaint proclaimed to the people, "Don't ever again pay any attention to what savage rebels will try to tell you. In this colony, there are more negroes than whites and mulattoes combined. And if any problems should arise, the French Republic will stand behind us as the strongest party. I am your commander in chief; I maintain law and order here."

Toussaint was embraced by Laveaux and loaded down with gifts. On April 1, Laveaux addressed what was left of the Assembly in Cap François. "We now have in our midst a savior, our only authority, the black Spartacus who, as Abbot Raynal predicted, has come to revenge all the evil done to his race. From this day forward, I shall undertake nothing without him and everything with him." This was Toussaint's triumph; he had taken power.

He was immediately appointed brigadier general and given permission by Laveaux to incorporate all the French troops into his ranks. The French soldiers fought for a place in Toussaint's honor guard, whose motto was, *"Qui pourra en venir about"* (roughly, "Nobody will be able to kill this man"). As an additional show of good faith with the French, Toussaint sought and received permission for his two eldest sons to study in Paris.

There was only one person who could still spoil things and who, in fact, did: Sonthonax. On May 11, the former commissioner arrived once more, heading a delegation sent by the Directorate. Having survived all the suits filed against him in Paris on grounds of unpatriotic and counter-revolutionary behavior, he was saved from the guillotine by the fall of Robespierre. He had been accused of being a staunch Brissotin and supporter of the military nationalism that Robespierre had classed with the imperialism of the Girondists. The fact that Sonthonax had freed the slaves barely seemed to count; and Robespierre had, instead, supported "Les Amis de la Convention" (Friends of the Convention), white Haitians who had come to Paris pretending to be radicals while they were actually reactionary planters.

Thermidor, the end of the Terror, made it possible for Sonthonax to explain how his actions in Haiti had, in fact, been correctly revolutionary without indulging either the left or the right; how he had been able to win over both the mulattoes and the slaves; and how he had greatly increased the likelihood that, now, the Big Island could be retained for the revolutionary regime.

The Directorate had decided that the best way for Sonthonax to redeem himself completely would be to act as its representative during a new assignment in Haiti. They could not think of a better test for his trustworthiness as well as for the chances that might still exist for France, now that the slaves were obviously laying down the laws in Haiti.

Among the men who accompanied him were Roume (once again), a moderate who, when cornered, could quickly turn into a yes-man, and Julien Raymond, a mulatto who had formerly hated the blacks but had developed an admiration for Toussaint.

The mulattoes had already gambled and lost their chance—now the future was Toussaint's. Toussaint, however, was extremely disappointed about the arrival of Sonthonax, who had even brought along the infamous Negro-hater, General Rochambeau, with twelve hundred troops—*Les Légions de la Liberté*. Toussaint had not forgotten that, on May 5, 1793, less than a year before the abolition of slavery, Sonthonax had drafted a new Black Code that prescribed how slavery as an institution could best be maintained.

It had been Sonthonax who had accepted the mulattoes into his armies in 1793, thus planting the seed for a fratricidal war between them and the blacks. Like many other blacks, Toussaint also believed that Sonthonax, in his Jacobin fury against Galbaud, had purposely ordered the destruction of a part of Cap François in June 1793; at that time as well, the mulattoes had been the third party that was standing by laughing. And finally, Toussaint begrudged Sonthonax that the people called him *"Père"* (Father) because the very first—limited—decree proclaiming the abolition of slavery had been issued under his name.

Sonthonax, who was a doctrinarian, had no liking for Toussaint, a man of principle and very religious. When he pretended to communicate his good intentions toward Toussaint, he used the rather ill-chosen words: "All the Negroes are only interested in jobs that will procure them enough money, rum, nice clothes and women. Toussaint is the only one with intelligence and an understanding of the true glory."

Sonthonax undertook things in the Jacobin manner. He immediately sent Vilatte, who had gotten away with a mild sentence, to France with his recommendation that the man should be executed. He then had dozens of whites arrested whom he accused of having sided with Vilatte's mulattoes. Toussaint, who had only talked to him briefly a few times, remarked, *"Doucement alle'loin, patience bat la force"* ("Easy does it. Patience wins out over force.")

Toussaint now decided to steer a twofold course. To the outside world it would look as if he were formally and faithfully following orders, while he would secretly be undermining Sonthonax's prestige. Although Laveaux was governor on paper, Sonthonax was again, ever since his return, dictating laws on behalf of the

Directorate. Hence the solution would be for both of them to disappear. Toussaint began by writing the following astonishing letter to Laveaux:

My General, my father, my good friend,

I am sorry to say that I foresee much unpleasantness for you in this unfortunate country, for which you have sacrificed your health and your family life. In the hope that you may be spared the sorrow of having to be a witness to a painful spectacle, I would greatly desire that you were chosen to serve as delegate in Paris. This would give you the satisfaction of seeing again your home country, your wife and your children. It would also save you from becoming a plaything at the mercy of the parties that are constantly opposing each other here in Haiti. At the same time, my brothers in arms and I shall have the advantage of being represented by the most devoted advocate we could possibly imagine. Yes, my general, my father, my benefactor, France has many excellent men, but where is the man who, like you, can always be counted upon to be a faithful friend of the blacks? No, there will never be anyone equal to you!

This sample of Machiavellianism alone shows how Toussaint stood head and shoulders above Sonthonax, the dogmatic politician.

While Toussaint proposed the faithful Laveaux for election to the Council of Elders in Paris, he suddenly pushed Sonthonax, who did not know what to do with this honor, into the foreground for election to the French Council of the Five Hundred. At this juncture, however, Sonthonax's position was even weaker because he had further worsened his situation with the mulattoes of the south. A mission led by the mulatto commissioner Leborgne had ended in complete failure as the result of a personal incident: Leborgne's abduction of one of Rigaud's mistresses.

The mulattoes in the south decided to disregard all orders to submit to the central authority and refused to join in the effort to drive out the remaining British.

Rigaud had the French disciplined, and ordered that their proclamations be dragged through the streets of Les Cayes attached to a donkey's ears. He had realized that neither Sonthonax nor

Toussaint was now in a position to take up arms against the south. This was the actual beginning of an independent mulatto state, in which slavery was preserved because the mulattoes treated both the whites and the blacks, who were free in name, as their slaves.

Sonthonax did his very best to project the image of being a friend of the Negroes. He fired Rochambeau, who had been governor general for a short time – during which he had immediately wanted to occupy Santo Domingo. Sonthonax also took a black mistress, Madame Villevaleix, a mulatto who later became his wife. The American consul, who had also married a colored woman, had assured Sonthonax that this would be extremely helpful in his negotiations with the blacks and that it would hence also improve Sonthonax's position with Toussaint. Finally, Sonthonax distributed two thousand guns among the blacks.

However, in December 1796, the relationship between Sonthonax and Toussaint reached its lowest point. For Toussaint this was mainly the result of one thing only: Sonthonax's proposal to deport or liquidate all the whites in Haiti and to continue on with the blacks alone. This was exactly what Toussaint did not want to do. "We are still living in the ninth century or about that time," he said, "and we need the whites in order to catch up somewhat. Furthermore, in the worst-case scenario, the whites will always be our trump card since they can be used as hostages." Toussaint added disingenuously, "Once I will have murdered all the whites and declared myself independent from France, what would your Honor the Commissioner then advise me to do with *you*?"

While Laveaux left voluntarily for Paris, where he became a consistently positive advocate for Toussaint, Sonthonax naturally continued to stall his own departure.

During "elections," which had been heavily controlled by Toussaint, Sonthonax had indeed been appointed as the person who should depart for Paris to represent the Council of Five Hundred. He had, however, absolutely no desire to go. He actually did dream of an independent black republic, of which he himself could become the president. With that powerful position as a base, he would then proceed toward negotiations with Paris about the conditions under which Haiti could be incorporated into the French commonwealth, while preserving a high degree of autonomy. Or did he still entertain the thought of setting a trap for Toussaint, whereupon he could execute a pro-French coup together with the mulattoes?

Toussaint's extraordinary new successes on the battlefield against the British, who were weakened by yellow fever, became the deciding factor. Toussaint took the initiative, acting on the principle "Shoot first, then negotiate."

Once more, Sonthonax made an attempt to persuade Toussaint to eliminate all the whites and then declare Haiti a free state; this time, he even promised Toussaint a personal fortune in the bargain. Sonthonax always denied having suggested this; but Jacques-Nicolas Billaud-Varenne, the terrorist who was to spend his last years living on Haiti, testified that Sonthonax did indeed admit to this in conversation with him. On the one hand, Sonthonax was obsessed with hatred against the Haitian whites, whom he continued to see as representatives of the pre-revolutionary regime. On the other hand, he foresaw that the blacks would definitely one day take over power completely. Wouldn't it then be best to reach for the pinnacle of that emerging power?

Once again Toussaint executed some skillful maneuvers. First, he offered his resignation, which Sonthonax could of course not accept due to the danger of total chaos ensuing. Subsequently, Toussaint staged a coup on August 16, 1797. He managed to keep just one step ahead of Sonthonax, who was at the same time in the process of engineering an intrigue against Toussaint within the army.

Sonthonax had promised higher salaries to the conspirators. Once the mutiny that resulted had quickly been suppressed, Toussaint circulated a rumor that Sonthonax, together with a new army elite, had been planning to reinstate partial slavery. Toussaint also saw to it that the whites received the message that Sonthonax had plotted to exterminate them. On August 16, Toussaint proclaimed martial law. Given the seriousness of the situation, he sent an ultimatum to Sonthonax, who did not have a leg to stand on because he had refused Toussaint's resignation. Hence Toussaint could now press forward as hard as he could.

The ultimatum demanded that Sonthonax finally depart for Paris in order to take up his assignment there. Sonthonax admitted

that he no longer had a choice. Until the last moment, he attempted
to get the people whom he had freed from slavery to support him.
While walking to the boat that would take him back to France, he
did indeed hear a few shouts of "Long live Father Sonthonax" from
among the masses lining the streets. But there was not one instance
of someone throwing himself at Sonthonax's feet and begging him
to stay. His charisma paled completely next to that of Toussaint,
who had at once ordered a *Te Deum*.

Never before had anyone seen Toussaint, who was always sober
and stiff, laugh and exult as he now did while congratulating
himself on becoming the sole ruler of Haiti. Now he had it within
his authority, first, to throw out the last of the British, and then to
chase the Spaniards out of the east.

Sonthonax's career was over at once and, in Paris, he was again
involved in all kinds of lawsuits. He fell into total disgrace with
Napoleon, whose invasion army would, a few years later, be so
scornfully beaten and driven out by the slaves whom Sonthonax
had liberated. Poor and vilified, Sonthonax died on July 13, 1813.

Had it been strictly his fault that the authority of the French
failed so miserably in Haiti or had Toussaint set a trap for him?

Sonthonax had not only had a falling-out with Toussaint, but
he had also driven away Rochambeau—who was later rehabilitated
in Paris. He had also had Desfourneaux, the general who succeeded
Rochambeau, arrested and cut off from all authority. He had driven
out General Michel, who had suppressed Vilatte's coup. Sonthonax
was hated by Rigaud and Beauvais, who, as has been shown by
letters, were even prepared during these final days to support
Toussaint against Sonthonax.

The ruses of history are complex. In 1838, years after the French
under the reinstated Bourbons had finally recognized the independence and sovereignty of Haiti, a stepson of Sonthonax became
the first representative of Haiti in Louis-Philippe's France.

*   *   *

At the beginning of 1798, the British still controlled Port-au-Prince,
Jérémie, L'Alcahaye, Laporte, Saint-Marc, Môle Saint-Nicolas,
Mirebalais, and even Croix de Bouquet, which was considered a
sacred spot by Toussaint because here there were said to have been

appearances of the Virgin Mary. However, raids by Toussaint and his generals, as well as bouts with yellow fever, had caused the British to suffer terrible losses, totaling twenty-five thousand men. All operations conducted in the Caribbean, including a difficult war in Guadeloupe, cost England an estimated total of some eighty thousand men, the greatest loss ever suffered by the British armies up to that time. And this had happened precisely at a time when so many troops were needed for the wars in Europe.

General Thomas Maitland, the last leader of what would become a military disaster for the British in Haiti, did not get a chance to develop any military counteroffensives after Toussaint began a large-scale attack on February 3, 1798. For the first time it became clear that the blacks were not merely successful in raids or guerrilla warfare or surprise attacks under cover of night. The British were now being defeated on open battlefields and in battles fought according to books of military strategy.

In a letter to Laveaux, Toussaint described one successful battle against a formidable corps of white creoles under the planter Dessources that was operating against the blacks in the west:

> The enemy had not taken the precaution to establish on the St. Marc road reserve camps to protect his retreat. I used a trick to encourage him to pass by the highway; this is how. From the town of Verrettes he could see all my movements, so I made my army defile on the side of Mirebalais, where he could see it, so as to give him the idea that I was sending large reinforcements there; while a moment after I made it re-enter the town of Petite-Rivière behind a hill without his perceiving it. He fell right into the snare, seeming even to hasten his retreat. I then made a large body of cavalry cross the river, putting myself at the head of it in order to reach the enemy quickly and keep him busy, and in order to give time to my infantry, which was coming up behind with a piece of cannon, to join me. This maneuver succeeded marvelously. I had taken the precaution to send a four-inch piece of cannon from Petite-Rivière to the Moreau plantation at Détroit in order to batter the enemy on his right flank during his passage. While I harassed him with my cavalry, my infantry advanced at great speed with the piece of cannon. As soon as it reached me I

made two columns pass to right and to left to take the enemy
in flank. As soon as these two columns arrived within pistol
shot, I served the enemy in true republican fashion.

He continued his way, showing all the time a brave front.
But the first cannon shot that I caused to be fired among his
men – and which did a great deal of damage – made him abandon first a wagon and then a piece of cannon. I redoubled the
charge and afterwards I captured the other three pieces of
cannon, two wagons full of ammunition and seven others full
of wounded, who were promptly sent to the rear. Then it was
that the enemy began to fly in the greatest disorder, only for
those at the head of the retreat to find themselves right in the
mouth of the piece of cannon that I had posted at Détroit on
the Moreau plantation. And when the enemy saw himself
taken in front, behind and on all sides, that fine fellow, the
impertinent Dessources, jumped off his horse and threw
himself into the brushwood with the debris of his army, calling
out, "Every man for himself."

Rain and darkness caused me to discontinue the pursuit.
This battle lasted from eleven in the morning to six in the
evening and cost me only six dead and as many wounded. I
have strewn the road with corpses for the distance of more
than a league. My victory has been most complete, and if the
celebrated Dessources is lucky enough to re-enter St. Marc it
will be without cannon, without baggage, in short what is
called with neither drum nor trumpet. He has lost everything,
even honor, if vile royalists are capable of having any. He will
remember for a long time the republican lesson that I have
taught him.

I have pleasure in transmitting to you, General, the praises
which are due to Dessalines. . . . The battalion of the sans
culottes, above all, which saw fire for the second time, showed
the greatest courage.

On April 14, 1798, there arrived for Toussaint the great day on
which he would make his triumphal entry into Port-au-Prince. It
happened to rain that day and it was a constant, hard, tropical rain.
But the entire population was out on the streets. A procession of
the clergy, headed by bridesmaids, came out to meet Toussaint.

Flogging of a female slave by a mulatto.

Flogging of a slave by another slave while the owner watches; a third slave pours something into a saucer that will be rubbed into the wounds of the disciplined slave to cause him agony.

Drawing made by a German colonist during the first few days after the
Night of Fire, when the slaves performed violent acts of revenge.

Whites massacring slaves in Cap François; in the background, the columns of smoke that rose up during the Night of Fire.

Above, left: Toussaint Louverture after his appointment as general by the French. *Right:* English print of Toussaint as a self-assured negotiator.

Below, left: An officer and two soldiers of the slave army. *Right:* Portrait by Anne-Louis Girodet-Triosin of Jean-Baptiste Belley, the member of the delegation from Haiti who, in Paris in 1794, received the official decree announcing the abolition of slavery. It is tragic indeed that he participated in the French invasion of Haiti in 1802, during which he lost his life.

Toussaint negotiating with the British in 1798. The print is by
Francisque-Martin-François Grenier de Saint-Martin, one of the French
painter Louis David's students.

Top: Antonio Canova's famous sculpture of Pauline Bonaparte as "Venus Victorious." *Bottom:* General Charles-Victor Leclerc, shortly before his appointment as commander of the French invasion army. The resemblance to Napoleon is remarkable.

Toussaint Louverture in a flattering pose on a Haitian stamp dating from 1801.

Napoleon as First Consul in 1803, the year of Toussaint's death.

Despite the entreaties of his wife and children, Toussaint accepts the treacherous invitation of the French that will result in his arrest and deportation.

The kidnapping of Toussaint Louverture, who is about to draw his sabre.

Battle in the Serpents' Ravine between Rochambeau's troops and those of Toussaint Louverture.

Facing page, top: Battle during the last slave war, in a sketch by D. P. Raffet. *Bottom:* Drawing by the Pole Suchodolski of a battle between Frenchmen and slaves in 1803.

Toussaint Louverture as he lies dying in his servant's arms. Toussaint actually died alone. His secretary had left Fort Joux several months before his death.

Mass executions of Frenchmen near Cap François, early in 1804.
Illustration from the eyewitness report by Marcus Rainsford in *Historical
Account of the Black Empire of Hayti,* published in London in 1805.

Above: Fort Joux in the Jura Mountains.
Below, left: Dessalines, first emperor of Haiti, in gala uniform.
Right: Henri Christophe, who rose from slave, cook, innkeeper and rebel to become king of Haiti (1811–1820).

Some people cheered him as King of Haiti. Whites, mulattoes and blacks knelt along the road for him and, as he walked, incense was burnt around him as if he were a god. The white bridesmaids, dressed in snow white, sprinkled his path with flowers. It had even been proposed that he would walk underneath a canopy and next to a priest, who would hold up the effigy of Our Lord; but Toussaint had drawn the line there. Devout, his features stiffened by emotion, Toussaint walked behind the canopy until the procession reached the church. There, the *Te Deum* was sung, exclusively for him this time. Toussaint was wearing a wig with short tails that seemed to dance along ever more enthusiastically during the singing of the hymn. He had donned his most beautiful French uniform, displaying signs of the highest rank.

Bernard Borgella, the mayor of Port-au-Prince, was a planter who had only recently been a collaborator of the British. He now handed Toussaint a medallion on behalf of the planters, including the infamous Marquis de Caradeu, an incredibly rich planter who used to throw uncooperative slaves into his ovens while they were still alive. There was an inscription on the medallion reading, "Second Only to God!" These were the words that Toussaint had once said to Laveaux to show his love and admiration. Now he himself had become the man who was second only to God and who must, could and would save Haiti for the blacks, for the whites, for the mulattoes. For peace and for the future!

* * *

A final British attack led by John Churchill ended miserably because by this time Toussaint's army had also learned the tactics of defense. General Maitland decided to execute a change in policy on behalf of the Empire. Toussaint had proclaimed an amnesty for all whites who had collaborated, but not fought, against him. This had started a great pro-Toussaint movement that could no longer be halted.

After discussions with Toussaint that were straight to the point, Maitland was glad to obtain an agreement that, at a time when France and England were still at war with each other, almost resembled a peace treaty. British ships were granted practically unlimited access to all of Haiti's ports, and a trade agreement was concluded that provided for extensive transport of food and weapons to Haiti. Later, when the British had stopped supplying weapons, Toussaint speeded up negotiations with the Americans, who had already participated in the British treaty with Toussaint on some minor points. In any case, in a matter of a few weeks eight times as many American ships as French were moored in the harbors of Haiti. Six months later, the Americans broadened their treaty with Toussaint, which allowed him to buy large quantities of guns. The famine that threatened the western part of Haiti for a short time in 1798 was completely eliminated by the import of American food. It was agreed that, in the framework of this pro-Toussaint policy, the British would also withdraw from Môle Saint-Nicolas and Jérémie. Toussaint also concluded non-aggression pacts with both the British and the Americans.

Toussaint, for his part, consented to refrain from undertaking anything in foreign politics without consulting the British. This allayed their fear that Toussaint would use his own example to begin meddling in other British colonies in the Caribbean. Ten thousand Negro slaves, who had been transferred by the British from Haiti to other colonies, especially Jamaica, were returned to Haiti as free people. They marched into Môle Saint-Nicolas just as Toussaint was making his solemn entrance there among the passionately cheering townspeople.

The British, now mistaking Toussaint for an ally, prematurely showered presents upon him. First, they had underestimated Toussaint the soldier; now they were underestimating Toussaint the politician, who would never become a vassal or satellite of England. The British even offered to crown Toussaint King of Haiti, stating that King George III was willing to give his approval. But Toussaint refused, saying, "Don't forget that I represent France and that the Revolution shall always continue to be a bond for us with the mother country."

In the end, unable to bribe Toussaint, the British agreed to give up their last toeholds in Haiti and, with very little regret, evacuated their army. Largely due to yellow fever, but also due to the skill and determination of the Haitian armies of black slaves, the British during this period suffered casualties on a scale that would not be matched in their history until World War I.

* * *

How did this mother country, the official French authorities, the Directorate, react to these negotiations of Toussaint with England and the United States, conducted as if he were at the very least his own Secretary of State?

Roume, who had already lived about ten difficult years on Haiti, had issued orders to arrest Maitland when Toussaint was first invited by Maitland to participate in negotiations. Who could have carried out such an order, and in such a climate of deceit how could Roume have prevented his own arrest?

While Toussaint was getting down to brass tacks with the British, no objections were heard from Roume. And he definitely did not object when, to his astonishment and that of many of the French, he saw the strongest army in the world withdrawing from its main positions. Objections *were* made, however, and a last strong French counteroffensive was initiated by a General Hédouville, who had landed in Haiti with a small staff, having been sent by the Directorate as another great hope from their roster of would-be dictators.

Born in 1755, Gabriel Marie Théodore, Count of Hédouville, was sent as special agent by the Directorate and they had complete confidence in him. Hédouville, who had almost lost his head under the regime of Robespierre, was one of the men who had brought the rebellious French region of Vendée under control. He had led the infernal columns of soldiers and was partly responsible for the war of terror against the army of rebellious peasants there, who had fought for the King and for Catholicism. This war had cost the lives of many thousands of innocent women and children. Of all the generals who had operated in the Vendée, Hédouville's reputation was greatest as a negotiator and administrator. After the disaster in Haiti with the radical hothead Sonthonax, it was hoped that this composed organizer, who could be rough if necessary, would restore the French hold on the island, all of which supposedly now belonged to France. He should be able to turn that "ugly old Negro," who was doing as he pleased over there, back into a follower of the Directorate.

Roume had warned Hédouville about Toussaint, "He is a man

of exceptional qualities and extremely intelligent."

From the very beginning, however, Hédouville openly acknowledged that he considered Toussaint nothing but a monkey with a cloth wound around its head. And the people the French count had brought along as his staff were just as unashamedly racist. Toussaint had already become suspicious when Hédouville, upon his arrival in the spring of 1798, had made contact with Rigaud. This happened while he had also invited Toussaint for a meeting during which the black leader had been told it would be all right for him to arrest Rigaud!

Certainly, the thing to do was to divide and conquer; but couldn't this intriguer Hédouville operate in a somewhat less gross and shameless manner? Had Toussaint and Rigaud still not earned respect after all these years? And all this time Toussaint was indeed negotiating with England and the United States about the situation in the Caribbean.

For his meeting with Hédouville, Toussaint had purposely brought along his two white secretaries, Guyber and Case. This, nevertheless, did not prevent Hédouville's staff members from subjecting him to continued racist treatment. At Hédouville's cynical suggestion, at one point during the meeting, that Toussaint travel to France to see his children, the black leader replied, "Your ship is too small for me." Pointing to a sapling tree, he added, "I will go as soon as this tree is full-grown."

If intrigues were called for, Toussaint would accommodate Hédouville, certainly given his own extremely strong position. He made the decision to go to greater lengths than anybody would ever have expected – he would meet with Rigaud. It was a short conversation, held in Port-au-Prince, during which Toussaint put up for discussion only one question – without anger and with great seriousness: Could they work together against this Hédouville? Could they make the decision that the authority of the Directorate should be terminated forever?

Toussaint and Rigaud decided that the two of them would meet with Hédouville and that the meeting would take place in Cap François.

As Hédouville and Rigaud stood talking for the first time, as the meeting in Cap François was getting off to a slow start, Toussaint managed to hide soundlessly behind a curtain. There he heard Hédouville say, "Rigaud, you are France's only rock in Haiti."

Toussaint, the political tactician, now executed a stratagem. After the meeting, he submitted his resignation – twice – knowing full well Hédouville could not accept because the Frenchman was in no position to be the "deposer" of Toussaint. Toussaint then made sure that news about his offer to resign became known, which made a very favorable impression. Rigaud felt obligated to follow suit; however, his offer was not refused. Hédouville subsequently suggested he leave at once for France, which, of course, Rigaud refused to do. The discussions had ended in total failure. It was clear that everyone was suspicious of everyone else – but who would strike the first blow?

*   *   *

After Hédouville's arrival, Toussaint simply continued his negotiations with the British. He would communicate the results of each discussion to Hédouville, who could not do much more than confirm the decisions meekly. At one point, having taken the initiative himself for a negotiating session with Maitland, Hédouville was told by the Englishman that he should first consult with Toussaint! It was clear that the British considered Toussaint the only trustworthy party in Haiti. The lifting of the British and American blockades suddenly brought food and some measure of prosperity, in the wake of rapidly increasing exports. As Toussaint put it, "Full stomachs always defeat empty stomachs." The only thing Hédouville could do to save face was to approve all Toussaint's treaties after they had been made. In any case, he did not oppose any of them.

Hédouville then attempted to pull out one more trump: the new labor contract. From then on, every worker would need a contract to work on a plantation, and this would bind him for a period of three years. Together with this Decree of the Sixth Thermidor, Hédouville proposed to expropriate the lands of all white planters who did not have a totally irreproachable republican-revolutionary record. This meant that he was reversing Toussaint's measures, which had resulted in the return to Haiti of some fifteen hundred planters. Finally, Hédouville's most obvious "declaration of war" came in the form of an attempt on Toussaint's life. The attempt failed, and Toussaint's spies were able to ascertain that it had, unmistakably, been the work of Hédouville. It was the last straw for Toussaint.

Once more Hédouville played into the black leader's hands in a sadly amateurish manner. Persuaded by members of his staff, he began to fire blacks who had high-ranking positions in the army. Toussaint now replied with an ultimatum, which simply came down to: "Leave!"

Hédouville now increased the wages of the troops in Cap François on whom he was convinced that he could count. He even ordered General Manginat to do the worst thing possible, the ultimate and fatal challenge: arrest Toussaint's "nephew" and deputy commander, Moyse. The result was an uprising against Manginat in Fort Liberté. Black soldiers who had been dismissed joined together with irregular bands that began organizing for looting and pillaging. When Manginat ordered that fire be opened on them, Toussaint decided to take action. He had waited long enough.

He began a campaign of rumors that always worked, spreading the news that Hédouville wanted to restore slavery. Hadn't his actions with regard to the army made this clear? Even his reminder of the Decree of the Sixth Thermidor had been a prelude to this.

"Away with Hédouville! Father Toussaint, save us!" the masses were now shouting in Cap François.

Toussaint played this last game astutely with the nominal power of France in Haiti. At one-hour intervals, he had cannons fired below the walls of Cap François. He kept completely away from the mutinous gangs that were attacking Hédouville's troops. Hédouville realized that he was caught like a mouse in a trap. After a coup by Moyse, who had been freed, the men of Fort Liberté were celebrating the liberation of their empty stomachs. Finally, on October 22, 1798, Hédouville boarded the ship *Bravoure*, which had been ready and waiting for him and which would take him back to France.

The last sally in the Toussaint-Hédouville duel was Toussaint's, who now dropped any pretense of political good manners in his desire to enjoy the aftermath. With biting sarcasm, he sent a message to Hédouville, on the *Bravoure,* advising him that the insurrection against his authority had been suppressed and that Hédouville could, therefore, return!

Hédouville did not take the bait. He knew that his mission had been a total failure and that the game was over for all forms of French diplomacy. The French would no longer be playing parties against each other in Haiti. He had gambled and lost all of his power and prestige to Toussaint Louverture, the man of destiny.

Hédouville's parting shot was a long and inflammatory letter to Rigaud, in which he tried to the best of his ability to incite the mulatto. He hoped that, as a result, Rigaud would even forget what he had been told by Toussaint – that Hédouville had asked him to stage an attack on Rigaud's life.

* * *

In Paris, Hédouville would conduct a most active campaign to destroy Toussaint's reputation. But Roume, who was left behind and whom Toussaint seemed to have ignored as too weak a man for him to worry about, could not find enough words to praise the "old Negro." In the name of the whites in Cap François, he declared that they thanked God that Toussaint had been saved.

At this time Roume made an attempt to exorcize the evil that Hédouville had wrought by inviting the various Haitian parties to negotiate their differences. Roume summoned Toussaint and Rigaud with all their generals to a meeting in Port-au-Prince at which to discuss the long-standing territorial disputes over areas in the south around Petit Goave and Grand Goave. The large numbers of blacks concentrated there had been complaining about the way they were being treated by the mulattoes. Rigaud, for his part, feared that Toussaint would use that area as a staging ground for a campaign against his forces. One major offensive with Petit Goave as a base could easily split the entire south in half.

The discussions in Port-au-Prince did not last long, but they were marked by several unpleasant incidents. At one point, Toussaint's general for the southern territories, a black by the name of Laplume, even drew his sabre against Rigaud. Rigaud reacted by falling into one of his hysterical fits, a tactic he would sometimes employ to get his way. He would fall to the ground and lie there jerking his arms and legs as if he were having a stroke.

During the discussions, Rigaud also drew his sabre several times; but he did so threatening to plunge it into his own heart. When Roume, as arbiter, announced the most important decisions, Rigaud left the meeting room, banging the door behind him. The decisions clearly established that Toussaint Louverture would be the number-one man in Haiti, and Rigaud number two.

As a result of these decisions, made in good faith by a well-intentioned mediator, the door was unfortunately now wide open for civil war.

◆ 7 ◆

The War of the Knives

━━──━━

A NDRÉ RIGAUD, BORN THE SON OF A FRENCH LAWYER AND A mulatto woman, was the most colorful hero of the mulattoes. Being a bastard, he was especially despised by his father because little André's skin color was so much darker than it should have been for the child of a completely white Frenchman and a light-colored mulatto woman. His father did have him educated in France, however, so that as a strictly pro-French mulatto he would later display little empathy with the black slaves in the south of Haiti.

In France, Rigaud developed an interest in jewelry making and became such a skilled craftsman that he could have earned his living as a goldsmith. A desire for adventure took him to North America, however, where he fought in the Revolutionary War against the British. Both the Americans and the British had formed several black brigades in their armies. Most of the soldiers were slaves who had escaped from the Caribbean. These unfortunate people were promised their freedom after the end of the war, but most of them would only be able to enjoy that freedom if they stayed in the army. They were primarily used in campaigns against various small uprisings in the Caribbean. They were nicknamed the "Swiss," after the bodyguards of Louis XVI.

The Swiss were hardly ever granted the freedom they had been promised, but as tools of the whites they also became abhorred by the mulattoes and resented by the black slaves. Rigaud's own hatred of the Swiss through his experiences in North America seemed to translate into an ill-feeling toward all blacks. In Guadeloupe, he once witnessed the Swiss march against rebellious blacks. "They are the lowest, most debauched and most traitorous race in the world," he declared. "They are fit to be one thing only: slaves." That the slaves did not rebel at the time of the failed revolt of Ogé and Chavannes in 1790 is due mainly to the enmity that existed between the mulattoes and the blacks.

Rigaud recognized only one power: that of the mulattoes. In 1791–92, he was the leader of the corps of mulattoes which, near Port-au-Prince, obtained one of the first important victories over the whites. It was at that time, too, that a horrible slaughter took place of three hundred Swiss, who had first been allowed to help the mulattoes obtain their victory. The Swiss were strangled, suffocated and drowned. News of this massacre reached the leaders of the slave rebellion, by now begun, who promised themselves that one day they would once and for all settle accounts with the mulattoes.

"Our souls retain something of the whites and of the blacks, and that is what gives us such intuition," Rigaud once said. He used that intuition to maneuver brilliantly in the south with an independent command while the slaves, on the other hand, first joined the Spaniards to fight against the French and then joined the French to fight against the Spaniards. Rigaud possibly saved Haiti by making a stand at that time against the British, who wasted their best men, during the earliest period of the invasion, in battle against the mulattoes while they might have been able to defeat the weakened French with those same forces. For a period, Rigaud's career seemed to parallel Toussaint's, though the latter's role in thwarting the mulattoes' coup attempt against Laveaux in Cap François made an eventual collision between the two leaders inevitable.

Through repeated shows of force, Rigaud was able to convince first Sonthonax and then Hédouville that the sovereignty of the mulattoes in the south was irrevocable as long as he was alive.

Kerverseau, a French officer who had been trying in vain to subdue the mulattoes for Sonthonax, wrote a shocking report in 1796:

Rigaud and his mulattoes maintain contacts with other mulattoes in Cuba, Saint Thomas, Jamaica, and in all the Lesser and Greater Antilles. These mulattoes dream of acquiring power over the entire Caribbean territory from their base of attack in Haiti. They are totally determined to take complete control of our Big Island. On the ruins of the feudal power of the white caste, they have erected a new caste of the aristocracy of their mixed blood, a more ridiculous aristocracy than all previous ones. The position they used to have under the whites is now that of the whites in the south, who are under their power. For the blacks, they maintain slavery in its most callous and pitiless form.

During Rigaud's "reign of terror," thousands of whites had fled to the north and east. Kerverseau was convinced that Rigaud was maneuvering toward a decisive war with Toussaint for the purpose of reinstating slavery, this time strictly for the benefit of the mulattoes. Based on the mulattoes' aspirations and their acquisition of power, Kerverseau advised against an alliance with them. Ever since his report, French policy consistently aimed at playing Toussaint and Rigaud against each other. Roume, the only French representative left to carry on the Directorate's policies after Sonthonax and Hédouville had been driven away by Toussaint, pursued such a policy as well, although he did it in secret and from behind closed doors. The treaties that Toussaint had concluded with England and the United States in 1798 and 1799, which even prohibited French warships from entering into Haiti's harbors, constituted a threat to Rigaud, but they were sanctioned in their entirety by Roume.

Rigaud was a man with a fierce disposition. This had led, several times during his life, to duels about women, whose favors he vied for without taking into account the husbands or lovers they might already have. Rigaud's amorous exploits had even played a part in several sudden, sharp political changes. Inclined to celebrate life, he was an exuberant man who wanted nothing to do with Toussaint's prudishness and frugality.

Rigaud loved to eat, and his favorite dishes were roasted parrot, broiled lobster, the extremely tasty mussels of Haiti, and *poules à créole* (creole chicken). He always walked around not only with sabres and pistols, but generally also had papayas, avocados, pineapples and bananas hanging on the belts around his waist and across his chest. At receptions or at the audiences he granted in his palace at Les Cayes, he would appear wearing two broad powdered braids, a green collar, multicolored plus-fours with pleats, white stockings with blue stripes, a two-cornered hat and with his hair combed to hang over his ears. He was extremely popular with the fashionable creole women whose lives were filled with parties and amusements and who, in Les Cayes, were sometimes called "the merry women of Tivoli."

Rigaud would suddenly halt a campaign when he felt a need for sexual amusement. When a French negotiator once proudly declared that he had been allowed to put his nose between the breasts of one of Rigaud's mistresses, Rigaud cut off the man's nose with one stroke of his dagger.

Hédouville, who probably preferred handing Toussaint over to Rigaud rather than the other way around, left a message for Rigaud when he departed that he hoped would amount to a revenge against Toussaint. He released Rigaud from all obligations ensuing from agreements with the powerful black leader, and stated that Rigaud was to consider himself free to act as he saw fit. It would have been better if Rigaud had paid attention to Roume's declarations of affection for Toussaint, who was now being referred to as a great sage, legislator, general and "another Solon." Rigaud instead adopted Hédouville's description of Toussaint as a monster with three heads who had caught the Americans, the British, the Spanish and the French in his traps. Even at the time of his conversations with Hédouville, Rigaud had scornfully mentioned Toussaint's insignificant stature and his ignorance of the ways of the world. He also remarked to Hédouville that Toussaint was "actually even uglier than one could possibly imagine the ugliest Negro."

And if Toussaint was so clever at writing letters and proclamations, he, Rigaud, could do so as well. The eventual military confrontation with Toussaint began, in fact, with a campaign of pamphlets, that had some success in tarnishing the black leader's reputation in the northern and western zones.

There were coups favoring Rigaud in Jean Rabel, in Fort Liberté and even in Môle Saint-Nicolas. Some black generals who suffered from an inferiority complex with regard to Toussaint defected to Rigaud. "The rats are coming out of their holes," remarked Toussaint, who foresaw another mulatto coup attempt, as in 1796, but this time directed against *him*. However, as he opined, "Rigaud is unfortunately a person who immediately falls off his horse when he breaks into a gallop."

The "ugly old Negro" reacted decisively, with enormous force. He ignored the south, where Rigaud had occupied Petit Goave and Grand Goave and the surrounding area that had so long been in dispute, and went on a lightning campaign to suppress the small uprisings in the north. In addition, he ordered mass executions performed in order to spread terror. Pétion, one of the mulatto leaders in Port-au-Prince, even chose to join Toussaint after hearing him give a stirring peroration from the pulpit for the benefit of mulattoes who had been rounded up and taken to a church in that city. Toussaint thundered:

Mulattoes! You have betrayed the blacks from the very beginning of our revolution. What do you want now? It is clear as day that you want to become the new rulers of this colony. You want to exterminate the whites and enslave the blacks. I want you to know that you will forever be considered depraved and dishonored because you first deported the black troops known as "Swiss" to the whites and then massacred them yourselves. You held the hatred of the "small whites" against the Swiss in greater esteem than the blood they had spilled for you. Why did you sacrifice them? Because they were black. Why does General Rigaud object to obeying me? Because I am black. He has sworn irreconcilable hatred against me because of my color. Why else would he not want to cooperate with me, a French general who has contributed so much to expelling the British? Mulattoes! As a result of your ridiculous pride and your pernicious faithlessness, you have already lost all right to any possible power.

As far as General Rigaud is concerned, he is lost. I see him lying at the bottom of the precipice even now. As a rebel and traitor to his country, he will be devoured by the troops who fight for freedom. Mulattoes! I look into the depths of your souls. You were ready to revolt against me. But, although I am now leaving the west with my troops, I will leave my eyes and my arms behind. My eyes will see you and my weapons will be able to find you.

The budding opposition of the mulattoes in the entire western and northern area soon collapsed. The situation that was supposed to have closed in on Toussaint and his men instead boomeranged into a consolidated base from which the blacks could take on the mullato south.

The power in all of Haiti, nominally still a possession of France, would in fact reside with either the blacks or the mulattoes. The former still fought for their freedom, while the latter now fought for their very existence. It became the "War of the Knives," the civil war-within-a-war in Haiti, which remains the one about which the most tales of unprecedented atrocities have been told.

In the towns and villages, blacks and mulattoes stood across from each other and fought until one was able to cut the other's throat. Even the corpses were torn to pieces, "so that the grasses would be drenched with their blood and grow more quickly." Thousands of old people, women and children were killed. Toussaint let his cruelest generals, Dessalines and Moyse, have free rein. He himself never took part in executions and childishly plugged his ears against any news he received about the atrocities that were committed, especially by Dessalines. When women would throw themselves in despair at his feet to offer their lives, this general would take pleasure in flinging their children into the fire in front of their eyes or splitting them apart.

Rigaud was no less degenerate in his methods. The mulattoes had a reputation for using a technique of killing that consisted of throwing their victims into the infamous "black holes." These were narrow, underground spaces, into which prisoners were tightly pushed together until they suffocated.

Commissioner Roume, who had received orders from the Directorate to stop the bloodbath, declared Rigaud an outlaw on July 3, 1799. This was the reason why one of the most heroic mulatto fighters, Louis Jacques Beauvais, gave up the fight; he foresaw the downfall of the mulattoes and called for reconciliation.

Beauvais had fought on Rigaud's side since 1791. Before then, he had been a teacher in France and had also organized instruction for mulatto children in the south. Toussaint, who liked to found schools, and enjoyed teaching as well, had hoped to work together with Beauvais in building a new Haiti.

Beauvais' change of heart had come too late. When an attack on Toussaint's life took place – which cost the life of his physician – he lost all interest in consultations and efforts toward peace, even with Beauvais. "You too are a leader of rebels and you act in accordance with Rigaud's orders," he said.

Beauvais fled the inferno with his wife and children, but the ship on which he hoped to reach Curaçao foundered. A small safety raft only held enough room for some women and children. Beauvais ceded his place and went under with the ship, waving until the very last to his wife and children on the raft. It seemed to symbolize the doom of the mulattoes' dream.

The battles now concentrated on the most important harbor, at the southern town of Jacmel, which was blockaded by British and American ships. Toussaint had his troops surround the city in late November and managed to close it off completely, positioning his men along the almost impassable rock wall and hills that encircled it.

Hundreds of blacks dragged the artillery – heavy American cannons, some of which had been used in the War of Independence – along the precipice above the town. Jacmel was fired upon day and night. There was famine, and people began eating rats and lizards. On the side of the mulattoes, the hero during the siege was Pétion, who had gone back to Rigaud after Beauvais had left and who had become his right hand. Nobody could know at the time that Pétion, many years after Toussaint's death and many years after the French had been expelled, would show up once more to save the honor of the mulattoes in their own free republic.

The name Pétion will, in fact, always remain linked to the siege of Jacmel, as its hero. When the last remnants of resistance among his men had dissolved, he had the flags torn into strips that he wrapped around himself and his men, saying, "If we die now, we will have remained true to our banners." Still, managing to miraculously elude the grasp of the besiegers, Pétion led his surviving men in a breakout through the black encirclement. This unleashed a new eruption of fury in Dessalines, who ordered the slaughter of all the mulatto prisoners then being held in the black camps. This time they were crucified in upside-down position, in such a manner as to give them only an excruciating release from their struggle. Dessalines wanted to see his victims die slowly.

The mulatto fighters did not yet give up, however. While Rigaud seemed to become mentally unstable at the imminent collapse of his power, and even attempted suicide, Pétion and another mulatto leader, Geffrard, continued to maintain the front until the summer of 1800. By then, Bonaparte was ruler of France and he sent a delegation of three to Haiti with the assignment to bring about peace. Two of these men were whites, Colonel Vincent and Pierre Michel. The third was the mulatto Raymond, who had been working the Paris circuit of antechambers since 1790 and had been a defender of slavery before switching to become a passionate supporter of Toussaint.

Toussaint had absolutely no intention of accepting further orders coming from Paris, where the power structure kept changing. He did not even wait until he could expel the gentlemen, but imprisoned them at once. Raymond and Vincent professed their pro-Toussaint feelings and were quickly set free. Vincent, in fact, was sent to Les Cayes to negotiate with Rigaud.

Rigaud had slowly been going insane. Heavily armed, he walked the corridors shouting with rage. His brother Augustin received Vincent, who communicated Toussaint's proposal, asking for complete surrender of the mulatto army to the blacks. Then Rigaud suddenly jumped out from behind a curtain and threw himself with a dagger on Vincent. Augustin Rigaud barely saved Vincent from what looked like certain death.

Near Jacmel, a final, terrible battle was fought, where blacks and mulattoes struggled for hours in hand-to-hand combat. But Rigaud had now played out his last cards. On March 1, 1800, Toussaint Louverture held his triumphant entrance parade into the mulatto capital Les Cayes.

Rigaud and most of the other mulatto leaders had fled to Cuba, from where most would go on to France. Toussaint heard from Hébécourt, his spy in France, how the mulattoes had been received by Napoleon. As it turns out, Rigaud had been allowed to tell the French leader his entire story, with all of his furious insults against Toussaint. At the end of the conversation, Napoleon had only one remark: "Everything you have said is probably true and, in any case, moving. You have made only one mistake. You lost."

◆ 8 ◆

The Conquest of
Santo Domingo

━━━┤━━━

CÉSAR TÉLÉMAQUE, MAYOR OF CAP FRANÇOIS, LIKED TO CONVERSE with Toussaint in Latin. When the news of Napoleon Bonaparte's successful 18th Brumaire (November 9, 1799, when he terminated the Directorate and created the Consulate) reached them, Toussaint had remarked, "This success is very encouraging for me, too." He had added, "The world belongs to those who are strong."

Such a strong man had indeed come onto the scene in France. As of 1800, after his campaigns in Germany and Italy, Bonaparte had emerged as the dominant figure in Europe. Toussaint understood that the future of the Big Island would, for better or for worse, remain for a long time to come linked to the destiny of France under the leadership of its great military commander. Toussaint was also firm in his resolve that, in any case, he would not let Haiti's destiny be determined by Napoleon's star alone. Without the need to officially break its bond with France, the entire island had to become an iron fortress of the slaves. After all, they had fought and succeeded in obtaining their freedom without the help of, and even despite, the French. "Bonaparte is a fine man," Toussaint admitted, "and France is his. But Haiti is mine. I am not in his way, so why would he come and block my way? And if he does, he will have to face a buck rather than a sheep."

On December 13, 1799, Napoleon abolished the decree issued by the Directorate that had nominally halted practically all American trade with Haiti. It was a decree that Toussaint had totally ignored when he had made his own treaty with the Americans. Napoleon's decision to abolish the decree signified an end to the war-like state that had existed between the United States and France, and that had played so strongly into Toussaint's hands. The decision was the first move in the duel that the white Napoleon now began to fight against the "Black Napoleon."

Toussaint reacted with his usual talent for improvisation and energy. On December 28, while he was still very much occupied with the siege of Jacmel, he requested that Roume grant him official permission to finally occupy all of Santo Domingo on behalf of France. At the same time, he presented Roume with one of his ambiguities: "I have always admired Bonaparte and consider him a true republican. I have no ambition other than to bring happiness to my country and, if someone else should be able to do this better than I, I will not hesitate to renounce the mandate that was given to me."

Roume, meanwhile, was playing several games. He maintained contacts with the Spaniards, who continued to engage in slave trading from Santo Domingo, and he even obtained profits from that trade. He had sent spies to Jamaica, where they were to test the mood among the slaves there to determine whether these could be persuaded to ignite the torch of rebellion against the British. If this could be accomplished, he would have been of great service to Napoleon. When two of his spies were apprehended, they stated, wrongfully, that they were agents hired by Toussaint to instigate riots. This led to British warships' capturing a large frigate filled with weapons while it was being conducted by sea to Jacmel on Toussaint's orders.

Roume now fawned upon Toussaint in a way that far surpassed even the most exaggerated compliments uttered earlier by Laveaux and Sonthonax: "We truly worship you like Jesus Christ on the altar." He also indicated to Toussaint that he would from then on always be supportive and well disposed to Toussaint rather than to the mulattoes, who by then were being suppressed by the black armies anyway. But he refused to give Toussaint permission to annex Santo Domingo. He pointed out that Generals Kerverseau and Chanlatte had already taken interim control for France. It would be better, he felt, to await the new "special regulations" for the colonies that had been announced by Napoleon.

Toussaint was furious and decided once more to use his old recipe for unrest. He had Moyse put pressure on Roume with a display of six hundred threatening cavalrymen. The news was circulated that an uprising had already occurred among blacks who were afraid that slavery would be reinstated from Santo Domingo. Roume remained obstinate for ten days while Moyse had him subjected to various mistreatments. He was hit in the face, dragged from room to room and, finally, locked up in a chicken coop. He was then told that he would soon be hacked to pieces and fed to the animals. Moyse also told him that the blacks could no longer be restrained and were at the point of massacring both the whites and all remaining mulattoes.

On April 17, 1800, Roume consented. On May 2, he received a message from Napoleon to have Toussaint make peace with the mulattoes as soon as possible. This seemed to indicate, at the very least, that there was no official sanction for an invasion of Santo Domingo. Even then, however, there were rumors that Napoleon was keeping two sets of records. On the one hand, he had ostensibly accepted the facts that had occurred in Haiti and even confirmed Toussaint in the position he held. On the other, he had struck Toussaint's name as a general of France and was even preparing an invasion of Haiti. Already in the summer of 1800, rumors were afoot that Napoleon's invasion fleet with twenty-five thousand men was on its way!

As soon as he heard this rumor, Toussaint sent a commando led by the white general Agé to Captain-General and Governor Don Joaquín García in Santo Domingo in order to negotiate an unconditional surrender without the shedding of blood. This turned into a disaster. There was grumbling among the Dominican citizenry, and they even showed up to throw rocks through the windows of the house where Agé and his men were staying. García replied that he would simply not submit to a regime operating by the force of arms. He pointed out that there were already two French generals to supervise affairs in Santo Domingo for France. García also felt that it would be tactically advantageous to emphasize the solidarity of the people of Santo Domingo with the brave mulattoes in the south of Haiti.

On June 18, Roume found the courage to revoke his permission to Toussaint. But Toussaint was able to strike while the iron was hot. He again imprisoned the Frenchman, who had meanwhile become ill, but gave orders not to mistreat him. Roume's imprisonment in Dondon became the immediate reason for his departure from Haiti, although Toussaint had not been planning to send him back, as he had done with Sonthonax and Hédouville. In fact, he wanted to keep him for possible use as a hostage in his dealings with Napoleon. And meanwhile he could turn Roume once more into a useful tool by putting him under pressure.

In late autumn, Toussaint received the news that Spain had officially ceded Louisiana to France as of October 1. It meant that a gun was being held to the heads of the United States and England, but for Toussaint it simply meant that Napoleon was already in the process of surrounding Haiti.

A letter arrived from Napoleon emphatically forbidding the annexation of Santo Domingo, but the letter did not get to Toussaint. It was sent from post to post, following Toussaint on his military campaign. Somehow, Toussaint managed to always stay just one step ahead of the letter. He was leading the invasion himself, while Moyse and Paul Louverture were operating in the north. In a flash, Toussaint's armies cut through the weak Spanish defenses. The Spanish General Guerra did not do honor to his name (which meant "war") as he quickly surrendered. The campaign became a military "walk" for the men who, only six years before, were slaves working as mercenaries for the Spaniards.

The Spaniards transferred the bones of Christopher Columbus to Cuba in their fear that Toussaint would take possession of these as well. Chanlatte fled to Venezuela. Toussaint wrote another of his adroit letters full of threats with double meanings to Don Joaquín García, the man who had once stated that he did not feel enough esteem for Toussaint to help him into the saddle:

I hope that you, Esteemed Gentleman, will not leave the Spaniards in uncertainty as to the fact that their persons and their possessions, as well as their religious customs, shall be respected. To this, I pledge my word of honor as a soldier.

At the same time, Your Excellency, please rest assured that I only insist on fulfilling my obligations so that the name of France shall continue to be respected and so that it shall be possible to preserve the friendly relations between France and Spain.

On January 24, 1801, Toussaint made his solemn entrance into the capital city of Santo Domingo after a military campaign that consisted only of a few skirmishes. Napoleon soon received news about the defeat of the once-so-famous Spanish armies. He already had a grip on Spain itself, but at this point became over-confident about the potential of Spanish resistance, wherever and in whatever form. This would lead to his mistake in trying to hold down the Iberian peninsula – a waste of troops in a protracted civil war, which, like the one in Haiti, would become a prelude to the terrible defeat of the Grande Armée in Russia.

García handed Toussaint the keys to Santo Domingo. The people had now erected triumphal arches and decorated their houses with garlands and Toussaint's banners. So, it seems, it had only been a small gang, specifically incited for the purpose by the Spaniards, who had thrown the rocks through General Agé's windows! The approximately fifteen thousand slaves in this eastern part of the island were at once given their freedom. Toussaint and Moyse expropriated a considerable part of the estates and divided them, together with the cattle herds that were the pride of Santo Domingo, among the officers of the campaign. García decided to make a lukewarm attempt to bank on the future: Could Toussaint possibly take Santo Domingo into his possession for Spain and conduct an interim government in the name of Spain?

"I am doing all this for the French Republic, officially," said Toussaint. "And, Your Excellency, please keep in mind that the French armies will shortly cross the Pyrenees just as easily as I crossed into Santo Domingo."

Now Garcia had to help Toussaint into the saddle. Now he had to sit behind the old Negro during High Mass. Toussaint also came face to face once more with Hermonas, on whose troops he had played such a horrible trick at the time of the trap in San Raphael, back in 1794. Toussaint could not refrain from telling him, "If you had done what I'd suggested at the time when we were still supporting you, the entire island would now have been Spanish."

With some twenty shots fired in salute by a cannon, the Spanish flag came down. Then twenty-two shots were fired as the French flag was hoisted while the *Marseillaise* was played.

Most of the Spanish officers left the island. Toussaint divided it officially into two provinces, and once mentioned in passing that he had founded a Greater Haiti for France. Paul Louverture and Clervaux were appointed to head the new provinces. In a sermon, Toussaint then impressed upon the men in Santo Domingo that they should marry their concubines or kept women as soon as possible. He also took various measures to intensify and strengthen the weak plantation system and to improve the primitive system of roads. He then made a long triumphal march back to Cap François.

Though Toussaint was achieving great victories, supposedly on behalf of France, to one Frenchman it had become clear that the Big Island had escaped the mother country's control. One month later, Napoleon Bonaparte ordered preparations made for the invasion of Haiti. He therewith stated that, for the moment, it would suffice to press vagabonds into service while assembling the invasion army.

◆ 9 ◆

Toussaint's Constitution

A FTER THE FALL OF THE DIRECTORATE, TOUSSAINT WAS SUPPOSED to wait for the "special regulations" that were to be issued by France's First Consul, Napoleon, for dealing with the situation in Haiti. In the new Constitution of the Consular Regime, there was an Article that reflected Napoleon's viewpoint, but it was vague, abstract and provisionary. The fact that it was officially effective as of Christmas Day 1799 did not make it any more definitive for Toussaint. The First Consul had advised that there would, of course, be a place in his colonial administration for the loyal blacks who had so consistently defended French interests. The generals, in any case, would be rewarded.

Through his spies, Toussaint already knew that early in the year 1800 followers of the pre-revolutionary regime, even admitted monarchists, had been appointed to the new French Council of State. One was Barbé de Marbois, the former lieutenant governor who had never given up hope, after his ignominious escape in 1789, of returning to power in Haiti. Another was Moreau de Saint-Méry, who was able to combine an inclination toward splendid poetic descriptions of Haiti, where his plantations were blooming, with a determination to retain slavery unconditionally.

On December 14, 1799, the quasi-war between the French and American republics that had lasted for years ended. Toussaint very quickly noticed the consequences of this event. He had reacted to the trade war of the Directorate with his economic agreement of April, concluded with those same Americans. This had essentially meant that Toussaint had become an ally of the Americans.

More than on anything else, Toussaint was gambling on the influence of American power for when the time should come that he would have to preserve his position in the Caribbean; whether this would be as an enemy of France or not, it would in any case be without France. He was planning to adapt to the circumstances and conduct a policy that would at times be somewhat more pro-American and at other times somewhat more pro-British, which would be expressed in the trade conditions. In any case, he had already made sure there was no longer any danger of a surprise attack from Santo Domingo, by whatever enemy.

* * *

"The history of the West Indian islands, and hence that of the Pearl of the Antilles as well, has been linked to France in a manner determined by destiny," Toussaint had said. From 18th Brumaire on, this bond with France meant for Toussaint that he had to stay constantly attuned to, or, at least, react to the course that Napoleon was taking. In so doing, Toussaint also happened to be, several times and in a number of respects, one step ahead of the French leader. Hence, if Toussaint must be called Napoleon's imitator, then Napoleon may also be considered an imitator of Toussaint Louverture.

Once he had defeated the mulattoes and subjected all of Santo Domingo to his authority, Toussaint knew that he had crossed the Rubicon. When he issued his Constitution in the summer of 1801, the implicit challenge of Haitian independence had become an accomplished fact.

On June 14, 1800, Napoleon had won a great victory against the Austrians at Marengo. On February 9, 1801, Austria accepted the Peace of Lunéville, which confirmed Napoleon's supremacy. Surrounding France, Napoleon had built a restricted military area such as he had envisaged in his dreams. It consisted of the Batavian republic, the Swiss republic, the Cisalpine republic and the Ligurian republic; all were, to a greater or lesser extent, satellites of France. Denmark, Sweden and Prussia, all being nations that endeavored to remain neutral, had been included in a Russian treaty aimed at protecting the area around the Baltic and North Seas. The relationship between France and Russia had improved to such an extent that Napoleon had even begun to dream of a campaign to the heart of India, together with the Russians. There they would fight Great Britain, the power that, despite the short interruption of the Peace of Amiens, remained the principal enemy.

Toussaint knew that Napoleon had to experience feelings of incredulity and respect for him because he had expelled not only the Spaniards, who were considered weak, but also the formidable British. Hadn't this been the reason that Napoleon had promised, shortly after 18th Brumaire, to confirm the ranks that Toussaint and his generals had been granted by the Directorate?

Considering himself to be in a strong position, Toussaint dared to write his most challenging letter to Napoleon, on February 12, 1801:

Now that peace has been restored to the colony and it has been rid of enemies, it is my duty to write and ask you to confirm the promotions that you had promised to the courageous soldiers who helped me during the difficult campaigns. They are all deserving officers who are worthy of the confidence and the gratitude of the nation. Citizen Consul, the soldiers of Haiti have indeed earned their right to be recognized by the government of France. You may put your complete trust in them. Led by able leaders, they are capable of performing in the most grandiose manner. During the last campaign, in Santo Domingo, which was not murderous but definitely exhausting, they displayed more stamina than horses. Several times, I was forced to slow down their marches in order to give the cavalry time to catch up with them. With the discipline that I demand from them, they would be an absolute match also for European troops.

Startled by my decision to place the Spanish part of the island under the dominion of the Republic, my enemies are going all out in their intrigues and in trying to put obstacles in my way. They succeeded in bringing citizen Roume, the representative of the government, to their side and in persuading him to revoke his decree, so as to invalidate the occupation of the Spanish territory that had been sanctioned by him. Determined to force the annexation by a display of arms, I had no choice but to request, before I undertook this campaign, that citizen Roume resign his mandate and withdraw at my command until further orders to Dondon, where the intrigues of my enemies could no longer turn his head so easily. He is at your disposal and, if you so desire, I will send him back to you.

Whatever defamations of character my enemies are spreading about me, I do not feel any need to justify myself toward them. While discretion obliges me to remain silent, my duty compels me to prevent them from doing any more harm.

My regards and deepest respect,
Toussaint Louverture

What a letter! What intuition! Barely a few months later, Napoleon would order Talleyrand to advise England (preparations were being made for peace between England and France): "My decision to destroy the authority of the blacks in Haiti is not so much based on considerations of commerce and money, as on the need to block forever the march of the blacks in the world."

Toussaint knew that there was more to it than Napoleon wanted the British to know. Haiti was to be a bridgehead for the furtherance of French power in the Caribbean and for influence in the United States by way of Louisiana and, subsequently, an even greater chance of punishing England. What happened, however, was that in Paris, on May 3, 1803, exactly one week after the death of Toussaint in one of Napoleon's dungeons, Louisiana was sold by treaty to the Americans. That Napoleon's dream ended this way was largely to the credit of the "ugly old Negro," whose legions had dealt Napoleon a disastrous defeat, in Haiti.

*   *   *

"I now feel as if I am soaring with eagles, but I need a rock on which to set down," Toussaint said after he had written his splendid letter to Napoleon.

From the beginning of the spring of 1801, Toussaint had been giving the opportunity to all the municipalities throughout the country to send in petitions relating to the new constitution then being drafted. The Constitution was ready on May 9, 1801. It had been written by nine men: Bernard Borgella, André Collet, Julien Raymond, Gaston Nogère, De Lacour, Carlos Roxas, André Muñoz, Juan Manceba and Etienne Viart. Six of them were whites and three were mulattoes. Borgella, the most important among them, a former mayor of Port-au-Prince and an ex-royalist, had fought with the British. His spiritual advisor was Father Molière, who had studied the American Constitution and had recommended it as a model. After Toussaint had worked several days and nights on the draft, it became the official Constitution of Haiti on July 7, 1801. The Central Assembly, which had been called together by Toussaint in February and had since been meeting in closed sessions, granted its approval. Special regulations relating to cultivation and labor, as well as a final decree on morals and religion, issued in the fall, rounded out Toussaint's creation. He himself read the principal core of the Constitution to thousands of people during a solemn gathering in Cap François.

"If I had been white, it would have been appropriate for me to feel that I am beyond praise, but I earn this praise even more because I am a Negro," he said.

Borgella had no trouble confirming to all the whites who supported him that this constitution was the noiseless, veiled and incognito declaration of independence with which even the royalists, who had been fighting the consequences of the French Revolution in Haiti since 1790, could agree. Toussaint, for his part, had considered it of cardinal importance to bind the whites, no matter what other expectations they might have, to a constitution that emphatically banned slavery from Haiti forever. "All people shall live, worship and die on this island as free Frenchmen," he stated. A second important point had been the granting of absolute executive power to Toussaint Louverture, who also had the right to name his successor, "as long as his glorious life shall last." Toussaint also formally claimed the title Governor General of the Republic.

The labor laws entailed that people who were employed on a plantation would be bound to that plantation for an extended period of time. The period would be determined by the state, and the obligation was in effect both for the owner and for the laborer.

By way of a system of excise duties, the laws provided in practice that one-third to one-fourth of the revenues went to the laborers, an equal amount to the state, and the remainder to the owner. The concept of bondage meant that people could not change plantations without permission from the state, which was represented by an officer in every municipality. Most of the officers would have one or more detachments of professional soldiers at their disposal to act as police.

To keep people from living as vagabonds, an employment card was adopted that could also be used for identification. In addition, Toussaint enacted a law providing that owners could only sell land in plots of more than fifty hectares. When estates were divided into very small lots, the immediate result was that production fell. Toussaint pressed for large plantations.

Plantations that had been abandoned by the whites during the wars or that had been vacated for other reasons became the property of the state, which gave them to officers to run. In all the municipalities, these men were also given the task of supervising the bookkeeping of the plantations. Out of obvious aversion for any explicit statement of "servitude," the Constitution stated that "citizens can only use the services of others if this is indispensable for the performance of their tasks."

One-third of the land had been devastated. More than a hundred thousand people had died. The streets had not been maintained, the aqueducts had been destroyed and the plantations had by and large fallen into decay. Haiti's national debt was huge and there was runaway inflation. In 1801, production was barely one-fourth of what it had been before 1791.

There appeared to be only one way to remedy the situation. There had to be a forced return to more regular production – economic stability – in which the entire population had to participate. The only authority remaining after all the years of fighting and the only entity capable of maintaining order and discipline was the army. Hence Toussaint's Haiti became, to some extent, a military state. The standing army consisted of more than thirty-five thousand men out of a population of barely half a million. Officers maintained discipline with pistols in their hands when necessary. From the United States, weapons were bought for enormous sums.

In addition to the standing army, another approximately hundred thousand men between the ages of fifteen and fifty-five exercised several hours daily, in addition to their work on the plantations. The fact was that the enemy of black freedom, under whatever guise, could return at any time. Vigilance remained essential.

In order to prevent any new incidence of stagnation in the interior while the country was in the stage of rebuilding, there was strict censorship and a prohibition on public gatherings. A new tax law was enacted, as well as a new regulation for the system of justice that was set up according to military principles. All voodoo practices were strictly forbidden and a concordat was concluded between church and state, the provisions of which basically meant that the Roman Catholic priests, who supported Toussaint with impressive solidarity, obtained considerable power – second only to the soldiers. Prostitution was outlawed and divorce was impossible. The system of concubinage, which Toussaint considered a typical remnant of the period of slavery, was also restricted. The slaves had been kept from contracting marriage, so that their owners could more easily sell them. According to Toussaint, the system of concubinage had had a disruptive effect on the honor and standing of women in society and it should, therefore, be discarded. Serving as a mirror to the state, the family would be the rock-solid social and moral base for the new society.

It was not possible for Toussaint to be in the island's now six provinces at the same time. He had to have faith in the soldiers who had won the war for him and in the former slaves, who would continue to think day and night how wonderful it was to be free, no matter how hard they had to work.

Where Toussaint could not supervise things himself, the checks on compliance with the labor laws at the plantations became, unfortunately, arbitrary hunts for vagabonds. Some of the officers, who suddenly found themselves landowners, conducted "reigns of terror." The system of bondage, moreover, was aggravated by the tax system, which was extremely complicated despite the new laws. The whites considered it more oppressive than the colonial system imposed by Paris that had existed before 1789. The blacks, who had had no prior experience with taxation, considered it a dressed-up form of slavery.

The generals and the officers sometimes turned their campaigns against the many vagabonds into punitive expeditions, during which beatings with a stick – since whips were strictly forbidden – were among the mildest form of punishment. Dessalines especially excelled once more when it came to inhuman acts. The so-called vagabonds were assembled in camps and, under pitiful circumstances, forced into bondage in accordance with the precepts of the Works Council.

Toussaint aimed at turning as many of the large plantations as possible into small, labor-intensive industrial enterprises so that all work activities would be concentrated in one place and so that, on and around the plantations, mature industries would arise that could produce sugar, coffee, cacao, wool, indigo and wood.

In theory, if not always in practice, Toussaint's system was sound given the circumstances. Maybe it was even the only possible one, especially because so many conditions would remain uncertain for a long time to come.

When, on May 4, 1802, French General Leclerc introduced his own system for the regulation of labor on the plantations, he had to admit that it did not need to be much different from the system that Toussaint had adopted earlier: "A very good system. I wouldn't dare imagine any better system under the circumstances. I will, in fact, use it in its entirety."

Though the reality of the countryside consisted of a difficult, uphill struggle for prosperity, this was belied by the extravagant spending that occurred in the nightlife of Cap François and Port-au-Prince. Even American merchants looked in amazement at the luxury, the entertainment and the amusements of some of the free blacks, who had become rich and were now living in peace next to the whites, who were also beginning to return to their old lifestyle.

There was progress in the area of education because it was handled by the church, which received the second largest share of the state budget, after the army. The roads were also improved and the cities beautified in accordance with the wishes of many a municipality to become "a little Paris." But as far as the economy was concerned, the new regulations had done not much more than "streamline the chaos," as Julien Raymond described it. Comments by contemporaries differed greatly. Even with all the regulations and the supervision by the army, many whites did regain prominent positions as owners on the plantations. This fact caused many blacks to wonder if Toussaint should not have effected a much more drastic social revolution.

The question is whether, in that case, there would have been a greater sense of solidarity and support for him among the people. Other contemporaries are of the opinion that Toussaint should have adopted a system much less controlled by his soldiers. He should have liberalized more, so that greater numbers of whites would have returned to preserve the plantation system, which the blacks could not save without them.

On the side of the blacks, arguments were advanced for an independent, entirely black republic. Some whites were so adverse to any possible new control from Paris that they, too, favored total independence under the leadership of Toussaint; they counted on him to keep the blacks in line until they, the whites, could gradually get the economy in their hands again. With, on the one hand, his system of bondage imposed on both blacks and whites and, on the other, a complete militarization, Toussaint attempted to find a middle road between the two options. His enemies have insisted up to the present day that there was social and economic chaos, a situation hardly better than slavery. His friends, on the other hand, maintain that the economy was gradually improving, that people were again acquiring a desire to live and work in peace and that this was, at the least, a unique historical experiment that needed and deserved to have time to develop.

The number of cattle was, in fact, growing spectacularly. And women were beginning to lead a totally different life within their families. At one point, they decided to organize a great Negro Ball to pay homage to Toussaint, the "Gilded Negro" and the "Black Alexander the Great."

Periès, Perrod, Vollée and Raymond, who were the most knowledgeable in economic and financial affairs, meanwhile, all made efforts to reduce the burdensome cost of the military apparatus. This naturally caused resistance within the army, where Toussaint's generals had views of their own. Christophe, for one, was always coming up with proposals for lowering taxes and, especially, for the reduction of assessments (that were sometimes as high as thirty percent). In his opinion, an extremely accommodating system of import and export duties should have been adopted, so as to procure more British and American trade and ensure that Haiti would again become the commercial "Pearl of the Antilles."

Moyse, who administered part of the northern zones, came to entirely different conclusions. Many generals were of the opinion that it was, in any case, a good idea to keep the whites and let them play a role so that they would be available as hostages in case France decided to attack. Moyse did not agree with this, and argued that the state should impose racism, meaning that all the land should go to the blacks, as well as all the power, and that all the whites should be expelled or executed.

Social uprisings occurred in Moyse's territory, but he did not have his police intervene. Next, bands were formed that began to attack plantations and murder whites. Moyse kept making references to the old feelings of solidarity that had existed among the slaves at the beginning of the rebellion and that seemed to be disappearing or wearing away.

Toussaint was ready for battle, however, and reacted quickly against this nostalgia for the Night of Fire. His guards had not lost any of their militancy, and the insurgent bands were hunted down and defeated. Then Moyse suddenly took quick action against the rebels and had those who fell into his hands summarily executed. Maybe they knew too much. Moyse's true sentiments were in any case already known. He had not only said out loud, but had also written, "Whatever they say about my old uncle, I cannot take the decision to become the executioner of someone my own color. It is always in the name of the interests of the state that he reproaches me. But his interests have become those of the whites. And I only like the whites when they have lost the light in their eyes during our battles with them."

From the interrogations, it became clear to Toussaint that Moyse had not only neglected to stand firm at the beginning of the rebellion, but had incited the rebellion himself—whatever his intentions might have been. Neither could Moyse deny that the rebels had called out, "Long live Moyse!" Toussaint had his favored nephew (actually cousin) arrested. He was by now convinced that the man had had the rebellious leaders executed because they had even more information, perhaps even about a coup planned by Moyse against himself.

Moyse did not have his day in court. Toussaint, who no longer desired to see or speak to him, made the brutal decision to have his one-time right-hand man put to death. Moyse's request to die without a blindfold and by giving the order for his execution himself was granted.

* * *

Shortly before the loyal mulatto Julien Raymond died, in 1801, he strongly recommended that Toussaint not pay any attention to Napoleon but rather pursue his own plans ambitiously. "Napoleon will disappear sooner than you will," Raymond insisted. Vincent, as general and representative to the First Consul, was assigned to present Toussaint's Constitution to Napoleon and elaborate on it. He had had several disagreements about it with Toussaint, and these had been so severe that Toussaint, several times, almost attacked him physically. After having in vain proposed all kinds of amendments, Vincent finally departed unwillingly for Paris. In British newspapers he would read that Toussaint had become King of the new Republic of Haiti. All that was left of France in Haiti was the currency, the flags and the national anthem.

Vincent's interview with Napoleon, who immediately displayed intense hostility and suspicion as he announced that he would settle accounts with that "black garden dwarf," ended with Vincent's banishment to the island of Elba.

But Napoleon did read Toussaint's labor regulations carefully, as became clear in 1801, when he issued his own labor booklet that workers had to carry with them. Also, his new policy with regard to émigrés, who were allowed to return in large numbers to work within the Consular system as functionaries, was clearly influenced by Toussaint's accommodating treatment of the white planters. In fact, the wording that set forth Napoleon's position as Consul for Life – his first step toward becoming Emperor – seemed to have come straight from Toussaint's Constitution. Religion and family were restored by Napoleon to an honorable position in society in his solemnly proclaimed concordat between the French state and the Catholic Church of April 18, 1802. Again, the wording was the same as that used for the same subject in Toussaint's Constitution issued a year earlier.

Chateaubriand's *Le Génie du Christianisme* (The Genius of Christianity) was published on April 14, 1802, an event that, nearly simultaneous with the concordat, symbolized the end of the French Revolution and inaugurated the new age of Napoleon. But, Chateaubriand asked himself, wasn't the white Napoleon imitating the black one?

• 10 •

The First of the Blacks

■——■

"**P**ARTURIUNT MONTES, NASCITUR RIDICULUS MUS," TOUSSAINT
once said. ("The mountains gave birth and a ridiculous
sparrow was born.") But that sparrow, that fragile stick, that pain
in the neck, that monkey with rags wound around its head was now
dictator, and he had the constitutional right to appoint his own
successor, even before Napoleon had gotten to that point in France.
Was Haiti on the eve of a dynasty of black emperors?

"*Patere quam ipse fecisti legem,*" Toussaint remarked after he had
taken the oath on his own Constitution. ("I will be subject to the
laws that I myself have drafted.")

"My desire for power is sincere," he said to Borgella, who had
been a feared royalist planter and was now the editor of Toussaint's
Constitution. "Your enjoyment of power constitutes the pure dynamics of your being," Borgella replied.

During consultations that lasted for weeks, Borgella had discussed the Constitution in all its parts with Toussaint. He was
amazed at Toussaint's shrewd ideas and numerous suggestions on
details. Toussaint was particularly concerned that there should be
no wrongful applications of any of its articles.

"I am in Little Paris," Borgella remarked. "Toussaint Louverture
is the Pericles of the Constitution of Haiti."

The women and girls who liked to consult Toussaint about their
personal problems and dilemmas called him their "Solomon the

Wise." The people believed that Toussaint "was always busy thinking." Pascal, Toussaint's secretary, once said, "He thought when he was galloping on his horse, he even thought when he was praying attentively and, therefore, he did not pray but he thought."

On the other hand, Toussaint also acquired the nickname "Chatterbox," which referred to his monologues. He was not good at conversation, but he listened, again according to Pascal, visibly invisible or invisibly visible. When he began to speak in a debate or discussion, it often seemed as if he wanted to confirm both points of view at the same time. He said both yes and no, which meant that he could remain impartial and make the decisions himself, as dictator.

Toussaint loved the theater. The first thing he did after the constitution had been adopted was to organize a big evening in Port-au-Prince, at a theater that had remained unused for years. Remarkable here as well was his resemblance to Napoleon, who, during his tensest days in Moscow, sat drafting, by candlelight, new regulations for the Théâtre-Français. Toussaint went even further in his love for the theater – he would have liked to have been an actor himself. "Those whom we love and those whom we hate live inside us," he once said. It was a cautious sophism for saying that he had no finite convictions. He had been able to make the greatest, most successful changes in his career by showing himself to be wholly or partly unpredictable: "People should be able to change their opinions often, sometimes a hundred times per day."

Toussaint never displayed any emotions at the death of friends or relations. "The death of a loved one never burdens me, but the absence of a beloved person who is still alive is always unbearable to me," he said. One of Toussaint's slogans was, "*Ça qui lans coeur gnannc, ce couteau seul qui comain*," which means something like "What is in my heart can only be removed with a knife."

He considered the fact that he could dissemble a virtue. Those who watched him in small, everyday routines were witness to the fact that his dissembling could also be a form of hypocrisy. There was always vanity in his boldness, egotism in his energy, sly hidden motives in his desire for order. As with all men considered truly great, his character was not simplistic or plain to any observer.

Toussaint also exercised terror during his reign – that is to say, he allowed massacres to take place with his knowledge and permission. When given cause, he had hostages and innocent people murdered without hesitation. He raged terribly against the mulattoes, against the Spaniards and against the whites after Leclerc's invasion. His opponents spread horror stories about him, and a defamatory pamphlet by Dubroca was popular in France a year before his death. For decades, historiography in Haiti itself was dominated by mulattoes who judged Toussaint negatively for the most part, even the careful record keepers Saint-Rémy and Thomas Madiou. On the other hand, there was limitless glorification as well as justification of his machiavellian deeds of terror, even during his lifetime.

Toussaint never personally killed or tortured innocent people; even his opponents could never produce any eyewitnesses to substantiate this, or even anyone who had heard such a thing. Numerous times he halted or intervened in executions or torturing. But there definitely were some settlements of personal accounts. A certain Blanc Cazenave once received clear indications from Toussaint that the liquidation of some twenty whites would be appreciated by him. After the executions, Toussaint showed great indignation toward his "father," Laveaux, and he had Blanc Cazenave executed without trial. *"Requiescat in pace,"* he wrote derisively to Laveaux.

Vollée handled Toussaint's personal administration for many years. Toussaint lived a frugal life and he never made any attempt to enrich himself arbitrarily or to embezzle state funds. But Toussaint did administer state funds as if they were his private wealth. During his best year, 1801, there really was a light on the horizon for the economy of Haiti. This was partly thanks to Vollée's administrative work. He knew a lot; he knew everything; hence he knew too much and, shortly after Leclerc's invasion, he was liquidated by order of Toussaint.

These sad examples are counterbalanced by many more examples of Toussaint intervening on behalf of victims of terror and arbitrariness. Even when Haiti had almost completely been returned to the authority of the French in 1802, the great majority of whites continued to prefer the protection of Toussaint's troops as escorts when they had to travel cross-country. Toussaint was famous, even during the first years after the Night of Fire, for those safe escorts – especially for the so badly harassed whites.

"The revenge is mine, but God will determine when," is a saying that Toussaint most assuredly did not honor. For example, he never held Dessalines accountable for his frequent cruel and arbitrary killings, when it could easily be determined how the Tiger raged. When whites called his attention to the atrocities that were committed, at least partly, in his name, Toussaint generally started talking about the atrocities in France. He was aware not only of Saint-Just's theory of the Terror ("It is impossible to reign without terror") but also of the atrocities that had been committed in the name of liberty, equality and brotherhood from the beginning of the French Revolution and, in waves of alarming extent, from the late summer of 1792 on.

In 1802, Toussaint learned that Louis Fréron, the French mass murderer who had accounted for so many hundreds of innocent victims in Toulon, among other places, had been included in Leclerc's invasion army (Leclerc's wife was the former mistress of Fréron). Through the black officer Laplume, Toussaint tried to make contact with Fréron, who had taken up residence in Les Cayes, because he wanted to hear the stories about the Reign of Terror in the provinces from Fréron himself. Even earlier, when Hédouville had come to Haiti, Toussaint immediately informed himself about the man and first heard about the dreadful bloodbaths that had been caused in the Vendée by the republicans, under the leadership of Hédouville among others. To Roume, Toussaint once held forth about the laziness of the republican army, which couldn't manage to defeat the British but had, with its superiority of numbers, settled with the armies of the unfortunate Catholic peasants in the Vendée – armies of peasants who were even poorer than the poorest republicans. "I would have totally defeated those armies of yours among all those hills and marshes," he asserted.

Of course, what happened in France during the September killings in the Vendée, and in the provincial cities subjugated to the Reign of Terror, was no less horrible than the bloodbaths the French perpetrated in Haiti. And even before the Night of Fire, the French in Haiti were already responsible for the first extensive massacres and torturings, generally in the name of the Revolution. When they made their last attempts to restore their authority, as well as slavery, in 1792 and 1802, they did so in the name of the Revolution.

* * *

Under the short-lived government of Toussaint there was terror. However, wildly contradicting reports can be read in the brochures and newspaper articles about Haiti from the days before Leclerc's invasion fleet set out. Some authors testified to order, quiet, peace, restoration of trade, courageous and massive attempts to restore cultivation of the plantations, commitment toward a new social structure and a remarkable solidarity among the various races and groups – for the first time in the context of an individual nation. On the other hand, there are the testimonies about a reign of strict military cruelty, about generals who, like maharajahs on their estates, squeezed and kneaded the last ounce of energy out of a people who, in reality, saw themselves as doomed to a new, fancified form of slavery.

There are also testimonies about an ever-worsening economy, ever-higher taxes, ever-lower proceeds. These opinions are even to be found in the newest books about this heroic period in Haiti's history, a period that can only be compared to that of the Mexican, Chinese or Russian revolutions of the twentieth century. No historian can draw definite conclusions from the numbers and statistics found in the greatly manipulated sources. In Toussaint's favor remain the bare facts.

The year 1801, when Toussaint's Constitution was implemented, was a year of peace for all of Haiti. During the year 1801, again there was importation and exportation of all plantation products on a scale that could be compared to the years before 1791. American, British and French ships came and went. The ports of Haiti were once more the busiest of the entire Caribbean. Toussaint had blacks brought in again on ships from Africa. But this time the blacks came of their own free will, their hearts full of expectations, as immigrants to the first free country for their race. These immigrants were also at once declared French citizens by Toussaint. He issued the most severe prohibitions against the display of any official sign of independence. Haiti was a nation but, as a part of France, it was a partner in the French commonwealth.

Toussaint represented France and he was France. The national anthem was the *Marseillaise,* the flag was the tri-colored flag of France, the language was French, the religion was Catholicism – at first the Gallic version of the republic and later the Catholicism of Napoleon. All French national holidays were also celebrated in Haiti; and the planters were allowed to take up all their old relationships with the French ports and trading companies.

It was the clear and obvious commitment of Toussaint that caused the poorest of the poor to have some hope again, even the expectation of an entirely new future, after so many years of war and terror. Toussaint's insatiable interest in everything that happened in his realm exhausted his dozens of secretaries and government officials. Around noon, they would fall asleep on their benches, behind the tables with the endless piles of papers and reports by and for Toussaint. Then suddenly he would be standing in front of them and would put everyone back to work. They never knew whether he was far away or nearby.

Within a period of days, he would show up in Cap François, in Les Cayes, in Saint-Marc, in Jérémie, in Léogane, in Port-au-Prince, in Santo Domingo. Some seventy horses of a carefully bred British–Spanish race were always kept at the ready for him. They could cover eighty kilometers in one stretch and Toussaint could remain in the saddle for twenty-four hours without tiring. A few times, he had ridden horses that showed signs of exhaustion until they dropped dead. Thanks to them, he was "omnipresent."

"Father Toussaint," the children said, "likes to ride over the clouds if there are clouds and, if there aren't any, he rides at night because he likes the dark." While Toussaint rode or walked, he constantly looked to the side. Another peculiarity of his was that his tongue could be seen almost all the time, as if he had a small snake in his mouth. It was so obvious because Toussaint did not have any teeth in his upper jaw and the teeth in his lower jaw caused him constant pain. His face showed all kinds of tics and twitchings and his laugh was always short, loud and sly. He could, as his secretary Pascal said, be horrible in his anger, so that even Dessalines would cringe before him.

Toussaint was wounded in battle seventeen times. At least ten attempts on his life were made and some of his doubles were killed.

There were false Toussaints going around, men who looked very much like him, at least in the dark. These were the ones who, instead of their leader, would attend meetings and gatherings that Toussaint did not quite trust. He himself regularly pretended to be someone else by taking on a disguise. At those times, his preference was to play the goat's head, *bouche abrit* (mouth covered).

Toussaint preferred to eat alone, quickly, in a dark corner. He considered eating a shameful waste of time. He did not eat meat and he was always wary of being poisoned. On the one hand, he simply ate as little as possible for safety's sake and he only ate a regular meal if some old auntie whom he trusted had prepared the food, two of his favorite dishes being callaboo and pumpkin soup. For entire days, however, he would live on hard biscuits, macaroni, oranges and bananas, which he insisted on peeling himself.

Every day, Toussaint took a bath at least once and, when he was on the road, he often took mud baths. While out on campaigns, he simply slept on the ground, in his clothes and with his boots on. Two or three hours of sleep were sufficient for him. Just like Napoleon, he was able to fall asleep, if he so wished, amidst noise, hustle and bustle, and with people talking all around him. He wore chicken legs attached to his boots by way of spurs. (With these he wounded the French General Rochambeau on both legs in man-to-man combat in 1802.) He was excellent at fencing and fighting with sabres, and he was unbeatable in precision throwing with knives. Toussaint was a fantastic horseman, but people would double up laughing when he mounted his horse. He would look like a little old lady—a condition probably caused by the premature aging of his hip joints, which, along with an old wound, also made it impossible for him to lie on his side when sleeping.

Toussaint wore a watch on a long chain around his neck, but he never looked at it to see what time it was because he always knew from the position of the sun. "I only use the chain to chase away flies," he would say. He was almost always dressed in blue, with white bands in his trousers. He very rarely wore epaulets, which were the pride and joy of Belair, labeled as his successor, who had his wife attach them to his bare shoulders. When Toussaint went to see a white man, he sometimes chose to put on a fancy hat with plumes rather than his usual madras. "Am I not a real Jacobin?" he would ask. Among blacks, he sometimes walked around dressed in a brightly colored chasuble, which he also wore when preaching Christ's passion. It was said that during the period of Easter he had celebrated Mass repeatedly, and had been one of those present at the altar during a Solemn Mass with three or more priests celebrating.

Toussaint set great store by his soldiers' showing themselves as devotedly Catholic as possible. Hédouville, who had spent much effort persecuting and exterminating the Catholics in the Vendée on behalf of the Reign of Terror, was stunned at one of the first letters he received from Toussaint. It read:

> You must punctually take care of the following: the army commanders shall be ordered to lead the men in morning or evening prayers, to the extent their service activities allow this. At the very next parade, the commanding generals must have a High Mass celebrated and a *Te Deum* sung in all municipalities of their province as a manifestation of gratitude to the Lord for having led us in our campaigns, for the enemy's departure without blood having been shed and for a safe return of thousands of people of all skin colors who had gone astray. And, finally, for the return to work of ten thousand workers. The sign for the *Te Deum* shall be given by a cannon firing twenty-two shots.

Toussaint liked to have fresh flowers around the house and he enjoyed gardening, together with his wife. His very ample Suzanne liked to have her husband push her around among the flower beds until they both rolled over in the grass. He had parks created, where the main theme would be busts and monuments of himself that he had erected, although there were busts of Raynal and of Spartacus scattered around as well. The new province of Louverture especially was full of these. All Saints' Day, Toussaint's brithday, had been declared a national holiday, the day of the beloved father of the people.

His British admirer, Rainsford, described how Toussaint moved freely among the people on feast days. At the Hôtel de la République in Cap François, he happily participated in games of billiards. He admired the unusual watches of foreigners and, if any of these would be presented to him as gifts, he placed them at once in the National Museum that he himself had founded. There, he also began to collect paintings that were offered to him by people dabbling in art, precursors of the famous primitive painters of 20th-century Haiti.

A few times, Toussaint ordered festive meals served in Government House in Cap François, which he had enlarged and restored, and also in Dessalines' palace in Port-au-Prince, where he sometimes stayed. During the meal, of which Toussaint himself barely partook, drummers continued to beat their drums. The orchestras of Dessalines and Toussaint sometimes played against each other with competitive enthusiasm so that guests had to shout to understand each other. ("At least they can't prepare a conspiracy," was Toussaint's view.) Every time a special toast was made, a cannon would fire a shot.

After these festive state dinners, Toussaint would grant an audience, during which he would prefer to stand in a rather dark spot or near a window or exit. People would find that he had an absolutely amazing memory, especially for faces. He could also repeat and mimic what someone had said at a previous meeting, which might have been years ago. The French especially would laugh themselves to tears when he imitated them. Toussaint thought French was an affected language and he was proud of his uneducated way of pronouncing it. He actually believed French was too beautiful and elegant a language for a people among whom there were so many scoundrels.

When people presented him with too many requests and asked too many favors of him while they were conversing, Toussaint would sometimes suddenly leave them standing alone. He would also become irritated the moment a guest began to talk about politics. He would then refer the person to his pamphlets and to the newspapers, *Le Cap François* and the *Gazette Officielle*.

He much preferred to talk about the catechism, which had been published under his supervision and with his imprimatur and, as people were saying, in his final edited version. He would point out to people that they should be sure to study Latin as used in the Catholic Church. Latin might possibly one day become the new, more convenient world language, once everyone had finally converted to Catholicism. Anyone who did not know the answer to a question like "What is the meaning of God's grace that saves souls?" would at once find Toussaint's back turned to him. Being amazingly well-informed about the most diverse subjects, he would also come up with questions such as "What is meant by cultivation by grafting?" "Can you name some different kinds of taproots?" "You mean you don't know all these things? You had better do some studying before you do anything else, you poor Negro!"

When Toussaint bowed, it always meant that he wanted to end the conversation. And he could slip out of a room noiselessly. While the audience continued on and people were merrily eating and drinking, Caribbean style, with many a toast to Toussaint, he would be miles away on his horse, thinking about other matters.

* * *

Toussaint always addressed white women as madame and black women as citizeness. Shortly before Leclerc's invasion, he was preparing to found a separate association for black women, where they were supposed to have been able to learn the grand manners of the Parisian drawing rooms. That he spoke more at length with whites than with blacks was simply a consequence of the fact that it was easier for him to start a conversation with whites about matters that occupied him or that he had read. In addition, he always liked to pump the whites for information. The encouragement of a greater interest in reading and in the use of libraries was one of the programs on his agenda. It has been estimated that, at the time of Toussaint Louverture, approximately ninety percent of the black population did not know how to read. Toussaint once said to Borgella, who had called his attention to the worrisome problem of illiteracy among blacks, "Oh yes, school and reading will be necessary. But don't forget that our people must now be soldiers first of all. They must think of their guns day and night. And, in addition, they must work constantly."

Some whites who began to act brazenly when they imagined that Toussaint gave them preferential treatment were immediately told off in a sarcastic manner. Toussaint was always a good judge of people's intentions. This remarkable ability to see matters objectively was reported by all whites who left testimonies about him as his most alienating and, at the same time, perhaps most valuable quality.

Bayon de Libertad, Toussaint's former master, whose family had been saved by Toussaint during the Night of Fire, returned to Haiti in 1798. Toussaint gave him all his lands back, as well as a special labor contract exempting his employees from all forms of bondage. Nothing that smacked of forced labor was to encumber any part of the plantation where the young Toussaint had learned to tame horses and had read Raynal for the first time.

Libertad then decided to attend an audience given by Toussaint. When his turn came, he was overcome with emotions of gratitude and attempted to embrace the leader. But Toussaint stepped back, as if stung by a bee. "Stand at ease, Mr. Planter, there is more distance between me and you now than there ever was in the past between you and me. Return to the Bréda plantation and administer it with justice and strength. Make the blacks work hard so that the general well-being of all blacks will be increased by the success of your property. This is the wish of the first of the blacks, who is now in command in Haiti."

Toussaint offered reimbursement of damages to many of those among the emigrated whites whose relationship to Haiti he deemed important. He did the same for Napoleon's Empress Joséphine, whose feelings of racism and indignation about the nationalization of her properties changed to a great appreciation for Toussaint. His sons Placidus and Isaac, who were studying in France, were received by Joséphine at the palace of Malmaison outside Paris. Isaac even wrote a poem for her there. She told him in confidence that Napoleon's hatred of the blacks was very similar to that shown by the "small whites" in the Antilles, which she herself had been able to observe in Martinique, where she was born. She also told him that Napoleon had been angriest when, in a newspaper article, he had been called the "Toussaint Louverture of the Whites."

Toussaint also remembered his former enemies. He made certain that Biassou's widow received a small pension. He also sent a warm letter of recommendation to Sonthonax, his former antagonist, when Sonthonax, upon his return to France, was again taken to court by his opponents in the Directorate.

The only topic of conversation about which Toussaint would become emotional was Africa. When it came up, his tics would change from little grins that interrupted his speech to sob-like grimaces. From the beginning of the year 1800, Toussaint had encouraged voluntary immigration of Africans to Haiti. He had only one wish for the time when everything would be functioning well in Haiti: he would go to Africa with a select army of one thousand in order to plant the French flag there and effect the Louverturian revolution for the benefit of all blacks.

Toussaint had supposedly declared to the slaves on the Bréda plantation as early as 1778 that, no matter how long it would take, black supremacy would be the future of Haiti, of the Caribbean and of the Americas. Again and again, Toussaint would pull out his glass vial with black and white kernels of corn. He would shake it and shake it until finally the moment would come when all the black kernels were on top and all the white ones at the bottom. Then he would beam and call out, "This is the way it will be here too, you can rest assured of that."

Toussaint often embarrassed blacks at his audiences by sharply pointing out their shortcomings and failures while praising the whites for their commitment and inventiveness. Especially Dessalines, who could neither read nor write but loved to dictate overly long letters, is acknowledged to have felt an enormous resentment of Toussaint for his pitiless sarcasm about stupidity and laziness. Dessalines liked nothing better than to have protracted meals, accompanied by music, wherein one brass band would drown out another and he would move along with the rhythm – singing along completely off-key because he could not carry a tune. Toussaint's generals often did not dare to look him in the eye because they were afraid of having to confess their carousing and wasting of time to him.

In conversations, Toussaint would also put the whites in their place even more brusquely, as Roume testified. Toussaint felt that, considering all the centuries they had had in which to study and develop themselves, their general culture had remained rather poor. What was the planters' favorite book? *Margot la ravadeuse* (Margot the Chatterbox), pornographic and insignificant.

Toussaint's most convincing strength was his complete fairness and impartiality. He was simply not open to any form of flattery, nepotism or corruption. It was something the blacks recognized and appreciated, and which became a source of widespread pride.

At one point, a white planter wanted to have the position of supervisor of a government-owned warehouse. He wrote to apply for the job, but did not get a reply. His wife's letters to Toussaint also remained unanswered. Shortly after she gave birth to a son, she went to one of Toussaint's audiences and asked him to be the godfather of her child.

"Why do you want to name your child after me? Your request has no purpose other than to influence me to help your husband get the job he wants, and your heart resists the request you make of me."

"How can you think such a thing, General? No, my husband loves you and all the whites are fond of you."

"Madame, I know the whites as if I were inside their skin. But I am black and I know their aversion for us. Have you given any thought to the request you are making of me? If I said yes, how can you be sure that your son will not reproach you when he has grown up and he sees that a Negro is his godfather?"

"But, General . . ."

"Madame," and Toussaint pointed at the sky, "only he who governs everything is immortal. I am a general, that is true, but I am black. Who knows if, after my death, my brothers won't be forced back into slavery to languish again under the whip of the whites? The things people accomplish do not last. The French Revolution has enlightened the Europeans and they now love and pity us, but the white planters will continue to be the enemies of the blacks. You want your husband to have that position. Well, madame, I will approve the request. Let him do his job well and remember that I cannot see everything, but that nothing escapes God's eyes. However, I cannot agree to become the godfather of your child. You would risk being reproached by the planters and, one day, maybe by your son."

In Port-au-Prince, Toussaint liked to go for walks with Father Mélenière on his right and the Italian priest Marini on his left. He would spend time with them particularly on liturgical feast days, when he would often ascend the pulpit himself. Using an abundance of Latin quotations, he would then talk about church and politics or spiritual and worldly matters as if they were all in the same category. According to Toussaint, people could only be good French republicans if they were good Catholics.

It was striking that Toussaint continued to use the names Port-au-Prince and Fort Dauphin instead of the new names, Port Républicain and Fort Liberté. It gave some whites the wrong idea that Toussaint would help them restore the pre-revolutionary regime. But Toussaint never talked about a return to the monarchy. Although his policies were indeed geared to the preservation of the plantation system, he made sure that one party would own and control all the land, namely, the state – represented by Toussaint, and with his soldiers as the officials.

Toussaint's policies were perhaps closest to those of an enlightened dictatorship, with some elements of populist democracy of a Bonapartist nature. He felt that there was no other stance for him since the country had to be in a constant state of military readiness and economic restructuring. For this reason, Toussaint preferred hard-working people, even if they were not pious, to pious people who did not want to work because, in Haiti, they could always live off what they could gather free of charge on the fields. People who were not pious but worked hard had his blessing: "Whoever does not want to go to church but does work hard has no need for a sermon."

Toussaint thought out loud and arranged for many of his thoughts to be recorded in letters. His most brilliant letters were written during the period between 1796 and 1800, the splendid years of battle before he came to full power. It had been the period in which he accepted the French Revolution, yet shoved Paris and the French planters aside (while Paris could not deny that he was in fact implementing the Revolution). Shrewd, witty and astute were the letters he wrote to the Directorate, whose lurches between left-wing and right-wing coups he had once cleverly described as "fructidorizing," after the revolutionary month Fructidor (August). In a letter of November 5, 1797, he lectured the Directors in France about their politics. It almost seemed as if a First Consul was addressing them!

It is your duty, citizen directors, to help us weather the storm that is being brewed in the shadows of silence by the eternal enemies of liberty. It is your duty to put laws in effect that truly enlighten. It is your duty to keep the enemies of our new order from swarming again over the coasts of our unfortunate island and defiling them with new crimes. Do not allow your brothers and friends to be sacrificed to people who want to rule, even if it is on the ruins of human civilization. We want to believe that your wisdom will help you to avoid the dangerous cliffs among which our common enemies are asking you to navigate.

* * *

From the time the Haitian Constitution had been enacted, about twenty-five men worked with Toussaint in the capacity, more or less, of state secretaries. Half of them were blacks, one quarter were whites and one quarter were mulattoes. The generals and colonels who monitored the plantations, a few hundred, were at least ninety-five-percent black.

Toussaint did not have friends with whom he could have a highly confidential relationship. Even Dessalines never became his friend. According to Toussaint, Dessalines was like the murdered French satirist Marat, just as superficial, and he lacked both tact and strategic insight. "When I ask him to cut down a tree, he immediately pulls out the roots." Toussaint often told Dessalines straight out what he thought of him. In the presence of Toussaint, Dessalines was constantly hissing between his teeth while keeping his eyes on the ground. Toussaint also reproached him about his gluttony: "A full stomach ties our hands and chains our feet."

Toussaint constantly emphasized a strict work ethic and he expected his soldiers, to whom he had in fact entrusted the entire top layer of society, to believe likewise. According to Toussaint, the blacks had to be able to keep themselves in perfect physical condition as soldiers from the time they were fourteen years of age until they were fifty-five. However, they also had to be able to monitor the books of the plantations, to distinguish among the various qualities of crops, to build roads and to read Latin.

Toussaint liked to participate in the work on his plantations,

Deks, Ennery, Beaumont and Sansay. Toward the end of 1799, there
was a report in the newspaper *Le Moniteur* about such a day: "With
Toussaint on the Plantation." Toussaint had established this uni-
tary newspaper that took the place of two former competitors –
La Gazette de Cap, which had supported Sonthonax as "our
Robespierre," and *Le Capois,* which continued to show a crypto-
liking for the marquis Borel and the pre-revolutionary government.
In this new paper, Toussaint liked to publish his proclamations and
decrees. A very faithful supporter of Toussaint was the journalist
Nathan, the only Jew on Haiti, who had a position in Toussaint's
administration. Toussaint once remarked to him, "Those who do
not have the strength to be hammers should be able to keep going
while playing the role of anvils." Nathan remained more faithful
to Toussaint than Huin, Toussaint's spy in France, who had been
praised by Toussaint for years. It later turned out that Huin was a
double agent, and he revealed himself as such during Leclerc's
invasion.

Pamphile de Lacroix, a general who fought with Leclerc and the
author of a standard work on the Haitian war of independence,
continued to greatly appreciate refined sensual pleasures until he
was a very old man. He wrote about the women of Haiti, "The
atmosphere of this country makes the women glow with love in an
extraordinary manner. They fetter the men with their loose morals.
They are sometimes gripped by erotic fury as if by a serious illness,
the *furor uterinus.* Just seeing a man, no matter who he is, stirs their
emotions. They provoke him, throw themselves at him and, with
their caresses, draw him into their own state of frenzy. Hence, the
men on this island have nothing to complain about and, thanks
to these women, the population increases."

Against this "fury," Toussaint set forth his pleas for chastity. He
championed matrimony and fought against concubinage. "I do not
understand how respectable women can act this way, against
common decency. Chastity should be the principal ornament of
their sex," he said. Toussaint therefore fought an intense campaign
against women's lewd or seductive ways of dressing. He was
especially irritated by the ever-advancing decolletage of women's
dresses. He proudly told how Napoleon was very much against
this as well: "In the drawing rooms, he has big fires going even in

summer because he is afraid that the ladies might otherwise catch cold, since they are almost naked."

At receptions and audiences, Toussaint made a point of turning away from women whose breasts showed too seductively, or he openly stated his indignation to them. One mother, who obviously had her daughter show off her charms on purpose, was told by Toussaint, "But, Madame, how can you let your daughter expose herself this way?" Toussaint once called breasts "the devil's holy-water font." Women eventually adopted the habit of wearing flowers, preferably roses, which were Toussaint's favorite, on their breasts.

Toussaint sometimes made vulgar remarks about women; for example, a pregnant woman had "a roll in the oven." According to Toussaint, the women in Haiti "calved like the cows." Although he definitely had a sense of humor and could be self-effacing, he always got upset if women laughed in his presence, perhaps due to self-consciousness about his appearance. "I know for sure that there is always one among them who is laughing about me."

Toussaint would get angry at Dessalines and Belair, who drank too much during lustful pursuits. "They only use rum and tafia so that they can grab under skirts without inhibitions." He forbade his soldiers to dress, as the mulattoes Rigaud and Beauvais liked to do, decked out in fancy clothes.

Despite all this and despite his simple way of life, Toussaint had no shortage of female admirers. The creole women especially considered him a mysterious hero who, perhaps, possessed the miraculous powers of a Mackandal. Gifts from women were delivered to Toussaint daily. Among these would be clothes and stockings that they themselves had made for him. Many of them became his girlfriends. Madame Valbrègue and also Madame Lartigue, a widow who had a position in Toussaint's administration, became his acknowledged mistresses. Madame Lartigue's daughter also became his mistress. Télémaque, the mayor of Cap François, often arranged for these encounters to take place in isolated houses.

In 1802, the French found a suitcase in Port-au-Prince that had belonged to Toussaint. In it were a large number of love letters, as well as ribbons, handkerchiefs, rings, baubles and locks of hair in various colors. Toussaint had written the names of some of the women on cards: Idé, Julie, Valentine, Léontine, Adélaïde, Angèle, etc. His pet names for some of the women were also included: Little Doughnut, Cinnamon Apple, Cream Puff, Honey Biscuit, Banana to Be Peeled, Oyster to Be Eaten, and so on.

Within the family, Daddy Toussaint was the favorite of his future daughter-in-law, Victoire Tuzac, and his niece, Louise Chancy. They regularly brought along children, who all liked to lie at Toussaint's feet, for he was good at telling at least one story: the adventures of a certain Ata Brigade. He probably meant this to refer to Attila, who was Dessalines' favorite historical hero.

Toussaint's wife, Suzanne, had an immaculate reputation, as did the wives of Dessalines and Christophe, respectively, Claire Heureuse and Marie-Louise. Madame Dessalines and Madame Christophe were active in the hospitals, which functioned rather poorly. Madame Dessalines would also appear shortly after a battle in order to help the wounded. Suzanne Louverture, a heavy-set woman who was always cheerful and pleasant, was totally dedicated to her husband. She enjoyed the reputation of keeping her door always open for anyone who wanted to have a meal or stay overnight.

According to a story told by an eyewitness, a certain Saint-Antoine, Toussaint once encountered a little girl who had neither mother nor father. She implored him, crying, "Daddy, Daddy, may I go with you?" She was a ten-year-old orphan, named Rosa, from Plaisance. Toussaint picked her up and put her on his horse, whereupon he rode home immediately. When he arrived, he said to Madame Louverture, "Look, another little orphan who has found her father. Please be her mother, too." Rosa stayed. She had been preceded by many other children, and many followed her as well.

◆ 11 ◆

Napoleon Strikes Back

■——■

O N MARCH 4, 1801, NAPOLEON WROTE A LETTER TO TOUSSAINT that was never sent. In this letter, Napoleon confirmed Toussaint's position as Captain General of Haiti. He also stated that the time was approaching when French divisions would be using Haiti as a base to project the continued glory of the republic in the Caribbean region. Surprisingly, the letter ended with the words "Most cordial greetings." The letter seemed to indicate that Napoleon was speculating whether to take his next step at that time toward realizing his great ambitions in the Americas. Although the Treaty of Amiens, establishing peace with England, was signed a year later, Napoleon was obviously counting on one thing remaining certain for the future: continued armed confrontation with England over power on the European continent and in the colonies. The situation seemed to be stationary otherwise. Austria had concluded a peace treaty; Spain had become a vassal state of Napoleon's and had ceded Louisiana to him. In addition, Spain and Portugal were waging a continuing war of economic blockades against England in South America. Russia was ruled by a tzar who admired Napoleon and who was ready to direct the League of Neutral Nations, of which he had become a member, against England rather than against France.

The ongoing and future battle against England was the crucial issue. Napoleon's plans included resumption of the fighting in

Egypt and the annexation of Malta for France. Expeditions to the islands of Réunion and Mauritius in the Indian Ocean were being prepared. Like Alexander the Great, Napoleon dreamt of marching on India. There he would repeat the Seven Years' War and this time win it for the French. The power centrum in Central America would be made up of Haiti, Martinique, Guadeloupe and Louisiana. The Guyanas would become the base from which to invade South America, which Spain and Portugal would one day be forced to cede.

It was a grandiose perspective on a global scale. In fact, the French war against England lasted practically without interruption until Napoleon's final fall from power. It was fought on so many fronts, situated all across the world, that it could be called the first world war, making the wars of 1914–1918 and 1939–1945 the second and the third, respectively.

It may be that Napoleon's American dream turned into a failure primarily because he did not send his March 4, 1801, letter to Toussaint Louverture. Instead of incorporating Toussaint's power as a hinge in the projection of French might and influence, he decided to destroy Toussaint instead. Later, during his exile on St. Helena, Napoleon confessed to French historian Emmanuel Las Cases, "My greatest mistake was to try to subdue Haiti by force of arms. I should have let Toussaint Louverture rule it."

Another reason the letter was not sent is that Napoleon had become exceedingly annoyed about the high-handed attitude of Toussaint, who called himself the "Black Napoleon" and who had once addressed a letter to Napoleon "From the first of the Blacks to the first of the Whites." The provisionary Constitution that Toussaint had enacted in the name of France, but of his own accord, had been another challenge to French authority, after the annexation of Santo Domingo, which had been done against Napoleon's will. And then there had been the brazen removal of Hédouville and, later, of Roume. These acts had really been veiled attempts at a coup or, as Roume called it, cheeky imitations of the Spanish *pronunciamientos*. Napoleon himself had, in fact, enacted a coup that had only barely succeeded and, at the decisive moment, there had been quite a bit of fumbling. He had reason to be jealous of Toussaint's much more resolute decisions.

There was yet another reason for Napoleon in 1801 to prepare the greatest invasion fleet of all time. The former planters, members of the resurrected Club Massiac, had convinced him that there was only one chance for a restoration of the economy in Haiti: the reinstatement of slavery. With France's prized colony under the control of an ex-slave who, while pledging allegiance to France, meanwhile signed treaties and conducted independent negotiations with the British and Americans, the need for a reassertion of French power was clear.

When Toussaint first heard from his spy, Huin, that preparations for the invasion were being made in France, he was bitter but not surprised. His reaction was, "I counted on this happening. I have known that they would come and that the reason behind it would be that one and only goal: reinstatement of slavery. However, we will never again submit to that."

*   *   *

Napoleon had no qualms about betraying some of the more luminous achievements of the French Revolution. On May 20, 1802, precisely fourteen days before Toussaint would be kidnapped, slavery was legally restored throughout French-owned territory. On top of this and to the disgrace of France, an imperial decree was issued on July 2 forbidding all blacks and coloreds entrance into France.

Napoleon had a ruthless secondary objective in mind with his decision to launch an invasion, and he did not hesitate to reveal it plainly in letters and conversations. In Europe, thousands of soldiers were without jobs who, after having fought for the Revolution under the leadership of officers with a firm belief in their ideologies, might become the core of a new longing for revolution or, in any case, for a countermovement to block the road toward the dictatorship Napoleon had in mind. These tens of thousands – among whom were Poles, Swiss, Spaniards and Germans who had been inspired to fight for France by revolutionary idealism – were nothing at that time but another problem for Napoleon to deal with. In Haiti, they could indulge their fighting spirit and, possibly, lose their lives in a climate that had already proved the undoing of so many British soldiers. And if they should succeed, Napoleon would at least hold the important pawn in the Caribbean that was the pivot of his American dream.

At the deliberations about Haiti during which the final decisions were made, Secretary Forfait was the only one to speak out against Napoleon's plans for the invasion. The First Consul shut him up by snarling at him, "There are sixty thousand men who will have to be removed."

England, in a secret agreement made earlier during the negotiations for the Treaty of Amiens, agreed to let the French invasion fleet cross the Atlantic unmolested. Napoleon knew that the British had no objections to his dealing with the upstart black nation. The continued independence of Haiti under Toussaint's leadership could unleash a dangerous new wave of slave rebellions in the Caribbean region, and both the British and the Americans feared such a wave. They might want to play Toussaint off against other powers when it suited their schemes, but they would never help him become truly powerful and thus an influence on their own slaves in Jamaica or in the American South. Through Talleyrand, the British were told that the invasion was being carried out in the interests of Western civilization and that it, therefore, deserved to be favored and supported by all nations with colonies and commercial interests in the American hemisphere.

Vincent, earlier sent as Napoleon's peace commissioner to Haiti, drafted a last desperate memo recounting the misfortunes that the rather formidable British army had suffered there. Napoleon was so enraged about this memo that he decided he never wanted to see Vincent again.

The mulattoes Rigaud, Pétion, Vilatte and Boyer were told that they could get themselves ready for their return home. They supported Napoleon despite the fact that they knew they would have to do the bizarre preparatory work for their mortal enemies, the colonists and former slave owners who were already busy dividing Haiti up among themselves once again.

Together with their guardian, Coisnon, Toussaint's sons Isaac and Placidus, both students at the Lycée Liancourt, were invited to the Tuileries by Napoleon. Bonaparte first let the young men enjoy a festive meal, in which Joséphine also participated. The two both knew Isaac and Placidus from several previous meetings. Then

Napoleon offered the boys splendid new suits, and told them: "Your father is a great man. He has served France excellently. Tell him that as first statesman of the French people I promise him protection, fame and honor. Never believe that France has plans to wage war against Haiti. I am not sending the army with which you will travel to Haiti in order to *fight* your father's troops, but to *join up* with those forces. You will travel fourteen days ahead of General Leclerc, whom I have appointed captain general, in order to prepare your father for the arrival of the army."

There was no need for this. Toussaint had already been informed about the imminent arrival of the French army. For months he had been making preparations. He increased the importation of weapons from the United States, he reinforced fortresses and casemates, he had pits dug in woods and undergrowth so that his men could entrench themselves there and his opponents fall into them. All young men, from the age of twelve up, had to participate in drills. A campaign of pamphlets and newspaper articles had been preparing his people for the worst-case scenario. "We must always seriously and faithfully welcome orders and envoys from the capital," he declared. "On the other hand, as a soldier I do not have to fear anyone. I only fear God. If I must die, it will be as an honorable soldier who has never had to reproach himself for anything."

The drums signaled to each other during the nights that the Christmas festivities just ended had been the last ones to be celebrated in peace. The irrevocable event was unavoidable – the French were coming!

* * *

Napoleon once gave as another reason for his invasion of Haiti that Toussaint would otherwise invade Jamaica before he could do it, and would start building an entire rebellious realm of slaves in Central America. In any case, Napoleon was definitely convinced that the invasion was a crusade against barbarians. He had Talleyrand inform the Spanish, who had to contribute three thousand men, that the purpose of the invasion was "the safety of the French colonies and of all the European powers in the two Americas; the uprising of the blacks has created a focal point of turmoil that could provoke disorders elsewhere in the world as well."

In the light of these words, the perfidiousness of Napoleon's letter to Toussaint, written a few weeks before the invasion, seems to be even more striking: "The fact that the French flag is still hoisted in Haiti is something we owe to your courageous blacks. Stimulated by your talent and helped by circumstances that you created, you put an end to the civil war, you silenced those tough characters who opposed you, and you restored the honor of our religion and our obligations to God, who is the creator of all things."

As early as the summer of 1801, Napoleon had completed his plans for the invasion. About eighty ships, carrying a total of approximately 35,000 men, would depart at the same time from Vlissingen, Le Havre, Cherbourg, Brest, Lorient, Rochefort, Cádiz and Toulon. After landing, the three main attacks would concentrate on the rapid conquest of Cap François, Fort Liberté, Port-au-Prince and Santo Domingo. The Batavian Republic (The Netherlands, as renamed by its French conquerors in 1795) had been ordered to provide 1,400 men. Vice Admiral Hartsinck was told to report to French Admiral Villaret-Joyeuse, who would command the fleet, despite a less than glorious track record. He had quite a few more defeats to his name than he had victories. When Hartsinck heard who was in charge of the invasion fleet, his comment was: "There has always been some problem with anything in which that man has ever participated. The result has never been good."

Most of the troops that sailed from Vlissingen in southwestern Holland on four Batavian ships were from Germany, supplemented by about one hundred Flemish. Napoleon decided to ignore the advice he had received from various sides suggesting an army of at least 80,000 men, and limited the number to 43,000. After Villaret-Joyeuse had departed with his fleet, he would send another 8,000 men as reinforcements, if necessary. It was still the largest invasion fleet in French history. Ten percent of all the soldiers who were shipped to Haiti were Poles, whose part in this endeavor will be discussed later.

*   *   *

Napoleon must have been goaded by his desire to personally settle accounts with the "First of the Blacks," who dared to have called

himself the "Black Napoleon" and who had been one step ahead
of him in defeating the British and in setting up a dictatorship.
Napoleon considered it too risky to lead the invasion himself after
the senseless adventure in Egypt, which had ultimately proved a
failure. He also felt that such a job was beneath his dignity, as he
stood on the threshold of being the sole ruler of half of Europe.
However, he did for a moment entertain the thought, maybe also
in light of the great American adventure, that he might be able to
crown the invasion with a French empire overseas. It was this idea
that led him to the decision of October 24, 1801, whereby he
appointed General Victoire-Emmanuel Leclerc leader of the
invasion and future governor general of Haiti. Leclerc was an
exceptional officer, the high point of whose career came during the
first Italian campaigns, where he participated in Bonaparte's initial
victories on foreign soil, and during which he came into Napoleon's
good graces.

There were two secondary, but curious, circumstances involved
in Napoleon's decision to send Leclerc as his replacement in this
historic duel with Toussaint Louverture. Leclerc was known as the
"little Napoleon." When comparing reproductions of portraits, the
resemblance between Leclerc, who was born in 1772, and Napoleon
is striking. Although he was blond-haired, Leclerc had the same
short, somewhat plump figure. He was only a little shorter than
Napoleon. His face seemed to have the same features as Bonaparte's
and he walked the same way, using short, jaunty steps. He also wore
exactly the same coats and hats as Napoleon. He would put his right
hand on his stomach inside his coat and let the left one hang on
his back, all in imitation of the French leader.

This was the first thing that was to surprise Toussaint. But there
was something else. On June 14, 1801, the short, blond Leclerc had
married Pauline Bonaparte, Napoleon's next-to-youngest sister.
Hence Toussaint, who had been so anxious to meet Napoleon,
would at least come face to face with the Bonaparte dynasty.

Napoleon accomplished yet a third objective with regard to his
invasion. He appointed the impoverished Stanislas Fréron deputy
prefect of Haiti. With his journal *Orateur du Peuple* (The People's
Orator), Fréron had been partly responsible for instigating the
Reign of Terror and, as an active practitioner, he had practiced what

he preached in Toulon and Marseille, the city he had punished by changing its name to Ville-Sans-Nom (City Without a Name). After the fall of Robespierre, he had led the "white terror" against the southern French royalists during Thermidor. In Marseille and Toulon, Fréron had imitated the "republican marriages" of Carrier, the most infamous murderer of the Reign of Terror; this entailed tying naked men and women to each other and putting them on boats with holes in them that were made to sink during the night. Now, Fréron would be exactly the right person to execute the mopping-up operations in Haiti as he followed behind Leclerc's front lines.

Still, Napoleon made sure that Fréron did not travel on the same ship with Leclerc and Pauline. The fact is that Fréron was Pauline's former lover, who had been rejected by Napoleon because he considered the man a kind of post-revolutionary "slavoyer," good enough to be used to do one's dirty work but not good enough to marry one's sister.

When Leclerc was informed of his appointment, he is said to have exclaimed, "Then I will have to go to those Negro serpents." When Pauline found out – she was rarely found in the same location as her husband – she reacted with the words, "But those Negroes who live there are something like insects, aren't they?"

* * *

Since the behavior of Pauline Bonaparte, often called "Our Lady of Trinkets," has become a legend in the literature of Haiti, she also deserves to be profiled briefly. Pauline, or rather Paoletta, Bonaparte was born in 1780 under the sign of Venus. Her mother, Laetizia, who bore thirteen children in nineteen years, indoctrinated her during her earliest youth with, "Don't ever cry, just do as I do; I suffer in silence. Corsica is the only country in the world where there will never be any luxuries."

Pauline's lean years occurred mainly during the time that she lived with her mother and some of her brothers and sisters in misery and poverty in a small, shabby apartment in Marseille. The extremely attractive Corsican girl had never learnt to read or write. She was a seamstress, but Laetizia, driven by her desperate need, may have possibly steered her and her sisters Caroline and Elisa into a more liberal profession. In any case, the house in Marseille was known as a brothel. During a performance at the theater in Marseille, Laetizia was once recognized by a commissioner. He immediately called out that a prostitute did not belong in the theater, and the entire audience stood and waited until Laetizia had removed herself. (At the time, Napoleon was still in the process of laboriously seeking his fortune in Paris. He had a tawny, yellowish skin, his uniform was far too big for him, he spoke French poorly and mixed it freely with his crackling Italian dialect.)

Pauline would often stand in line at the butcher's in order to buy the only items for which she had enough money: horse blood and meat from cattle either butchered in emergencies or partly rejected for sale. At some point in Marseille, during Fréron's reign of terror, she was noticed by him.

Fréron went around in a coat with enormous collars, wearing a heavily powdered wig and dressed in red silk trousers, white stockings and pointed shoes, while carrying a walking stick with a tip made of lead – the symbol of executive power. Among the Thermidor terrorists, Fréron was known as the most poisonous scoundrel. It was said that, if he were bitten by a snake, he would simply bite back; the snake would die and Fréron would live. This forty-one-year-old serpent fell desperately in love with the fifteen-year-old Pauline, who even then knew how to present her attractions to best advantage. Leclerc, too, was intrigued by her when, introduced by Napoleon, he got to know her in Marseille. Napoleon himself sometimes walked arm in arm with her in such an intimate manner that people took brother and sister for fiancés.

Fréron, who had met Napoleon at the siege of Toulon, and Pauline, who was considered a sensational natural beauty, were soon writing fiery letters to each other. After a lovemaking session with Fréron, who was married and a father but who did not confess to this, Pauline wrote to him, "The water from the river has not been able to cool off my love. I must have drunk nectar, because I am feeling warmer all the time." Next to Fréron, the young officer Leclerc seemed homely and indecisive. But he was the one who would end up in her arms. When Napoleon's star continued to rise, Fréron, who was in disgrace and forever short of money, was scratched as a marriage candidate. When Leclerc once casually brought a conversation around to the topic of Napoleon's little sister, the French leader assured him, "I shall make you a little younger again and give you more of a future. You will marry Pauline."

By then, Pauline had already been around the world as far as the art of love was concerned. In her drawing rooms, people could only whisper in her presence, so overwhelming were her charms. She had so many lovers that, in order to distinguish them more easily from each other, dressed as they were in uniform, she gave them the names of classical heroes. Without exception, her lovers were generals, who, serving and following Napoleon, were climbing their way up the ladder of the new France. The soldiers even had a song: *"Pauline s'empare des coeurs / Quand Bonaparte prend les villes"* ("Pauline conquers the hearts / After Bonaparte occupies the towns").

Pauline was not exactly excited at the prospect of marrying Leclerc, whom she was to cheat on from the very beginning. However, she barely protested against it either. "Marriage," she once told Napoleon, "is a custom that we can't avoid, but love is something else altogether. Love is a right all of us should have, but women are obviously not yet at liberty to take advantage of it. When will we obtain our freedom, brother?" On April 20, 1798, Pauline and Leclerc became the parents of a child who was named Dermide after one of the heroes in Scotsman James Macpherson's Ossianic poems.

The happiness Pauline spread to men was balanced by the grief she imparted to women, since she felt free to seduce any woman's husband. Her perfect beauty, which stimulated the great Italian sculptor Antonio Canova to produce his most lovely Venus, was marred by one blemish only: Her ears were too big. In her drawing room, she once happened to hear a woman whisper, "What a pity that her beauty is ruined by such a disfigurement." Pauline fainted, and did not find out until later that the reference had been to her ears. From that day on, she was never again seen by anyone with her ears uncovered.

* * *

In November 1799, after Napoleon had returned from Egypt, he was challenged by the moment of decision. He had not yet been able to make a dent in the British world empire or even find an Achilles heel, as he had hoped, but circumstances did allow him to make his bid for power in France. A new, large-scale change in the Directorate seemed to be imminent. However, this time it was not one whereby the beacons would be moved somewhat more to the left or the right, as had happened in 1797 and 1798. Instead, it was one whereby a military dictatorship could be established.

The generals who had earned their laurels in the revolutionary wars—Augereau, Macdonald and Lannes—were at the ready. Lucien Bonaparte, who was a more astute politician than his brother, was totally committed to Napoleon and so was Murat, another brother-in-law, and Leclerc. The politicians Barras, Siéyès and Talleyrand decided to take a chance on Napoleon in order to topple the Directorate, which was tottering, hoping to turn him into their vassal afterward. While Napoleon was in the process of impeding the coup in the Council of Elders as well as in the Council of the Five Hundred by giving a stuttering speech, Murat and Leclerc appeared with perfect timing and, with the usual shouting and screaming of soldiers, they had their men harass and disperse the representatives. The Directorate was exchanged for the Consulate and Napoleon became First Consul.

Leclerc had hoped for a position as Secretary, but it did not happen. First he was ordered to Spain, where he was to finish the primarily commercial "War of Oranges" instigated a few years earlier by a royalist Portugal. The war was over before Leclerc even became a part of it, and then, until he received the call to go to Haiti, Leclerc was dissatisfied and restless. He thus considered his new assignment an unexpected windfall. Leclerc was an excellent choice for the Haitian expedition because he was both a competent tactician on the battlefield and a thorough, strict administrator. While Leclerc was inspecting the troops that had been assembled for the invasion, however, he was assailed by doubts. Did Napoleon want to get rid of soldiers who were now revolutionary trouble-makers and whom he had, therefore, already written off? Was Napoleon cynically letting him play the "Little Napoleon" against that old Negro who deemed himself another Bonaparte?

A total of four thousand guns had been loaded aboard the ships and Napoleon had promised to procure the rest shortly. Leclerc, who was indeed a diligent administrator, found that half of the four thousand weapons were defective. In a separately delivered, secret letter, Leclerc was told how to proceed with his assignment. First, he was to sweet-talk the black generals so as to pacify them, then he was to capture them by surprise and deport them to France. Finally, he was to reinstate slavery and, he was especially reminded, he should not forget to deport any white woman who had had relations with a Negro.

Eighty-six ships sailed for Haiti with 35,000 soldiers who had acquired fame in the Alps, along the Rhine, the Danube and the Nile. Leclerc hoped that he would be able to conquer Toussaint's most important bulwarks by making fast raids on Cap François, Fort Liberté and Port-au-Prince, avoiding large-scale battles. Surprise could be achieved, he believed, by the simple artifice of neglecting to issue a declaration of war. His foremost generals were Rochambeau and Kerverseau, both of whom were ferocious racists and veterans of Haiti, who felt intense personal hatred for Toussaint; others were Boudet, Hardy, Dugua and Pamphile de Lacroix.

*   *   *

On February 1, 1802, the first ships approached the coast of Santo Domingo. Toussaint, who had hoped to have another month of time, had ridden to the hills around the bay of Samana. He wept when he saw the massive swarm of white sails approaching on the horizon. "Friends, we are doomed. All of France has come. Let us at least show ourselves worthy of our freedom."

There is no agreement among the sources about Toussaint's subsequent movements. His generals had been ordered to set fire to entire cities and bulwarks if it looked as if they would have to surrender them to the enemy. Toussaint had already announced this scorched earth policy in the summer of 1801. The hope was that yellow fever, intensified by the rainy season, would sweep through the invasion army as it had at the time of the British attacks. Toussaint and his men would keep up a guerrilla war from the countryside – forever, or until the French succumbed.

When Napoleon's army came ashore, the killing that had so devastated Haiti for the previous ten years resumed. Rochambeau did indeed find Fort Liberté practically burnt down. He was so infuriated that he immediately began mass executions of men, women and children. The Bay of Manceville ran red with the blood of those blacks and mulattoes who dared to call out, with their dying breath, "Away with the whites! Away with slavery!"

Dessalines laughed as he himself set fire to his splendid palace in Saint-Marc. Maurepas allowed Port de Paix to go up in flames. Port-au-Prince was saved as a result of treason by blacks, who defected to the French. Toussaint wrote to Dessalines:

> Try as much as possible to set fire to every city that you have to give up. Most of our towns consist of wooden buildings, as you know, so a handful of determined men will be sufficient. Oh my worthy general, what a misfortune about that traitor in Port-au-Prince, which made it possible for our orders to be ignored. But don't forget that we can always destroy and plunder while we wait for the rains, which will perhaps hasten the fall of our enemies. Remember that this soil, saturated with our sweat and and our blood, should not be allowed to produce a grain of food for our enemies. Wherever possible, set up ambushes so as to keep all roads under fire. Kill all and throw the bodies of people and horses in the wells; destroy everything and burn everything in order to ensure that they who have come to enslave us again will see opening up in front of their eyes, wherever they may turn, the gates of that hell that they so richly deserve.

Quick as lightning, the black armies withdrew into the woods and among the hills. All over the countryside, independently operating bands of new maroons, who had fled from the plantations, took part in the resistance. French units that dared to advance too far into the countryside moved irrevocably on a path to their doom.

* * *

Was Toussaint himself in Cap François when Leclerc issued his first set of demands to Christophe? Still drafted in courteous and careful words, Leclerc's letter asked for the surrender of the city. Did Toussaint harbor suspicions against his General Christophe even

then and, therefore, hide behind the curtains while Chrisophe
spoke with Leclerc's envoy?

A few months later, Christophe would be the first of the
important black generals to defect. But, in the meantime, he became
the hero of Cap François. Christophe was a former innkeeper and
cattle buyer from Grenada, who had not participated in the slave
rebellion itself but had only joined the slaves in 1793, fascinated
by the rising star, Toussaint. While dozens of French cannons were
pointed at Cap François, Christophe received a second letter from
Leclerc, this time an ultimatum. Totally in accordance with the
spirit of Bonaparte's plans, this letter consisted of a mixture of
promises and threats:

> To my indignation, I have been informed, Citizen General, that
> you refuse to receive the French squadron and army under my
> command on the pretext that you have not received any orders
> from your governor-general.
>
> After having concluded peace with England, France has
> now sent troops to Haiti in order to punish the rebels, if any
> of them still exist here. As far as you are concerned, Citizen
> General, I must confess that I should greatly regret having to
> count you among the rebels. I want to warn you that, unless
> you surrender the forts of Picolet and Belair and all the coastal
> batteries to me today, 15,000 men will be disembarking tomor-
> row at dawn. At Fort Liberté, 4,000 men have landed already
> and, at Port Républicain, 8,000. In my proclamations, I have
> clearly set forth the intentions of the French government. Keep
> in mind that, no matter how much I respect what you have
> done for this colony, I shall now hold you responsible for all
> the consequences.

Christophe had firmly decided what he would do, and this
resolve helped him to express himself eloquently: "Go and tell your
general that the French will march here only across piles of ashes
and that the ground will burn under their feet. Only the force of
arms will enable you to enter a city that has been burnt to ashes
because, even on those cinders, I shall continue to fight!"

Christophe had first entered Cap François on June 21, 1793,
fighting on the side of Macaya. At that time, 15,000 Negro slaves had

been called to arms by Sonthonax, who had promised them their freedom. During that night, sometimes called Haiti's second Night of Fire, they drove out the whites who, led by Galbaud, were making a last effort to maintain their power. Sonthonax had allowed the slaves to give vent to their rage for several nights. They entered the areas where the slave hunters had lived and the harbor where the ships were moored that, for years, had imported slaves from over the seas. Christophe's quick skill with torches had become legendary. Now a third Night of Fire would soon ensue.

On the evening of February 4, 1802, a delegation of citizens of Cap François presented Christophe with a petition. Old men, women and children begged him with tears to spare the city. Christophe promised to think it over that night. Leclerc's ultimatum would end at dawn. If they should hear three shots of a cannon fired, he told the unfortunate people, they should flee the city as fast as they could.

Christophe used the night, which thousands of citizens spent in tormenting fear, to have his men make preparations for the big fire. At six o'clock exactly, not three but twenty thundering shots were fired from Fort Picolet. Christophe and his men began at once to set fire to the houses, buildings, churches, warehouses, army bases, courthouses, stores and offices. Even the hospital, from which all the patients had already been removed, was not spared. Thousands fled the city, which seemed to slowly rise up like a gigantic torch.

The people fled in the direction where they hoped not to be hit by Leclerc's cannons. They stumbled, whole families together, over paths along steep rocks and ravines. A few hours after the fire had started, most of the unfortunate crowd had reached La Vigie, a mountain where they felt they would be safe. The French needed some time to get over their consternation, but then they finally began to shoot at the burning city. Meanwhile, as night fell, the thousands on the mountain stared at the dying capital. They held on to each other—blacks, mulattoes, former slave owners and former slaves.

While the French troops marched into the city, the sea of fire caused a rain of ash to descend over it just as the Night of Fire of 1791 had done. With this gruesome ritual the slave rebellion had begun and, in this same way, the rebellion now reached a new climax. It was difficult at this moment to imagine that true peace and freedom would ever come for Cap François.

* * *

In the first days after they landed, the French conquered almost all their original objectives: the most important coastal towns and harbors. From these bridgeheads, their army could start out on its crusade. Compared to Toussaint's, the French army was better armed and it was still in reasonably good condition.

Now Toussaint used one of his old tactics again, but in this new battle it misfired: He sent two different letters at the same time to his generals, one that contained the true message and was meant to reach them, and one that contained a false message and was supposed to be intercepted by the enemy so as to create confusion in the enemy camp. Both letters, to his brother Paul Louverture in Santo Domingo, ended up with Kerverseau, who made sure that the letter with the false message was the only one sent on to Paul. The letter with the true message had ordered him to stand firm until the end and to burn the cities, while the one with the false message had requested him to open negotiations with the enemy. Paul Louverture capitulated to the French. Afterward, Toussaint would never believe the story of the capture of the letters and never again reconciled himself with his brother.

The opposition against the French, wherever they appeared, was so intense and so complete, however, that Leclerc wrote in his first report to Bonaparte, "These people here are beside themselves with fury. They never withdraw or give up. They sing as they are facing death and they still encourage each other while they are dying. They seem not to know pain. Send reinforcements!"

This call for help continued to go out until Leclerc's death in November. Thereafter, Rochambeau conducted a pure war of destruction with his reinforcements, obeying Napoleon's last message: "Destroy all the blacks. They are the cause of our misfortunes."

On February 12, the president of the Colonial Institute, Coisnon, arrived at Ennery with Toussaint's sons Isaac and Placidus, whom he had been in charge of. A meeting with Toussaint had been set, and Leclerc knew about it. It had been six years since Toussaint had last seen his children. They threw themselves in his arms. Isaac argued fervently for France and the sincerity of Napoleon's intentions.

Coisnon asked, "Is this really Toussaint? Is this really the friend of France whom I embrace?"

"How can you doubt that?" Toussaint asked as he embraced Coisnon as well, with tears in his eyes.

"General! In your children you now see reflections, respectively, of the First Consul and the Governor General of the colony. Trust their innocence and the purity of their feelings. They will tell you the real truth."

Isaac insisted that, as a faithful servant of France, he would never take up arms against his country. Against his pleas stood the words of Placidus, "I am yours, poor father. I fear the future, I fear slavery, I am ready to wield the sword for the cause. I renounce France."

Madame Louverture was able to persuade Isaac to change his mind so that he too could serve his father's cause, which he later would describe so movingly. Toussaint took Placidus outside and addressed the men of his guard who were deployed there, "I bring you my son. He is ready to die for you."

Coisnon presented Toussaint with a sealed letter from Napoleon. Was this the kind of letter that could have averted the large-scale conflict after all? Toussaint had to look for support so as not to be overwhelmed by emotion when he finished reading it. Napoleon thanked the good Negroes who had so often served and saved the cause of France. He expressed his respect for Toussaint, who had allayed the civil war and, upholding law and order, had saved religion and the honor of God. Toussaint could consider himself one of the greatest men of the greatest nation on earth. However, the letter very specifically stated that Leclerc was now the new governor general and the first magistrate of the colony. In addition, Bonaparte wrote:

Although there are some excellent points in the constitution that you have enacted, it contains clauses that signify the opposite of what the French people are owed in dignity and sovereignty. And the people of Haiti are, after all, part of the people of France. You were surrounded by enemies, but you should now be the first to restore all the honor again to the sovereignty of our people. Tell the people of Haiti that, if they consider freedom their greatest possession, they can only enjoy it as citizens of France. Tell them that, in accordance with their duty to obey the new governor general, any action that conflicts with the interests of the country shall be considered an offense that wipes out all their good deeds and shall irrevocably turn Haiti into a theater of war, where sons will rise up against their fathers and fathers against their sons in order to kill each other.

Were these the conciliatory words for the future that had been so "cordially" emphasized by the force of arms displayed by Leclerc? Toussaint's reaction to this letter – the only personal letter he ever received from Napoleon – was, "How can this letter from the First Consul be reconciled with the behavior of General Leclerc? The one proclaims peace to me, the other makes war on me. Leclerc has hit Haiti like a bolt of lightning. He has announced his mission only by conquering the capital, by massacring the inhabitants of Fort Liberté and by armed attacks everywhere on our coasts. If General Leclerc sincerely wants peace, he should halt the march of his troops."

Did Toussaint know through his system of spies what Napoleon's special instructions to Leclerc had been? They were so much more inflexible than the letter to Toussaint. Toussaint's vision was, therefore, correct when, shortly before he was kidnapped, he wrote, "I knew that, in appearance, this letter offered all kinds of solutions but, in reality, none."

He was absolutely right. Napoleon's first instruction had been to come to an agreement with the Haitian generals by bribing them and promising them that they could continue in their positions. The second was to isolate the generals, to play them out against each other and to let them stumble, one after the other, in the treasonous actions they were then sure to commit. The third instruction was to disarm the entire black army and to deport the generals and all mulattoes and whites who had cooperated with them, despite the general amnesty that was to be proclaimed for all inhabitants of Haiti. The fourth decree, finally, of the Senate's decision with which Napoleon had entrusted Leclerc read: "All the Negroes, except the ones to whom special articles apply, must again be governed by the laws and regulations of the Black Code of the planters that was in effect before 1789."

A separate note from Napoleon urged his brother-in-law once again to transfer all white women who had ever had relations with Negroes or mulattoes to France, where they would be considered prostitutes.

* * *

Toussaint's health had deteriorated. He limped badly due to the problem with his right hip. At night, he had bouts of fever that caused him to sweat profusely. He no longer managed to sleep even the three hours that he generally reserved for himself every night. Only his incredible willpower kept him going.

It is hard to determine from the letters he wrote during this period whether he really believed in a victory over the French. But he wrote, again and again, the following words of encouragement, "We shall die with honor. We shall have remained true to our calling; we are the eternal enemies of slavery." He encouraged blacks and whites to maintain the alliance between the two races that he had tried so hard to foster, although the whites in most of the territories conquered by the French immediately joined the enemy again. "Children," he liked to say when he preached to blacks, mulattoes and whites, "children, yes, you are all my children." When speaking from the pulpit, he never tired of reminding everyone of the horrors of slavery and pointing out the delights of freedom.

Toussaint remained a master in deceiving his opponents with fast marches, ambushes, surprise attacks, raids at night and feigned skirmishes. Like Napoleon in 1814, during his last battles against enemies who had carried their attacks onto French soil, Toussaint was probably strongest, most brilliant and most imperturbable during this defense. Like the best and the strongest of his men, he had, after so many years of dedicated service, an exceptional capacity to withstand hunger, thirst and fatigue. Christophe in the north and Dessalines in the west remained his supreme deputy commanders.

But some other facts gradually became known as well. Rumors circulated that Christophe negotiated too frequently and too long with the French, and without Toussaint's permission. Dessalines acquired the nickname "Minotaur." The Tiger had not lost his fighting spirit, but he was sometimes out for days hunting down groups that had separated because they did not want to obey him. He exterminated them as if they were the same kind of scoundrels as the French. Toussaint's system of labor laws, with its forced bonds to the plantations and its strict supervision of exhausting labor that continued day and night, had also provoked resistance and dissatisfaction. "We are free but in worse shape than during the time of slavery," some blacks said. "Toussaint has replaced our old bonds with new ones."

An additional factor was that, in the areas conquered by him, Leclerc was taking energetic measures and issuing one proclamation after another stating that slavery would not be reinstated. By proclamation, Toussaint and Leclerc also declared each other outside the law. This meant that captured Frenchmen did not have to be treated as military prisoners, but could be summarily executed. Toussaint did not give his permission for this. He had the captured Frenchmen assembled in camps, together with large numbers of whites who had been interned after the start of the hostilities. There, many died from exhaustion and undernourishment. The descriptions left by the conquering French soldiers, who found dozens of bodies in such camps, are gruesome. The war was beginning to turn into genocide.

Hope and despair seemed to balance each other for the blacks. Hope ensued from the battle near Serpents' Ravine, not far from Gonaïves, where Toussaint managed to lead Rochambeau into a trap in the heart of his own territory. Despair ensued from the battle near Crête-à-Pierrot, which, after so many sacrifices, ended in a defeat for Dessalines.

Near Serpents' Ravine, Toussaint first managed to evade an encirclement that could have ended in a decisive defeat. Flexibly arraying his forces, he turned the apparent rout into a sudden victory. Above Rochambeau's columns, as if on flying carpets, plantation workers suddenly came floating in from the trees and, in contempt of their own lives, fell upon the French with their axes and cudgels. While this furious action from the trees kept the French occupied, Toussaint attacked separately with his smaller units. He himself used his sword like a gladiator. At one point it seemed as if Toussaint invited death in a hand-to-hand duel with Rochambeau, the worst of all the French Negro-haters.

Dessalines became trapped in the fort near Crête-à-Pierrot that had been built among the rocks like a monstrous bastion and that seemed to invite a new Thermopylae. Toussaint could not help Dessalines because he needed all his reserves to try to help Maurepas. But this attempt ended in failure and Maurepas had to surrender—a terrible blow for Toussaint, who considered Maurepas his most unflagging brother-in-arms. Further, Dessalines remained caught with his men for days. When hunger and thirst had become pure torture, Dessalines declared, "I want to have only courageous men around me. All those who would like to become slaves of the French may leave the fort." Everyone, including the heroine Marie-Jeanne, remained. Dessalines then grabbed a torch and held it close to a barrel of gunpowder. "Then I will tell you now, I shall blow up anyone who admits a Frenchman into the fort."

The bombardments of the French, who had almost 12,000 men surrounding the fort, continued day and night. Dessalines managed to escape in an attempt to call on the help of the guerrilla bands of Sansouci and Macaya that were supposed to be somewhere in the area. Rochambeau and Dugua meanwhile attacked with their best regiments. The battle became a duel of prestige—whoever would win here would win the war. Here it would have to be shown whether the slaves had become soldiers who were indeed as strong as the conquerors of Italy, the Rhine valley and Egypt. The slaves held their own. The wounded allowed their companions to push them out so they would no longer be in their way. It was a rare battle in Haiti in that mutual respect, even gallantry, became evident between the two sides. Later, the French would honor every black who could say, "I was at Crête-à-Pierrot," with the reply "Then you are a courageous man."

When Dessalines did not succeed in finding Macaya's and Sancouci's bands, he managed—incredibly—to return to the fort.

He then approved that all should evacuate and try to save themselves. Rochambeau himself would later describe it as follows: "Their retreat, this miraculous escape from our trap, was an incredible feat of arms. With our twelve thousand men, we had them completely in our grasp. But half of this hellish legion managed to escape–the other half was found dead among the rubble." The Haitians lay in each other's arms, starved, seriously wounded, dead, but looking as if they had won a victory.

* * *

One last time, Toussaint's indomitable desire for freedom was displayed in a brilliant campaign, along the Artibonite River, where he tried to separate the French troops in the north and the west from those in the south. He meant to keep them separated until the heaviest rains would arrive and yellow fever could do its destructive work.

Leclerc's situation meanwhile had become critical. He had already lost more than 5,000 men and another 5,000 lay pining away in poorly equipped medical stations. Leclerc was also faced with defeatism. The Polish, Italian, Dutch, Spanish and Flemish soldiers who, in Europe, had fought while inspired by their belief in revolutionary ideals now realized that they were being used in a barbaric civil and racial war. They no longer dared to sing their revolutionary songs, nor the French the *Marseillaise*, when they had to march against the poor Negro slaves. The slaves themselves were singing the *Marseillaise*, shouting it out joyously as they attacked the Europeans with an unimaginable disregard for death. What kind of glory was there to be had from the conquest of towns that had already so often been plundered and where only women and children were found under circumstances that were worse than they had ever encountered before? The First Consul had sent them here to die, instead of to gather new glory!

In addition to an increasing scarcity of food, there was now the new wave of yellow fever (none too soon, for Toussaint and his side). The illness was transmitted by flies, and the strain that occurred at this time in Haiti probably carried a sexual disease. The illness struck extremely quickly; some victims would suddenly fall ill and die at once. These were the fortunate ones, because in other cases the illness could also progress exasperatingly slowly toward its inevitable climax. In these latter cases, the victims would suffer a thousand pains, cramps and fears. They felt as if their head and brains would burst. They would vomit an appalling black vomit, known as black soup. They suffered burning thirst while they could not bear to drink even a drop of water. Their eyes would be bloodshot, their ears would buzz and their faces would become dark red and glow. Phlegm dripped from all the openings of the body and their gums turned black. Constant nightmares prevented sleep. When the victim began to turn yellow, the gruesome end would be near. Stench would emanate from the victim's body, so much so that it resembled the stench of the plague. The lips would stiffen and the victim would start vomiting blood in waves. Life shrank away to its last pathetic proportions.

No white man was safe from this tropical scourge. Once the wave of fever hit, some Frenchmen were already overcome as they were leaving their ships to set foot ashore. When a convoy finally arrived bringing reinforcements of more than 1,500 soldiers, all of them died miserably within fourteen days. And this was only the beginning. The summer and the fall would bring an intensification of the wave so serious that even the blacks, who had previously seemed almost immune to the illness, died by the thousands.

The imminence of death and the shortage of tomorrows had the side effect of stimulating a fierce desire to live. From the very first days that they set foot onto this languorous island, the lasciviousness of the French had already increased to an unusual extent. Toussaint had said that Haiti was the light beacon of lust, but the tomb of lasciviousness. People drank and tried to enjoy themselves on their way to meet death. Doom made people more anxious to enjoy the sensual pleasures while they still had time.

Meanwhile, the war continued, a terrifying guerrilla war that seemed to take place for the most part at night. The French saw their enemies more and more rarely out in the open. The campaign became for them a desperate target-shooting at blacks running away like hares. They would be pursued by the French, who would then stumble into the marshes and be decimated there. When Leclerc had André Rigaud deported to France again, he lost the support of practically all the mulattoes who had arrived with the invasion army and who had been able to persuade some of their brethren in the south to fight with them against Toussaint. The mulattoes in the south were now waiting, ready to change sides shortly, for the last time.

Christophe, who had at first courageously rejected an attempt by Leclerc to bribe him, finally gave in. On April 26, he met with Leclerc, from whom he received a letter for Toussaint. Christophe delivered it without telling Toussaint that he had already come to an agreement with Leclerc. With 1,200 cavalrymen and all his ammunition, Christophe defected to the French.

Although Toussaint did not know any details about the treason committed by Christophe, he knew he had been stabbed in the back. If the effect should be that of a spreading fire, Toussaint would lose all initiative. He decided to act fast in order to be one step ahead of Christophe. At this point, he could still negotiate from a position of strength, threatening at least a stalemate. He had to try to achieve a breathing space so that he could retreat and prepare to hit back once more with renewed power.

Leclerc sent his negotiator and, after a three-hour discussion, Toussaint reached an agreement. The freedom of all blacks in Haiti would continue to be maintained and guaranteed. The generals would keep their positions and all the black officers and soldiers would go into the service of France. Toussaint would be allowed to retire to his own estates with a small staff of his own. Louverture's Constitution and Leclerc's "special regulations" would be integrated after consultation with Paris. Leclerc invited Toussaint to a conciliatory meeting in Cap François.

* * *

What motives compelled Toussaint when he made the decision to travel to his own capital, Cap François, for something that was a reconciliation but also, at the same time, a surrender? Even Leclerc and his advisors had never counted on Toussaint's coming to meet with them. Was he so curious to see the "Little Napoleon," the man whom he had heard resembled Bonaparte so closely that it had been an element in the decision to send him to the Big Island?

On May 6, 1802, Toussaint left for Cap François with Isaac and four hundred dragoons. The artillery of the forts around the city fired a salvo for joy and the ships set off fireworks. Women lifted their children up to see Toussaint. Everywhere, blacks and mulattoes knelt and cheered for him. Under Toussaint's reign, the taxes had gone up to 25 percent, but Leclerc was raising them to 50 percent! Under Toussaint's reign, the whites had been afflicted with the labor regulations. Under Leclerc, famished soldiers plundered the plantations, violated the women and ate up all provisions. There were even whites who condemned Toussaint for returning to Cap François to treat with the invader.

He was received at the Carenage palace in a room set aside for honored guests. His favorite flowers, red roses, were delivered for him. His favorite music, that of Lully, was played. Pauline Bonaparte greeted him in a snow-white dress that constantly threatened to slip from her body. Toussaint was no longer in a position to reprimand her for the almost total exposure of her breasts. Reconciliation and more reconciliation was the password, even at the table where the generals sat, making toast after toast while Toussaint remained silent and consumed nothing other than some water.

Finally Leclerc appeared. He was wearing precisely the same uniform as Toussaint, since they were both generals of France, except that instead of a general's hat, Toussaint wore the Madras cloth that gave him his most fearful appearance. Toussaint observed the "Little Napoleon." The weeks in Haiti had already taken a heavy toll on Leclerc and he looked weary and despondent. He spoke an extremely articulated French and his movements were slow and formal. Toussaint asked him several times to speak slowly, since he was a little deaf. A conversation did not ensue. They sat down at the table next to each other. Leclerc ate and drank with gusto. He probably suffered even then from the tapeworms that made him so remarkably gluttonous until the time when, finally, he contracted yellow fever.

Toussaint ate nothing, but just sat staring into space. Very loudly, Leclerc asked why Toussaint had not reacted more conciliatorily at the time of Leclerc's arrival in Haiti. Why had he commanded Christophe to burn the city when there had not been a declaration of war?

Toussaint sat up and denied loudly, so that all of the guests at the table could hear, that he had given that command; it had been Christophe's own decision. Was this his revenge on Christophe, who, like all the other black generals, had not been invited to this historic meeting? Avoiding an answer about the war that had erupted without a declaration of war, Toussaint brought the conversation around to Dessalines.

Leclerc had advised that there could not be any amnesty for Dessalines, who had had so many whites murdered, and thus also no acceptance into the French army. Toussaint pronounced a halting, but unmistakable plea for Dessalines. He appeared to become irritated and stood up from his chair a few times.

Leclerc definitely did not want any problems at that point. Flushed with wine, he briefly put a hand on Toussaint's shoulder and communicated his agreement: Dessalines would become a general in Leclerc's army.

There was a last question that Leclerc could not keep from asking: "If the war had continued, where would you then have obtained your provisions and weapons in the long run?"

Toussaint looked up with the old grimace of irony on his face. "I would have come, Citizen General, to get them from you."

Toussaint said goodbye before the meal was over and before festivities began under the direction of Pauline, who had not participated in the meal but who planned to lead a ball. All that time, Isaac had remained outside with Toussaint's horse, Bel-Argent, on which he now rode off surrounded by his four hundred dragoons.

◆ 12 ◆

Toussaint Falls
Into the Trap

■——■

TOUSSAINT RETURNED TO MARMELADE AND SAID GOODBYE TO
his bodyguard, the famous Blue Cossacks, many of whom
sported the mustaches and beards that would later become the
well-known badge of the veterans of Napoleon's Old Guard. (One
thinks of Napoleon's own farewell to the last of his faithful soldiers
at Fontainebleau.) Toussaint's bodyguard now went into the service
of the French. His grenadiers left for Plaisance, where they, too,
would continue their terms of service under French generals. The
dragoons left for Cap François.

One by one, Toussaint shook hands with his men. They
watched him mount into the saddle with more difficulty than ever
before. Without once glancing back, he rode away in the direction
of Ennery. On the Sansay plantation, his wife was waiting for him
with Isaac and Placidus, as well as Mars Plaisir and Father Simon
Baptiste. An old man of almost 110, Father Simon Baptiste fell to
his knees, pleading, "Dear Toussaint, have you forgotten us?" "No,
children," Toussaint replied, "all the brothers remain under arms
and we are ready at our posts."

Toussaint never shared with anyone his hidden thoughts and
intentions when he accepted the deadly embrace with Leclerc.
One thing at least was clear: The two now had each other in a
hold. Did Toussaint speculate that there would be another night

of killing, maybe to occur on the night when the great autumn rains would burst? Did he hope that collaboration with the French, in which he did not participate, would turn out to be fatal to his earliest lieutenants, Dessalines, Christophe, Maurepas, Belair and Clervaux, who had all become gilded gentry, busily enriching themselves? Did he hope that this collaboration would provoke a new revolt among the entire population, a revolt that would usurp the ruling powers, and a revolt that he would again be able to lead?

Toussaint knew that Leclerc was turning more and more whites into enemies as a result of the renewed expropriations of land. At the same time, Leclerc's new regulations of servitude for the blacks were beginning to look more and more as if they were aimed at restoring slavery, which in fact had become general practice again throughout the Caribbean.

Pauline actually said it out loud: "Now the whip can be used again on the blacks." She felt that slavery could be reinstated even before the new reinforcements, promised to be coming from France, would arrive. She was already inviting friends from Paris to return to the estates and plantations assigned to them. In France, dispossessed noblemen from the Vendée were preparing to set off for new lands on Haiti. Leclerc was conducting a consistent policy of disarmament of the blacks. Not only were entire black brigades being sent home (within a matter of weeks 10,000 former soldiers were unemployed), but the black generals had orders to requisition all arms from the free bands that operated on their own – such as those of Sulla, Sansouci, Lamour de Rancé and Petit Noël.

The black general who was most eager to comply with Leclerc was Dessalines. He had restored discipline by physical punishment on his own plantations, and his wooden clubs inflicted more damage than whips, which, as symbols of the past, remained forbidden. In the countryside, he organized large-scale hunts in pursuit of the free bands. He had acquired a new nickname, "The Butcher of the Blacks," given to him by Leclerc. His preferred mode of execution had become strangling and he regularly handled such cases personally. After their raids, Dessalines, Maurepas, Laplume and Christophe handed a total of 30,000 guns over to the French.

Even Rigaud thought he had a chance to make a comeback with his mulattoes. He arranged to be received festively in Les Cayes, and the whites in the south opted for a new cooperation with the mulattoes. Leclerc, however, sought to nip this in the bud immediately. The former situation could not be allowed to return. Leclerc wanted a whole new slave society to gradually be erected, ruled by the white caste, the French, and protected by a strong army. In their hearts, the French had already written off the slaves of yesterday, in whom the poison of revolt and the intoxication of freedom could never again be extinguished. An entirely new wave of blacks, freshly imported from Africa, would submit to the system willingly. In this scheme, there was no place for the return of Rigaud and the dangerous artifice of his mulattoes. Rigaud was arrested and deported to France.

Leclerc did not appoint any more blacks to officer positions. Meanwhile, he had Toussaint's base in Ennery gradually surrounded by his troops until it was hermetically sealed. When Toussaint encountered Frenchmen during rides across his own plantations, they made it a point not to greet him. Friends came to warn Toussaint that at least twenty French officers were spying on his activities and connections, every day, everywhere. Toussaint knew that his letters were being intercepted and checked. In fact, he took to drafting them in as obscure a manner as possible, in almost a kind of secret language. A number of these letters, which were impossible for Leclerc to understand, and which for precisely that reason gave the impression of a conspiracy, became the deciding factor for the insidious plot that the French general resolved to enact against Toussaint.

Leclerc could not afford to wait for the height of the rainy season, as could Toussaint, who had calmly projected himself as the new Cincinnatus and who, as Leclerc suspected, was secretly planning a future fraught with treason. As long as yellow fever plagued the French, Toussaint, "like a ram without horns," could quietly work on gaining back his strength. Gradually, the fever would weaken his opponents. In fact, Leclerc called the plague the "illness of Siam," referring offhandedly to the cloth that Toussaint had worn around his head during their meeting. "He probably wanted to come across as a feared old pirate, wearing that headdress," Leclerc had stated.

Even before the summer of 1802, Leclerc had already lost at

least 5,000 of his men to the fever. His physicians did not consider it impossible that at least twice that many would die during the rainy season. In that case, Leclerc's army would be totally decimated. However, he expected heavy reinforcements in the fall: Napoleon had promised him some detachments of Poles who were living on the French army's budget but currently idle.

The Polish nation had been wiped off the face of Europe by Austria, Russia and Prussia. The French Revolution and its executor for the territory beyond its borders, Napoleon, on the other hand, held up the vision of a reinstated, free and independent Poland, causing Polish volunteers to flock to service in the French army by the tens of thousands. They earned their stripes on campaigns in Italy, Germany and Switzerland. They kept to a strict and serious way of life and were in much better shape than the troops with which Leclerc had arrived for his invasion. The Poles would at least be better able to cope with the fever.

Leclerc was sure that the unstable condition of many of his soldiers had stimulated and intensified the force of the plague. Badly nourished and given to drinking, his troops had also begun to suffer from the many strains of malaria immediately upon their arrival in the tropics; ill with sexual diseases, too, and burdened by their heavy packs, they had of course become victims of the climate, often before seeing any kind of action. The weakened Europeans easily attracted the insects and vermin that carried disease. Once fall came, yellow fever could be expected to come to the natural end of its course, as had happened earlier with the English, and at that time Leclerc could expect his new Polish reinforcements. But until then, Toussaint should not be allowed an opportunity to make a countermove.

*   *   *

Through his spies, Toussaint was extremely well informed about the way yellow fever was spreading through the cities. He was heard to remark, in fact, that the French army was already being defeated without the need for anyone to take up arms.

Especially in Cap François and Port-au-Prince, the consequences of the fever had an extremely demoralizing effect on the French. Their government seemed doomed. Preceded by lantern bearers mournfully waving their lamps, funeral corteges traversed the streets at night. The bodies of dead and dying victims that had been placed on the side of the road or left at the doors of houses were thrown onto carts like so much garbage. Gigantic pits were dug in which the corpses were dumped and then covered with lime. Funeral pyres of corpses often were lit, and the sweetish odor of death and decay would spread for miles.

Leclerc's best general, Hardy, succumbed to yellow fever. Now Leclerc had to act before it became too late. He ordered Colonel Pesquidon, with about one hundred cavalrymen, to conduct a campaign of terror against some maroons under Sulla, who were operating in and around Ennery. When Toussaint protested the measure, he was accused of having ordered his own dragoons not to hunt down Sulla's bands, who had been getting more and more bold in their attacks and ambushes on the French. Toussaint was also accused of scheming to escape to Santo Domingo in order to commence guerrilla actions against the French from across the border.

Dessalines was assigned a key role in the trap set for Toussaint. Leclerc hoped that the result of this traitor's behavior would cause Dessalines, Toussaint's former blood brother, to at once lose all that was left of his authority and reputation with the population. "Ever since the French Revolution, there is no longer such a thing as a word of honor," Dessalines was wont to say. That conviction came in handy now that he wanted to consider himself released from his word to Toussaint.

Like Dessalines, Maurepas, Christophe and Clervaux were afraid of Toussaint's power and his revenge that might come one day. They would feel more assured of the future if they, like Alexander the Great's generals, could divide Haiti amongst themselves. They reacted positively when Dessalines sounded them out about help in getting Toussaint deported. Indignant reactions, however, were displayed by others who were approached; these were Belair, who was Dessalines' mortal enemy, Paul Louverture, who so desperately wanted to get back into his brother's good graces, and a loyal mulatto general, Vernet. Dessalines, who had also suggested to Leclerc that Toussaint was planning to immobilize the Blue Cossacks who had gone into French service, wrote Leclerc that he was willing, personally, to act against Toussaint.

* * *

About this time, in Cap François, a strange incident happened: On the street, a planter encountered one of his former slaves wearing a uniform. Furious, he grabbed the soldier's epaulets and ripped them off while shouting, "Don't you know that times have changed, you miserable wretch? You are going to work on my plantation, again, as my slave."

This incident kindled the indignation of Boudet, who, after Hardy, was Leclerc's most capable general, and who was fond of his black soldiers. He forced Leclerc to arrest the planter and put him for an entire day in the pillory in Cap François wearing a sign "Supporter of Slavery."

Despite this action, rumors that the French were up to something and, especially, that slavery would indeed be restored, began to spread rapidly. They were reinforced by Leclerc's sub-sequent decision to send Boudet to Guadeloupe. There he assisted in the ruthless quelling of the last slave uprising on that island, the desperate revolt of the hero Delgrès. Rochambeau was now ap-pointed chief of the French army on Haiti, which was perceived as a clear challenge since he was noted for his hatred of blacks. His view was that blacks had no souls, very little feeling, and were best dealt with by setting hounds after them.

The fact that Dessalines was suddenly allowed to make his entrance into Cap François clearly showed that he and Leclerc were hand-in-glove for the moment. The blacks welcomed him exuber-antly, however, mistakenly hoping that Dessalines was using this show of power to put pressure on the French on behalf of the blacks.

Isaac Louverture, whom Toussaint and Leclerc had used in the past as a messenger to deliver their letters to one another, was now used as a spy by the cynical French general. Leclerc showed Isaac letters written by Dessalines that seemed to say he was preparing an attack on Toussaint, and suggested to Isaac that it would therefore be better if Dessalines and Toussaint sat down to discuss all their problems with each other. Leclerc also entrusted Isaac with a letter to Toussaint stating, "Since you, Citizen General, remain stubbornly convinced that the troops stationed at Ennery frighten your people, I have ordered General Brunet to have a discussion with you about transferring these troops to Gonaïves and Plaisance."

Meanwhile, a letter written by Toussaint to his agent Fontaine – intercepted by Leclerc – had become the deciding factor in the French commander's mind. The letter was vague and the question of its authenticity has never been resolved. Why would Toussaint have written the following? "I want to ask you if there is anyone close to the commander who can be persuaded to dedicate himself to procuring the release of D. . . , who could be extremely useful for any influence I may have in Nouvelle and elsewhere. Let Gengrembre know that he should leave Borgne, where the people should no longer go to work."

Who was D. . .? Who was Gengrembre? Who or where was Borgne? The French were all too aware of the black leader's penchant for writing in code. Toussaint later denied having written the letter, although the signature was his. In his administrative duties Toussaint signed a stream of blank letters on which the text had yet to be written, so forgeries were not difficult to acquire.

Isaac implored Toussaint not to believe in Leclerc's good intentions, but Toussaint was utterly depressed, especially at the thought of Dessalines' possible treachery. He entered a church and suddenly destroyed a cross by breaking it in half, exclaiming, "I can no longer believe in this God who favors such opponents." It was said that Toussaint was so plagued by doubts that, for the first and last time in his life, he consulted a voodoo priest. More substantially, Paul Louverture weighed in with a warning to Toussaint as well.

Leclerc did not hesitate. He ordered Brunet to write a false letter to Toussaint and, at the same time, Lieutenant Ferrari was ordered to make all preparations for kidnapping the black hero. Early in June 1802, Brunet wrote Toussaint from the Georges plantation:

The moment has come, Citizen General, to give General Leclerc positive proof about the people who are trying to mislead him about you. They are maligning you because your aim is solely to restore order in the district where you reside. I need your help in restoring the communication with Cap François that was disrupted yesterday after three people were murdered between Ennery and Coupe à Pintave by a band of fifty brigands. Please send some soldiers whom you trust completely to these localities and pay them well; expenses will be paid by us.

There are, esteemed General, some issues we must discuss together and which cannot possibly be dealt with by letter, but for which a conversation of a couple of hours between the two of us would suffice. If I weren't overwhelmed by work today, I myself would have brought you the answer to your letter. Now I will have to invite you to honor me with a visit. Here you will find not only the entertainment that I have long wished to offer you, but you will also find a straightforward man of honor who only desires to further the well-being of you and the colony. I should deem myself particularly honored if Mme Toussaint, whom I will be utterly delighted to meet, could accompany you. If she wishes to use horses for the ride, I will be glad to send some. Never will you, General, meet a more sincere friend than myself. As a result of your trust in the Captain General and your friendship for all those who serve him, you will be able to spend your life in peace.

"Suspicion is the mother of every confidence," Toussaint had once said. Did he really believe Brunet's words now? To the amazement of many, Toussaint's reaction was, "Have you seen this, all of you who keep saying that they want to arrest me? Those whites, those French, they still need me!"

On June 7, Toussaint set out for the Georges plantation together with Placidus and César, his adjutant. On the way there, a white woman threw herself in front of Toussaint's horse and begged him to turn back. The French were camped all around the Georges plantation, and when they saw Toussaint, they smirked at each other and did not salute him.

Brunet received Toussaint politely. Toussaint told him that he left his wife at home because she was generally loathe to travel. If Brunet should want to come by for a visit, however, he was welcome to do so. Toussaint also brought Leclerc's letter, his last message to Toussaint. Did Toussaint succumb to his eagerness to find out what it was that they were going to propose to him? Did he perhaps see all this as the beginning of his return to the political stage now that the black generals were played out as collaborators? Or was

Toussaint ill and in doubt? According to Placidus, his senses were dulled after having lived in peace on the land for five weeks, following ten long years of fighting.

Brunet asked Toussaint to excuse him for a moment before they began to discuss business. A few seconds later, the door was thrown open and Ferrari burst into the room together with a dozen soldiers with drawn swords. "General, the Captain General has ordered me to arrest you," Ferrari announced. "Your aides have already been taken into custody. The building has been surrounded by our men. If you resist, you will be killed. Your power on Haiti is over. Give me your sword."

Toussaint considered for an instant whether he should throw himself once more at the enemy with his weapon, and die fighting. Then he thought of Placidus, who would in all probability be killed in reprisal. "The righteous heavens will revenge me," were Toussaint's last words to his captors while he sheathed his sabre. The duplicitous Brunet quickly took possession of Toussaint's horse, Bel-Argent.

That same evening, Toussaint was transferred by Brunet, who at once received the nickname "Policeman," to the frigate *La Créole*, which sailed on to Cap François. There, the ship *Héros* was standing by, ready to sail for France as soon as possible. Toussaint was given lodging in one of the lower holds.

In the early morning hours of June 8, the French raided the plantation where Isaac, his mother, and little Saint-Jean had been taken. The three were brought to Cap François as well, and then to the *Héros*, where they were allowed to see their father one more time. During their transfer to the *Héros*, their French captors shot several times at people who tried to stop the group.

As he looked at Haiti for the last time before he was taken underneath the deck of the *Héros*, Toussaint said, "Now they have felled the trunk of the Negroes' tree of liberty. However, new shoots will sprout because the roots are deep and many."

Leclerc issued a proclamation in which he justified his coup and expressed his thanks to Dessalines and Christophe, "who were the first to expose Toussaint Louverture's schemes." By now Leclerc had been told that the supposedly treasonous letters from Toussaint to his agent Fontaine were probably false. Leclerc had already had

Font'ine arrested and executed, however, stating, "I have sufficient evidence against him." This evidence was never submitted. And no charge was ever brought, nor were legal proceedings ever instituted, against Toussaint Louverture, who was still a general of France when he was arrested.

♦ 13 ♦

The Last Slave War

■——■

AFTER HER FIRST NIGHT IN HAITI, PAULINE BONAPARTE LECLERC had complained, "All night long, I had the feeling that I was lying on nails; in any case I did not sleep at all." But after only a few days, as the writer-general Pamphile de Lacroix expressed it so floridly, "the sun of the tropics was surprised at the fire of her pleasures." Back in France, Pauline had already acquired the reputation of a formidable nymphomaniac. Lots of tales went around about Pauline, not all verifiable, but that reputation remained with her until the end. She loved to party and, at these parties, she constantly flirted. In Haiti, during her parties with the "Mamelukes" (her term for black dancers), Pétion, Christophe and Boyer frequently lavished attention on Pauline. Later they boasted of having practically taken turns at being her lovers. There are also varying reports about her respect for and commitment to Leclerc. When Napoleon caught wind of her behavior in the tropics, he wrote to her in his characteristically cynical manner, "I am happy to hear that my sister behaves this way. Now she no longer needs to fear death, since it cannot but be glorious, in the company of such an army and such a husband."

Together with Leclerc, Pauline started two botanical gardens. In consultation with him, she sent specimens to Paris of different kinds of animals that were unknown to her, so they could be placed in the zoo. Two ships full of such animals arrived in France.

Leclerc actually turned out to be the administrator that Napoleon had hoped he would be. He reorganized Haiti's finances and set up a system of public health where practically none had existed. He even made certain that postage stamps were printed again so that letters could be sent. He organized, for the first time in Haiti, a system whereby official documents could be drawn up by notaries; and he instituted the use of passports. Every day his new administrative measures could be read in *La Gazette de Saint-Domingue*, all of which gave the impression that Leclerc and the French were succeeding in their reorganization. But, since the news about the kidnapping of Toussaint had become known, a tense atmosphere that signaled the last explosion to come pervaded the Big Island.

On July 16, 1802, slavery was officially reinstated in Guadeloupe. At the same time, rumors were going around that Toussaint had been murdered on board the ship that was to take him to France. While Dessalines, Christophe and Clervaux were still hunting down hidden weapons, small uprisings suddenly took place all over the island. New names were heard, of fresh black commanders such as Gange, Valemo, Janvier, Lafontaine, Guingamé, Corrigole, Théodat, Wagnac, Bergerac, Eca-poule and Va-malheureux, as well as a fighter who called himself Toussaint Brave.

Leclerc received warnings from all sides that a new wave of uprisings was developing—this time, one that promised to bring blacks and mulattoes together into one great force. Leclerc now had to retake the offensive. He had to call upon the Negro generals, who already considered themselves in the same position as Alexander's would-be successors. Dessalines even traitorously quashed the insurrection with which Belair had tried to join the new rebellion. Belair had written an enthusiastic letter to Dessalines about the Louverturian Revolution, which they were now duty-bound to unleash for revenge, now that Toussaint, as they believed, had died a martyr's death for them.

Dessalines then wrote a letter to Leclerc about this former companion who wanted to change course. According to Dessalines, Charles Belair and his malicious wife, Sanité, had been responsible to a large extent for barbaric acts "that have been committed among our unfortunate comrades, the friends and defenders of the French government. Charles and his wife must be punished for this. I remain, totally dedicated to your authority, with the deepest respect, Citizen General Dessalines."

Belair and his wife were executed in a horrible manner. Until her last sob, Sanité, a strong woman, encouraged her husband to hold up under the torturing: "Husband, it is so sweet to die for freedom."

But those who sowed the wind would reap hurricanes in Haiti. Maurepas now revolted as well. He assembled a substantial little army of blacks and mulattoes, where the women also fought along, fully as feisty as the soldiers. Leclerc had gotten to the point where it was everything or nothing. Only the worst kind of terror could halt the spread of the new fires of rebellion. Dozens of blacks were executed. Soon bodies were floating everywhere in the harbor of Cap François.

Dessalines continued to be Leclerc's ally, nevertheless. Did he want, first, to see all the other generals eliminated while awaiting the hour for a new act of treason? Dessalines behaved as if possessed. He himself would cut open women's bellies. He had people locked up in their huts, which then would be set on fire. At one point he killed a woman who wanted to protect her children by cutting her in half with one blow of his sword; he then had the children seized and thrown into a fire.

When Clervaux and Christophe heard what Leclerc was now openly saying – that all adult blacks and mulattoes must be consistently exterminated and replaced by new slaves from Africa – they suddenly made contact with Pétion, the leader of the rebellious mulatto bands, to form an alliance against Leclerc. This was concluded on October 13.

At this point, Dessalines realized that the winning hand might get away from him. He also found out that Leclerc was seriously ill and might become a victim of yellow fever. In that case, Rochambeau would succeed to power and Dessalines' role as top collaborator would come to an end. The final turning point of the last slave war in Haiti took place on October 21, 1802, when "the Tiger" Dessalines chose the side of the rebellion. He saved face by proclaiming a dramatic call to arms: "A splendid war! We are anxious to obey every command. We will astonish everyone with our courage and we will dispel this horrible dictatorship, this prelude to death, forever from Haiti."

At about the same time, Leclerc wrote one of his last desperate letters to Napoleon, who had promised him reinforcements again and again without ever sending them. Although it would be another six months before France and England would resume their duel, Napoleon had already written off his grand schemes for North, Central and South America, influenced in part by Leclerc's continuous reports. Leclerc now wrote: "Ever since I am here, I have seen nothing but fires, uprisings, massacres, the dead and the dying. My soul is withered and debased. No other thoughts can make me forget the images of horror. Here I must fight the blacks, the whites, hunger, illnesses and my own army, which is becoming more and more discouraged."

He had come, on behalf of the "First of the Whites," in order to destroy the "First of the Blacks," and his power and all his ideas. Now the blond "Little Napoleon" was staring into the face of catastrophe. Of the 35,000 men he had at his disposal at the beginning of the campaign, 20,000 had died. Several thousand lay close to death in miserable so-called hospitals, where so many black women were still making the rounds and caring for them as sisters of love. His army actually consisted of no more than 8,000 men who were prepared to fight. He had only Cap François, Port-au-Prince, Môle Saint-Nicolas and Saint-Marc securely in his possession. And the new rebellion was gaining ground.

* * *

Pauline's passion to continue living was intensified at the prospects of doom and death. She had herself carried in a palanquin through the luxuriously blooming tropical vegetation around her little palace. The woods that emanated lovely fragrances provided her with sweet memories. She kept little Dermide with her all day long. In the evening, it was reported that a large black carried her from bath to bedroom where she would then entertain the lovers who waited patiently in line outside her door. She organized get-togethers in the rooms that she called "my death rooms." This is where the balls took place and the festivities that were marked by constant drunkenness – all on the edge of the grave. "We are living our last moments, so let us spend them pursuing pleasure," she said. In Cap François, on November 2, Leclerc died in Pauline's arms. He had become a skeleton, almost a corpse even before he emitted his final breath. His last words were, "I loved you, Paulette, as I love France." He was only thirty years old when he died.

Together with a doctor, Peyre, Pauline washed the body, embalmed it and laid it in a casket made of lead. She then had all her hair cut off except for a small area on the crown of her head and with the hair, after having opened the casket one last time, she covered Leclerc's face. On the ship *Swiftsure*, she traveled back to France. Both she and her son Dermide were already showing the first signs of yellow fever. However, once out to sea, they quickly recovered. In her joy, she began to flirt again, this time with General Humbert and Admiral Huber. Following her arrival in France, Napoleon proclaimed ten days of nationwide mourning, starting on January 9, 1803. His statement contained the following words: "I have lost my right arm."

In the Sainte-Geneviève Church, a funeral monument was erected for Leclerc. His mortal remains would later be placed in the dome of Les Invalides. Thus he remained in the vicinity of the "Big Napoleon" after all.

"You are twenty-four years old. You must now become truly a mature adult," Napoleon said to Pauline. She remarried and, in accordance with his wishes, her new husband was Camille Borghese. This stiff man with absolutely no erotic interests was completely unable to satisfy her desire for love and adventure. She traveled from one spa to the next, now plagued by a mysterious illness that could not be cured even by experimental operations.

Pauline was the only member of the family who would remain true to Napoleon after he was banished for the first time. In Elba, she tried to cheer him up, and she encouraged him to make his glorious return of "the one hundred days." Later, she also wanted to go to Saint Helena, but she was forbidden by Metternich, Austria's powerful Prince, who desired her. "She was as beautiful," in Metternich's words, "as it is possible to be beautiful. She was only in love with herself and her one profession was sensuality."

Pauline Bonaparte died on June 9, 1825, in the Strozzi Villa near Florence, Italy.

* * *

Donatien de Rochambeau became, as expected, Leclerc's successor. He was forty-seven years old and liked to be called marshal, a title that had been bestowed upon him by the Americans in recognition of his services to them at the end of their War of Independence against the British.

He had, years before, been interim governor in Haiti, but had been ignominiously deposed and ordered to depart from the island by Sonthonax. His coming to power meant that the war had openly become a racial war, fought without pity. As far as Rochambeau was concerned, the blacks were no longer even to be subdued back into slavery, but were rather to be liquidated one and all. Admittedly, he did respect the blacks militarily, witness his remark "It is a superior race of fighters that lives here in Haiti."

After Dessalines had joined the rebellion, he was recognized as supreme commander by all the blacks, all the mulattoes, the handful of whites who still participated in the rebellion – among these a German colony in Bombarde which had at first cooperated with the British – and all the dispersed groups of maroons across Haiti. Dessalines' command began as early as November 1802 and was officially recognized at the Treaty of L'Alcahaye in May 1803. The Tiger, who had been "The Butcher of the Negroes," an admirer of Attila and the "Minotaur of the Blacks" – a man who had again and again betrayed and terrorized his own people – was now regarded by the rebellious Haitians as the personification of the "Black Fury" who would settle once and for all with the French.

Although Rochambeau went on desperate offensives a few more times, bolstered by the reinforcements that had finally arrived from France, it became increasingly obvious that the French position was doomed.

His reinforcements consisted mainly of regiments of Poles that Napoleon wanted to get rid of in Europe. Rochambeau's soldiers had to manage on a few oranges a day during the campaigns. No other foods could be trusted, because the blacks were poisoning everything they could lay their hands on. Dessalines and his men waged a grim scorched-earth war. Whatever was left of the once great plantations was now being destroyed. Whatever was left of the woods, which had assured the fertility of the soil for centuries, went up in flames. Desert-like plains were created in Haiti, forerunners of the endless battlefields around Verdun that would remain forever sterile. The soil of the island was eroding with incredible speed. The ruined landscape began to be seen which would one day doom Haiti to be among the poorest nations in the world.

Rochambeau, who called himself mockingly "The White Negro from Europe," decided to make an example of Maurepas to show the black generals what was in store for them. Maurepas, who had been captured, was tied to the mast of a ship together with his wife and in front of his children. Then the process of torture and crucifixion began. But while they were dying, they encouraged each other with the following words: "Never, my beloved, will our children be slaves again." The children, who had watched their parents' suffering, were drowned afterward.

The French would also tie blacks together and then throw them in the rivers, dozens at a time. When some of the unfortunate victims, struggling desperately, managed to get back to shore, the French held races, while laughing and joking, to be the first to beat the poor people to death. The blacks were also burned with sulphur and suffocated, or were tied to cannon balls that were rolled into the sea. Others were whipped until their skin was completely raw. They were then tied to poles and left in the burning sun to become the prey of greedy insects.

Simple hanging was far too tame for the French. They did hang the blacks, rows of them even, but first the blacks dug their own graves below their gallows. After long hours of suffering in the hot sun, the blacks were lowered into these graves.

The French also remembered the hellish customs of the French Revolution. As they had done in the Vendée, they tied blacks to rafts and boats that were made to sink very gradually. Fréron, who knew these tortures from Toulon and Marseille, was not to be a participant this time. Pauline Bonaparte's former, seedy lover did not live long in Les Cayes. He died there of yellow fever, in solitude and praising the rebellion of the Negroes.

Rochambeau, who had become completely depraved after all his assignments in the Caribbean, seemed to have fallen into a maniacal, bloodthirsty trance. As long as he still found himself in Haiti, he felt that his only workable policy was to sow death and terror irrationally and desperately, and in so doing revenge himself for the tolerance that he had had to show toward the blacks for so many years. He had, meanwhile, reinstated slavery everywhere on the plantations that still remained under his authority.

Rochambeau had gallows erected in the remains of Dessalines' former palace in Port-au-Prince. He then assembled, in a room with walls completely covered in black hangings and lit by funeral torches, the wives of murdered blacks who were lying in an adjoining room in coffins below the gallows. Suddenly the torches were extinguished one by one while a large door was opened, through which the women were pushed. They were then led to the gallows on which they had to die, hanging above their own husbands.

The French general had heard that the uprisings of maroons in Jamaica had been quashed quickly and easily with the help of special bloodhounds from Cuba. These gruesome hunters had been particularly trained to hunt people. Kept in cages from the day they were born, they were continuously starved – and then let loose on dummies the size of people that were filled with blood and the intestines of animals. Thus trained, they were marked by small Spanish crosses that they wore around their necks.

Rochambeau had hundreds of these dogs brought to Haiti. When they arrived, they were cheered by white women who, according to one report, even licked the foam that dripped from their muzzles. In this degenerate atmosphere, Rochambeau had an arena built. As great numbers of spectators arrived, slaves were driven into the arena; there they were ripped to pieces by the dogs who were set at them. As one black was driven into the arena, the dogs only bit him but did not tear him to pieces – they were sated. One planter who was an avid spectator thought of a solution. He rushed into the arena and, with his sabre, he slashed open the slave's abdomen so that his intestines showed and blood flowed freely. Now the dogs could no longer be restrained. Throughout this arena torture, the whites were disappointed that the victims seemed to suffer so little pain. They held up so well through their torments! Those blacks had to be possessed by something, maybe by the devil.

All the more reason why they should die!

For Rochambeau, however, the sands ran out in July 1803, when England recommenced the war against the French in the Caribbean. British ships blockaded the harbors and Rochambeau was caught like a rat in a trap. The territories around the cities were entirely in the hands of the rebels, who left the French in peace only in Santo Domingo, where a few were still living.

In November 1803, Rochambeau surrendered to the British after his last bulwarks, Môle Saint-Nicolas and Cap François, had fallen. Neither he nor his officers gave a thought to the whites who had to remain behind. They were far too busy dragging along crates full of confiscated jewelry and gems. Captured as a prisoner of war, it was not until 1811 that Rochambeau was transferred to France, in exchange for a British general. In 1812, he took part in Napoleon's campaign against Russia and then died afterward, on the battlefield of Leipzig.

* * *

The vicissitudes of the Poles, four thousand of whom arrived in Haiti only in the fall of 1802, formed a strange interlude in the war. They were part of the Polish legion in the service of France that had been founded in 1797. The Poles had fled to France after the great Polish uprising under Kosciuszko had been suppressed in 1794.

In Haiti, they had been placed under the command of the pro-French mulatto Clervaux, shortly before he defected and joined the rebellion. At first they had been enchanted with the island—the exuberant vegetation, the exotic flowers, the birds with their colorful markings, the fruit, the fish, the delicious alcoholic beverages and, not to be omitted, the frivolous Creole women and their passionate rivals of mixed blood. "If there were only peace, this land would be superior to all others because of its women, its vegetables and its fragrances," thought the Poles.

Things changed quickly, however, when the Poles discovered that they had also arrived in the promised land of insects and reptiles, which meant that they hardly ever got a good night's sleep. Furthermore, it turned out that the fruit, which looked so deliciously inviting, was usually poisoned in this Land of Cockaigne. And they could never take a peaceful walk among the flowers and the birds because the dangerous pits of the blacks were everywhere.

General Brunet, who had engineered the arrest of Toussaint, was full of praise for the dexterity of the Poles in mountainous terrain. As agile as goats, they clambered among the rocks. But three-quarters of the weapons that had been provided to the Poles were found to be useless. And the French economized as much as possible on the minimal rations that were allotted to these men. It was not long before the Poles made an even more disappointing discovery: Their fight was to be against an unfortunate people whose only goal was to escape slavery. The Poles ended up feeling a sense of solidarity with the struggle of the blacks, almost all of whom, in addition, ardently practiced the faith of the Poles: Catholicism.

At least five hundred of the four thousand Poles joined the rebellion. Dessalines was very fond of these and he even formed a separate army corps for them, Les Polonais. When the British, now active again against the French, imported more Africans to help Dessalines fight the war, these were assigned to the units of the Poles, who, after all, spoke a language no more comprehensible to the Haitian blacks than it was to the Africans.

As reprisal, the Poles still with the French army were subjected to harassment. After Rochambeau's surrender in November 1803, their lot as prisoners of war was also the worst. They were not taken to England but instead to Cuba and Jamaica, where they were put to work on plantations where many of them died. Some of the Poles escaped and set out to sea, forming bands of pirates who fought both the French and the British. Only about one thousand returned to France after years of wandering, and most of these died on the battlefields of Prussia and Austria.

About fifty families with Polish names are still living in Port-au-Prince, the descendants of Poles who settled in Haiti after serving Dessalines. Since the Constitution forbade whites to ever again settle in Haiti, a separate Article that made an exception for the Poles was included. (A similar Article also existed for the small colony of Germans in Bombarde.) In 1926, an American of Polish descent, Faustin Wirkus, married a girl from Haiti who was also of Polish descent. Wirkus settled on the Haitian island of Gonâve, where, shortly thereafter, he became a crowned king. The King of

Gonâve, who kept a beautiful harem, died in 1945. When the Pope visited Haiti in 1983, the Haitian descendants of the Poles offered him a book called *Présence polonaise au Haïti* (The Polish Presence in Haiti).

* * *

More than 50,000 people died during the final slave war, of whom 30,000 were blacks. Only 4,000 of the French survived the disaster. The total number of victims of the wars and civil wars in Haiti between 1791 and 1804 is estimated at 350,000, of whom at least 200,000 were blacks and mulattoes.

In Gonaïves, former headquarters of Toussaint, on January 1, 1804, Dessalines and his generals proclaimed the Free Black Republic of Haiti. Haiti, then the Big Island, a mountainous land the size of Ireland, became the first country in the history of the world to be founded on the triumph of a slave rebellion.

But the French had not yet been driven out completely; remnants of the original white population still remained, mostly in the towns and cities. Dessalines decided that there was a simple solution for the problem of the remaining whites in Haiti: All had to be killed. His hastily formulated draft for a constitution did not allow for the possibility of whites to live in the new nation. Exceptions, as a rule, were made only for priests and physicians.

Again gallows were erected. The executions lasted from January through the middle of March. Approximately five thousand whites—men, women and children—were killed. The gallows were erected on the highest points along the coast, so that passing ships could see that this was the true and final Bartholomew's Night for the whites in the Free Black Republic. The gallows could not process all the victims and, in the municipalities, recourse was had to butchering the last whites any way possible.

Of course a mad exodus to the coast took place as whites desperately raced to escape the slaughter. For once, hostilities at sea were forgotten as American and British, as well as French, ships arrived offshore to take on white refugees. In one incident, a French ship became overloaded with nine hundred civilians and then promptly ran aground. Dessalines' army came up to the shore and began unlimbering their cannon to blow the helpless vessel to pieces. Suddenly a British ship, the *Hercules,* sailed into the harbor and realized the massacre that was about to take place. A British officer rowed furiously to the French ship, took down its flag and raised the Union Jack on its mainmast; at the same time, another officer rushed ashore to remind Dessalines of the consequences of firing on a "British" vessel. Dessalines held his fire and this particular group of refugees was saved.

By the end of March, no more than forty whites were still alive in Port-au-Prince. Most of them were women who had agreed to marry blacks. They had been encouraged to do so by Creole women who, during the period after Toussaint's Constitution – that short-lived period of peace and tolerance between whites and blacks in Haiti – had married blacks and mulattoes out of their own free will and for reasons of love.

In July, the news reached Dessalines that Napoleon had become Emperor of France. So, on October 8, 1804, he had himself crowned emperor as well, Jacob the First. His wife, Claire-Heureuse, became empress. On May 20, 1805, the Imperial Constitution was enacted. Various Codes were adopted that were directly based on Napoleon's Codes. Dessalines also now made an unsuccessful attempt to expel the last of the French from Santo Domingo. They held out there until 1809 and, during all that time, they preserved slavery. Then the Spanish, who had meanwhile joined the British in their war against Napoleon, returned.

Dessalines governed with terror. Whatever was left of the plantations was added together and then divided in the form of estates among his generals and officers. He hoped that, in so doing, economic recovery would follow. But Haiti's plight was serious. France as well as England and the United States had proclaimed a boycott against the island. Aside from feelings of distaste for Dessalines' method of governing, they were afraid that anti-slavery feeling would be transported from Haiti to the British colonies and to the plantations in the south of the United States.

While Dessalines had monuments in his honor erected everywhere, he forbade any talk or writing about Toussaint. His end arrived in the fall of 1806.

At that time, an uprising finally took place against "the Tiger" Dessalines and, at Pont Rouge, he fell into a trap. While he thought he saw his allies approaching among the undergrowth, these generals and their soldiers turned out to be rebels.

"It is not possible," Dessalines called out. "I must have been betrayed!" He had no other weapon than his whip. But armed with this, he boldly threw himself at the rebels and lashed out at their faces.

"Fire!" the officers called.

But the soldiers were afraid to shoot at the tyrant and they retreated, shrinking before the demon-like Dessalines. Grinning, he at once shot and killed a soldier with the man's own pistol, which he had snatched from the soldier's hand. He then spurred his horse on savagely. A young soldier managed to gather all his courage and fired on Dessalines' horse, which collapsed, trapping the Emperor's legs under its body.

"Help!" Dessalines shouted.

No one had ever heard Dessalines call for help. Now the spell was broken. They rushed at him and they hit and kicked and hacked at the now helpless victim. The generals arrived and emptied their pistols into his body. They cut the fingers off the twitching body so as to get hold of Dessalines' jewelry. His body was then tied to a horse and dragged all the way to Port-au-Prince.

Everywhere people wanted to spit and kick at the body. A black woman in the city, however, took pity on Dessalines' remains and buried him. For a long time, she continued to lay flowers on the grave daily. Dessalines was forty-eight years old when he died.

Just a few years later, Dessalines' star began to rise again, next to that of the Father of the Nation, Toussaint Louverture. After all, Dessalines had been the actual founder of the free nation of Haiti. The national anthem and the bodyguard of the president were named after him. The practitioners of voodoo also worshipped him, as can be seen from the following song.

Pito mun pase m'kurti.
Desalin, Desalin demabre,
Viv la libeté

(It is better to die than to flee.
Dessalines, Dessalines the powerful,
Long live liberty!)

*   *   *

After the fall of Dessalines, what we know today as Haiti split into two parts, namely, a mulatto republic in the south under the leadership of Pétion and the realm of President Christophe in the north. In 1811, Christophe had himself crowned King Henri the First. This great rebel who betrayed Toussaint Louverture had reached his zenith.

Like Dessalines, he ruled through terror. He created a party of loyalists by appointing many counts, dukes, princes and barons. Whoever belonged to the Order of Saint Henri was safe. King Henri had a formidable citadel built in the mountains near Laferrière – truly one of the wonders of the world. In this bastion on the rocks, the king would sometimes sit for hours staring at the sea. He himself wanted to see the French approaching, if they should come back. His castle, Sanssouci, was built completely in the Bourbon style. King Henri wished to be just as learned a king as the King of France (the pre-revolutionary regime had returned with Louis XVIII in 1814–15). So Christophe began to read and study. And he promoted improvement of the schools, the fight against illiteracy and the codification of law (in the royalist manner). He also became interested in the medical profession. Under the reign of King Henri, there was a gradual increase in the number and the qualifications of physicians.

But his realm, too, was doomed. Precisely at the time when an insurrection against him was gaining ground, he became the victim of a mysterious illness. "I had prepared for everything so to be able to quell an uprising at once," he is said to have declared, "but it never occurred to me that I might become the victim of an illness precisely at the time of that uprising."

An affliction, probably a stroke, paralyzed his entire left side. He was not able to do anything other than lie down. Christophe's thundering speeches could no longer keep his sovereignty intact. On October 8, 1820, after isolating himself from his wife and children, he committed suicide in his palace, which had been surrounded by the enemy. He shot himself through the heart with a golden bullet.

* * *

By his conquest of Santo Domingo in February 1822, Boyer, a mulatto who had come to power, was able to establish the Big Island one last time as a unified country. In 1843, that unity ended definitively.

In 1825, King Charles X of France declared himself willing to renounce French sovereignty over Haiti for a payment of 150 million gold francs. Haiti paid a total of thirty million on this debt. Jacques-Nicolas Billaud-Varenne, a former representative of the Reign of Terror and later a Thermidorian, was another who became a participant in the discussion about the definitive independence of Haiti. After many years of being banished from France, he had finally settled in the island nation. "At least my bones will lie in a land that has fought for its freedom," he said. His written contribution to the confirmation of the independence and freedom of Haiti was: "[As far as the] question of the rights of people [are concerned], the republicans of Haiti possess the necessary qualities to obtain the ratification of their independence – by an observer, who is a philosopher."

In 1840, during the reign in France of the good "Citizen King," Louis Philippe, plans were made for a new invasion and conquest of Haiti. The plans were then changed to a campaign of aggression that would be aimed instead at North Africa. Haiti had escaped, finally and irrevocably, from the designs and clutches of its mother country.

◆ 14 ◆

Death in a Dungeon

■■ ■■

O N JULY 12, 1802, A CLEAR DAY, THE SHIP *HÉROS* ARRIVED AT THE
port of Brest. The voyage from Haiti had been made in record
time, taking only twenty-six days.

"*Vae victis*" (Pity the vanquished) were Toussaint's first words.
Asked by the sailors what he was mumbling, he replied, "You now
have my life and my head but, believe me, you do not have my tail
as of yet, and, at some point, you will be sorry about that."

He asked for a new uniform, since he was still wearing the same
one he had on when he was arrested on June 7. He was promised
a new uniform but, in Paris, on July 23, he was told that Napoleon
had forbidden him to have one. Toussaint also found out only then
that the rank of general had been taken away from him by Napoleon
even before Leclerc set out on his expedition.

In his wrinkled old uniform, he was to be transferred to Fort
Joux, in eastern France, together with his secretary, Mars Plaisir.
Immediately upon arrival in Brest, he had been separated from
Suzanne, Isaac, Placidus and Saint-Jean, as well as his niece and her
companion, all of whom had been deported from Haiti together
with him. Even during the voyage he had not been allowed to have
any contact with them.

Upon their arrival in France, Placidus was taken to the fortress
of Belle Ile and Suzanne and her other two sons to Bayonne in the
south. There the little Saint-Jean pined away and finally died from

sorrow and from the whites' "continental disease," as Isaac sarcastically described it, which he had caught after his arrival in France. The money that Suzanne had managed to give to Toussaint in Brest just before they were separated (he would never see her again) was stolen from him after his arrival in Fort Joux. While he was on his way there, he also had three letters still with him, among these one addressed to Leclerc. These letters were stolen from him as well.

Toussaint gave the impression of being calm and composed. In a coach with closed curtains and surrounded by twelve military police, who brought along a piece of artillery, he was transported in the direction of the Jura Mountains. There were several delays as they stopped at military posts and encampments. There, the soldiers thronged around the coach and cheered Toussaint. They all wanted to see the hero of Haiti! Toussaint got out of the coach and shook hands with some of them.

At one stop, in Paris, Toussaint was housed in the Temple. He spent the night in the room where Louis XVII, the young uncrowned king, son of the beheaded Louis XVI, must have lain. Toussaint was told that Pinchinat had spent the night there only recently. Pinchinat was the mulatto who, in 1796, had persuaded Vilatte to attempt a coup against Laveaux!

Toussaint was never to receive the news that would have eased his last days so greatly; namely, that all the blacks as well as all the mulattoes, all the former slaves and all the free blacks were finally marching triumphantly against the French in an alliance that could no longer be defeated.

After one last overnight stop in Besançon and a long detour, the coach finally reached Fort Joux. The fort had been built on a rocky, fifteen-hundred-foot mountain in the Jura range. Behind it towered peaks that were covered with snow nine months of the year. The fort consisted of five sections that were separated by ramparts. In the fifth section, which could be reached only by a small bridge across a moat within the fort, were the prisons. These consisted of damp, dark and chilly underground dungeons where the ground was practically always covered with a thin layer of water. The cells and the casemates that were located along the prison had extremely small windows that were all provided with heavy bars. These windows were covered at about one hour before sunset. One hour after sunrise, the poor scanty light was allowed to enter again, together with the cold and the rarefied stillness of the Jura Mountains.

The prisoners in Fort Joux were forbidden to speak at any time. Baille, the commander, would regularly come to spend the night in the fort so he could check on whether the men observed the rule of silence. The fort had been built by the Romans and it was an impregnable stronghold. On the one side was the river Doubs and on the other the road to Besançon. It seemed as if Fort Joux, like a gigantic crouching predator, would be able to reach the peaks of the Juras in just a few leaps.

In the Middle Ages, the French knight Amaury had locked his seventeen-year-old wife, Berthe, into this fort when he set out for the Crusades. She remained there until her death at the age of twenty-seven, by which time she resembled an emaciated old woman with gray hair. Her dungeon's only window looked out upon a skeleton rattling in the wind. It was that of the young knight who had committed adultery with Berthe and who had been killed by Amaury. In Fort Joux, there were also the Spanish Wells. These were pits into which prisoners, among them Spanish mercenaries during the French religious wars, were lowered and then left to die. Count Mirabeau had also temporarily been a prisoner at Fort Joux when he was anonymously accused and taken there on an arbitrary warrant of imprisonment. He miraculously succeeded in starting a relationship with a young girl, who died from sorrow after Mirabeau, once he had finally been freed, left the fort without leaving a trace. With him went a pile of manuscripts, mainly pornographic novels, that he had completed during his confinement.

When Toussaint entered Fort Joux, he knew that he, like Moses, would never enter the Promised Land. However, a shadow from his country of origin was very near him, although he did not know it. When he arrived in Fort Joux, his old rival, Rigaud, was imprisoned there as well. Set free in 1810, Rigaud later managed to escape from France. In 1811, he was again in Haiti, where he fell upon his sword after a terrible row with the new leader of the mulattoes, Pétion, who was then fighting another civil war against the black king, Henri (Christophe), who claimed to be a successor of Toussaint's.

When, after many long years of shedding the blood of hundreds of thousands of people, Napoleon himself was banished to the British island of St. Helena in the South Atlantic, his first words upon arrival were: "I have been condemned without having been given a trial or a sentence, which testifies to contempt of all divine and human laws. To make my misfortune even worse, they are also keeping me separated from my wife and my son."

These could rightfully have been the words of Toussaint as well, when he entered Fort Joux and realized that he had to give up all hope. He would never be able to survive the twenty degrees below freezing that one had to bear during the winters in that location. The additional safety measures that had been taken, after some of the imprisoned Vendéans had escaped in August, were superfluous for him.

Toussaint handed to Commander Baille his sealed "letter of introduction" from Leclerc, which read: "I am sending you this totally perfidious man; you know, of course, what you will have to do with him." Separately, Leclerc advised the Secretary of the Navy and the Colonies, "You must make sure that this prisoner is kept especially far from the sea and in a dungeon that is as isolated as possible. This man has made Haiti so fanatic that his presence there, at any time, would again cause enormous turmoil. I think that it would be wise to make him, in some way or other, disappear from the scene forever."

(Leclerc did not understand that the news of Toussaint's kidnapping and transfer to France would cause even more turmoil. After they had rebelled again, Maurepas, Belair and Paul Louverture were brutally murdered. But, within six months of Toussaint's death, Dessalines, Christophe and Pétion had joined hands in an alliance that led to the final downfall of the French.)

During the first few weeks of his imprisonment, Mars Plaisir shared Toussaint's cell. It was not until September 1802 that Toussaint received another set of clothes to replace the rags that were the remainder of his old uniform. They were prison clothes. Toussaint also had to give up his boots. As a result, his legs were daily exposed to the humidity, moisture and mist, which seemed to be transfer directly from the wet ground into his bones. Toussaint was, furthermore, searched several times a day and sometimes also at night; the only purpose of this was to terrorize him and keep him from sleeping. In the morning, he was handed cold food, placed on a board, with which he had to make do all day. It consisted of rusk, cheese, salted meat and sour wine. He was not allowed sugar or coffee.

From his first day at Fort Joux, Toussaint pleaded for coffee. At the beginning of each month, Baille carefully divided the food meant for Toussaint in thirty portions. In an account to the Secretary, he wrote, "I have complied with your intentions by carefully preparing all the details of his meals with the greatest frugality."

It was not judged necessary for Toussaint to know the time, and so his watch was taken away from him. It was sufficient that he heard the fort's clock loudly striking each quarter hour.

During the few weeks that Mars Plaisir (who was subsequently transferred, heavily chained, to a prison in Nantes) was allowed to remain with him, Toussaint wrote letters to Napoleon and also something like his memoirs. He was doing the writing himself now, scrawling the words with pointy letters and using an ingenuous phonetic style. "*Premire Consul, pere de tout de militre, defenseur des innosant, juige integre, prononce donc, sure un homme qui e plus mal heuere que coupable*" ("Dear First Consul, father of all soldiers, defender of the innocents, upright judge, please pronounce a sentence over a man who is unfortunate rather than guilty"). Following is an excerpt of what Toussaint wrote on September 17, 1802:

> If I committed any crime while I did my duty, it was definitely unintentionally. If I committed an offense by boldly drafting a constitution at an early date, this was done as a result of my great desire to do right by the people and still please the government. I had the misfortune of seeing your wrath descend on me, but my conscience is clear because I remained faithful and honest. You never had a more honest servant. I have now been wretchedly ruined and dishonored. You are too noble and just to delay making a decision about my fate. In the report that I sent you, I have opened my heart to you.

Only a few fragments have been preserved of this report where, in any case, Toussaint again laid all the blame for his actions on Leclerc's brutal invasion. When no reaction from Napoleon arrived, Toussaint wrote, on September 29:

> Allow me, First Consul, to say to you with all due respect that the government has been completely misled with regard to Toussaint Louverture, one of the most diligent and courageous servants the government ever had in Haiti. I toiled long and hard to win honor and fame from the government and to earn the respect of my fellow citizens. And now I am being rewarded with thorns and gross injustice. I do not deny the mistakes that I may have made and I ask forgiveness for these. But those failings do not deserve even one-fourth of the punishment that is meted out to me, nor the treatment to which I am being subjected.
>
> First Consul, it is my sad fate that we never met! If you had gotten to know me well when I was in Haiti, you would have treated me with greater justice. My heart is good. I am not a learned man and there are not many things I can do. But my father, who is blind now, taught me to walk the path of virtue and honor; my conscience is at ease on this point. If I had not been faithful to the government, I would not be here – that is a fact. Now I am miserable and wretched, a victim of the services that I rendered. Ever since August 10, 1790, I have continuously been at the service of this country. Now I am a prisoner and powerless. And, to make matters worse, my health is seriously damaged. I have begged you for my freedom, so that I may work again and earn a living for myself and my poor family. I hope that you, who are a great man and a genius, will make a decision about my fate! May you relent and your heart be touched by my wretched condition.

Napoleon never reacted to this letter.

*   *   *

Toussaint was visited by two people in Fort Joux. The first was Dormoy, a former abbot, who probably managed to get by Baille's military guards with the excuse that he was sent from Paris to act as father confessor for Toussaint. He professed that he had come to discuss the possibility that Louverture might be freed.

Toussaint quickly realized that the man was a priest who had fallen from grace and, moreover, someone who had not even mastered any Latin. Toussaint never showed any interest in having a father confessor while he was in Fort Joux. The unfortunate trap into which he had fallen did not seem reconcilable with Toussaint's belief in a God the Father who supported him, a belief that had kept him going for so long. The only item representing the Christian faith to which he still clung was the Bible. Fortunately, this was provided to him by Baille, given the fact that France was a thoroughly Catholic country at the time of Napoleon. Toussaint liked to hum the Psalms in his cell.

The second visitor, General Caffarelli, came by orders of Napoleon himself. On September 9, Bonaparte had written to Caffarelli and remarked the following: "You should go by Fort Joux one of these days. You know that I have considered Toussaint a rebel from the moment he published his Constitution, and he added enormously to that crime by taking up arms against the republic. Also, we only found out through London about the nature of his treaties with Jamaica and England. You must now try to determine more precisely what the British were up to and also obtain definitive information, especially about the treasure that Toussaint has hidden."

At the end of September, the first of seven conversations between Caffarelli and Toussaint took place. At the time, Toussaint's physical condition was already very poor. He was plagued by headaches and coughing spells. He had turned gray and he had trouble walking. Nevertheless, Toussaint politely helped the general to sit down. Caffarelli was lame, his left leg having been crippled during one of the battles he had fought for Napoleon. He had, in fact, more trouble walking than Toussaint, who was suffering from his old hip injury.

Toussaint replied to every concrete question with abstract generalities. He did not provide any details, nor did he give any insight into the actions he had taken at the times in question. When asked about his treasure or the money that had been stored in chests and hidden in the Haitian mountains, he replied, "I earned treasures other than money."

His answer to questions about his contacts with the British was, "I only opened up a new horizon for the black race."

"But you must have invested your money somewhere in business?"

"I never conducted any business, sir. I am an agricultural worker," Toussaint replied.

"In your memo to the First Consul, you mentioned having 648,800 francs before the Revolution. What happened to those?"

"When the colony became more and more impoverished and France did not send us supplies, I used my money to pay the soldiers. Haiti is a treasure-chamber but, if people want to find that treasure, they will have to work and the Negroes must be able to live in peace and freedom."

"But what about those treaties?"

"You are familiar with them. They were all co-signed by Hédouville and Roume."

The myth about the treasure of gold that Toussaint was said to have hidden in Haiti's Cahos Mountains was so persistent that he has even been suspected of having ordered that all those who knew where the treasure was hidden should be murdered. For Napoleon, in any case, Toussaint was a kind of early version of the Count of Monte Cristo. Napoleon subsequently asked Caffarelli twice whether he wasn't able to get something out of Toussaint about that treasure. Toussaint stated instead that Haiti still owed *him* money, since he had spent all his money on the army. "All I owned were my horses and my land."

After seven tries, Caffarelli gave up on these conversations. As it was fall and the weather was getting colder all the time, he was suffering too much from the penetrating chill in the cell. "This introverted man," he wrote to Napoleon, "who is shrewd, subtle and concerned only with himself, talks as if he is totally sincere. But he says only what he has prepared in his head and not what should come from his heart or what we do not yet know."

* * *

In early 1803, Toussaint became more seriously ill. He lost his last teeth, which caused him great pain. At night, the temperature was far below freezing. The small fire in his cell was extinguished in the evening and he generally slept sitting up, with some shoddy blankets and old bags pulled around himself.

According to Baille, however, "the Negroes have a totally different constitution from that of the Europeans"; hence he did not permit a physician to visit Toussaint. In the heart of winter, Toussaint was so racked by rheumatism and fever that he was hardly able to walk. He would sit stiffly on his small bench in front of the fire that, due to the scarcity of wood, only burned for a few hours a day. He had a dry, racking cough, and he was unable to lift his left arm. During the few hours that light entered his dungeon, he would try to read the Psalms. But his eyes were watering too much as a result of his illness, his loneliness, his anguish.

Then Baille was succeeded by a new commander, Amiot, who was even grimmer and more insensitive, as well as more suspicious. He increased the number of nightly visits to Toussaint's cell, noting in the record that Toussaint's face had begun to swell badly, that his voice sometimes gave way and that he coughed incessantly.

In the beginning of April, Amiot had to go to Neuchâtel, in Switzerland, for a few days. His duties were taken over by a Captain Colomier, who was extremely indignant about the condition in which he found the prisoner. Not only was the man seriously ill, but he was apparently also starving. Flour had been his only food! Colomier gave Toussaint his first cup of coffee since his arrival at Fort Joux. When Amiot returned on April 7 and entered Toussaint's cell that morning, he called out mockingly, "Toussaint, I have a delicious meal for you today."

Only then did he see that the Haitian leader was dead. Toussaint had been in a half-sitting, half-lying position. Saliva and blood dripped from his mouth. Amiot quickly left the cell to get some food, so that he would be able to say that Toussaint could not have died from hunger.

Toussaint probably had had a heart attack or perhaps a stroke. But it is just as plausible that he died as the result of starvation and a broken will to live.

Captain Colomier and the mayor of Pontarlier, the municipality where Fort Joux was located, refused to sign the official report on the postmortem. Soon after, the rumor went around that Toussaint had committed suicide or, much more probably, been murdered. A physician discovered a large quantity of foul fluids in Toussaint's head, near his brains. "It is his anguish that has collected there," he reported.

* * *

Joséphine wrote to Napoleon, "What is it that you have always had against this leader of the blacks? I am afraid that your numerous family will become a source of much greater misfortune one day." In her memoirs, she talked about an assassination in connection with Toussaint's death. And she compared Napoleon's liquidation of Toussaint Louverture with the kidnapping and execution, a year later, of the Duke d'Enghien, an innocent pretender to the throne of the Bourbons, who was not even on French territory at the time. That same year, Pichegru, a general who had conspired against Napoleon, was found strangled in his cell in Paris.

With murders and terror, Napoleon Bonaparte prepared the way for his crowning as emperor. After the murder of D'Enghien, the writer Chateaubriand, who would one day call the Corsican an imitator of Toussaint, refused to accept an appointment as ambassador that he received from Napoleon. He remarked, "The heavens hear the voice of innocence and misfortune; sooner or later, the oppressor and the oppressed will stand at the foot of the same judge's chair."

Toussaint was buried in the chapel at Fort Joux, after a Funeral Mass had been celebrated where a priest was the only person present. The grave was not marked. When changes were made to the fort between 1876 and 1880, the chapel had to be destroyed. The remains from the graves that were found were used in the construction of a new wall of the stronghold.

Every year, representatives of the Republic of Haiti hold memorial services at the spot on the mountainside in France that holds the mortal remains of the greatest man in their nation's history. In 1926, Colonel Nemours, president of the Council of State and author of the two-volume *Histoire militaire de la guerre de l'indépendance de Saint-Domingue,* was the first to organize a memorial service for Toussaint Louverture in the little church at Pontarlier, France.

People of every color continue to honor the life and achievements of Toussaint Louverture. They continue to present this story of a tragedy – that was a triumph as well – to all those for whom William Wordsworth wrote the following poem in February 1802, when he envisioned Toussaint Louverture's death and resurrection:

> Toussaint, the most unhappy man of men!
> Whether the whistling Rustic tend his plough
> Within thy hearing, or thy head be now
> Pillowed in some deep dungeon's earless den –
> O miserable Chieftain! where and when
> Wilt thou find patience? Yet die not; do thou
> Wear rather in thy bonds a cheerful brow;
> Though fallen thyself, never to rise again,
> Live and take comfort. Thou hast left behind
> Powers that will work for thee; air, earth and skies
> That will forget thee; thou hast great allies;
> Thy friends are exultations, agonies,
> and love, and man's unconquerable mind.

Bibliography

Alexis, Stephen. *Black Liberator: The Life of Toussaint Louverture*. New York, 1949.

Benot, Yves. *La Révolution française et la fin des colonies*. Paris, 1988.

Besson, M., and R. Chauvelot. *Napoléon colonial*. Paris, 1939.

Buch, Hans Christoph. *Haïti Chérie*. Frankfurt, 1990.

—. *Die Hochzeit von Port-au-Prince*. Frankfurt, 1984.

—. *Die Scheidung von San Domingo, wie die Negersklaven von Haiti Robespierre beim Wort nahmen*. Berlin, 1976.

Caffarelli, Comte L. de. *Toussaint Louverture au Fort-de-Joux*. Journal presented to the Vicomte de Grouchy.

Césaire, Aimé. *Toussaint Louverture, la révolution française et le problème colonial*. Paris (?), n.d.

Cole, Hubert. *Christophe, King of Haiti*. New York, 1961.

Crêté, Liliane. *La Traité des nègres sous l'Ancien Régime*. Paris, 1989.

Dalmas, A. *Histoire de la révolution de Saint-Domingue jusqu'à la prise de Jérémie par les Anglais*, 2 vols. Paris, 1814.

Debien, G. *Les Colons de Saint-Domingue et la révolution, essai sur le Club Massiac*. Paris, 1953.

Dorsainville, Roger. *Toussaint Louverture*. Paris, 1965.

Dubroca, B.M.J. *La Vie de Toussaint Louverture, chef des Noirs insurgés de Saint-Domingue*. Paris, 1804.

—. *Vie de Jean-Jacques Dessalines*. Paris, 1804.

Duffy, Michael. *Soldiers, Sugar and Seapower: The British Expeditions to the West Indies and the War Against Revolutionary France*. Oxford, 1987.

Fregosi, Paul. *Dreams of Empire: Napoleon and the First World War 1792–1815*. London, 1989.

Frostin, Charles. *Les Révoltes blanches à Saint-Domingue aux XVIIe et XVIIIe siècles.* Paris, 1975.

Geggus, David. *Slavery, War and Revolution: The British Occupation of Saint-Domingue 1793–1798.* Oxford, 1982.

Girod, F. *La Vie quotidienne de la société créole de Saint-Domingue au XVIIIe siècle.* Paris, 1972.

Glissant, Edouard. *Monsieur Toussaint.* Paris, 1961.

Gragnon-Lacoste, T.P. *Toussaint Louverture, général en chef de l'armée de Saint-Domingue, surnommé le premier des Noirs.* Paris, 1877.

Grégoire, Abbé H. *Mémoire en faveur des gens de couleur ou sang-mêlé de Saint-Domingue et des autres îles françaises de l'Amérique adressé à l'Assemblée Nationale.* Paris, 1789.

Griffith, Anne. *Black Patriot and Martyr: Toussaint Louverture of Haiti.* New York, 1970.

Hassal, Mary. *Secret History of the Horrors of Saint-Domingue in a Series of Letters Written by a Lady at Cape François to Colonel Burr, Late Vice President of the United States.* Philadelphia, 1808.

James, C.L.R. *The Black Jacobins: Toussaint Louverture and the San Domingo Revolution,* rev. ed. London, 1982.

Korngold, R. *Citizen Toussaint.* New York, 1965.

Lacroix, Pamphile de. *Mémoires pour servir à l'histoire de la révolution de Saint-Domingue.* Paris, 1819.

Laurent, Gérard. *Toussaint Louverture à travers sa correspondance.* Port-au-Prince, 1953.

Lothrop Stoddard, T. *The French Revolution in Saint-Domingue.* Boston, 1914.

Louverture, Toussaint. *Mémoires,* edited by Saint-Rémy. Paris, 1953.

Madiou, Thomas. *Histoire d'Haïti,* 3 vols. Port-au-Prince, 1981.

Mannix, Daniel. *Black Cargoes: A History of the Atlantic Slave Trade 1518–1865.* New York, 1962.

Métral, A. *Histoire de l'expédition des français à Domingue, avec les mémoires d'Isaac Louverture.* Paris, 1985.

Mézière, Henri. *Le Général Leclerc, 1772–1802 et l'expédition de Saint-Domingue.* Paris, 1990.

Nemours, A. *Histoire militaire de la guerre de l'indépendance de Saint-Domingue*, 2 vols. Paris, 1925–1928.

——. *Histoire de la captivité et de la mort de Toussaint Louverture*. Paris, 1929.

Nicholls, D. *From Dessalines to Duvalier: Race, Colour and National Independence in Haiti*. Cambridge, 1979.

Ott, Thomas O. *The Haitian Revolution 1789–1804*. University of Tennessee, 1973.

Parkinson, Wenda. *This Gilded African, Toussaint Louverture*. London and New York, 1978.

Pauleus-Sannon, H. *Histoire de Toussaint Louverture*, 3 vols. Port-au-Prince, 1920–1933.

Pluchon, Pierre. *Toussaint Louverture, de l'esclavage au pouvoir*. Paris, 1979.

——. *Toussaint Louverture, fils noir de la Révolution Française*. Paris, 1980.

——. *Toussaint Louverture: Un révolutionnaire noir de l'Ancien Régime*. Paris, 1989.

Poyen, Colonel de. *Histoire militaire de la Révolution de Saint-Domingue*. Paris, 1889.

Rusch, Erwin. *Die Revolution von Saint-Domingue*. Hamburg, 1930.

Saint-Amant, Joseph M. *Histoire des révolutions d'Haïti*. Paris, 1860.

Saint-Rémy. *Pétion et Haïti*. Paris, 1956.

Sainville, L. *La Captivité et la mort de Toussaint Louverture*. Paris, 1970.

Schoelcher, Victor. *Vie de Toussaint Louverture*. Paris, 1889.

Stein, R.L. *Légér Félicité Sonthonax: The Lost Sentinel of the Revolution*. London, 1985.

——. *The French Slave Trade in the Eighteenth Century: An Old Regime Business*. Madison, WI, 1979.

Tardon, R. *Toussaint Louverture: Le Napoléon noir*. Paris, 1951.

Tyson, G. *Toussaint Louverture*. Englewood Cliffs, NJ, 1973.

Vaissière, P. de. *La Société et la vie créole sous l'Ancien Régime*. Paris, 1909.

Vandercook, John. *Black Majesty: The Life of Christophe, King of Haiti*. New York, 1928.

Waxman, Percy. *The Black Napoleon*. New York, 1931.

Wilson, Reuel K., and Jan Pachonski. *Poland's Caribbean Tragedy: A Study of Polish Legions in the Haitian War of Independence 1802–1803*. New York, 1986.

Index

v